D0958840

Also from the Modern Library Gardening Series

Old Herbaceous by Reginald Arkell

The Gardener's Year by Karel Čapek

The American Gardener by William Cobbett

We Made a Garden by Margery Fish

In the Land of the Blue Poppies by Frank Kingdon Ward

Green Thoughts by Eleanor Perényi

My Summer in a Garden by Charles Dudley Warner

The Gardener's Bed-Book

RICHARDSON WRIGHT

THE GARDENER'S BED-BOOK

Short and Long Pieces to Be Read in Bed by Those Who Love Green Growing Things

MICHAEL POLLAN
SERIES EDITOR

Introduction by Dominique Browning

THE MODERN LIBRARY
NEW YORK

2003 Modern Library Edition

 Published in the United States by Modern Library, an imprint of The Random House Ballantine Publishing Group, a division of Random House, Inc., New York, and simultaneously in Canada by Random House of Canada Limited, Toronto.

This work was originally published in 1929 by J. B. Lippincott Co. This edition published by arrangement with HarperCollins Publishers, Inc.

LIBRARY OF CONGRESS CATALOGING-IN-PUBLICATION DATA

Wright, Richardson Little, 1887–1961
The gardener's bed-book: short and long pieces to be read in bed by those who love green growing things / Richardson Wright; introduction by Dominique Browning.
p. cm.—(Modern Library gardening series)
Originally published: Philadelphia: J.B. Lippincott Co., 1929.
ISBN 0-8129-6873-5
1. Gardening. I. Title. II. Series.

SB455.W83 2003
635—dc21 2002045172

Modern Library website address: www.modernlibrary.com

Printed in the United States of America

2 4 6 8 9 7 5 3

Contents

Introduction to the Modern Library Gardening Series *by Michael Pollan* xv
Introduction *by Dominique Browning* xix
Foreword xxxiii

THE GARDENER'S BED-BOOK

JANUARY *has Thirty-one Nights* 3
1. Blessed Be God!— 2. Trees of Life— 3. Laying Down an Elm— 4. Domesticalities— 5. The Possessive Blue— 6. As for Maid Servants— 7. A Plant for Satellite Cities— 8. Fragrances— 9. The Truth and Antiquarians— 10. Prophets Without Honor— 11. No Wonder They Wilted— 12. The Beam in Thine Eye— 13. *La Chaise Pierce*— 14. Buxus Gets into the Social Register— 15. Those Little Slits— 16. Liliputian Loves— 17. The Height of Floral Luxury— 18. Garroting Wires— 19. Of Violas— 20. Bed and Board— 21. How to Look a Seed Catalogue in the Eye— 22. Howitzers— 23. Rushing Lilies— 24. Single-Track Gardening— 25. Death Comes for the Gardener— 26. Costumes for Coffins— 27. A Note on Obesity— 28. The Second-Story Habit— 29. Horticulturists' Gar-

dens— 30. The Contemplative Gardener— 31. Unregarded Folk

LONG PIECE: Scents of Domesticity 27

FEBRUARY *has Twenty-eight Nights* 31

1. Spare the Rod— 2. A Bouquet of Barks— 3. Novelties— 4. Table Centers— 5. A Prolegomenon to Gardening— 6. Taking It from the Chicks— 7. The Fuchsias of Yesterday— 8. Saith a Grocer of Troyes— 9. The Ultimate Revenge— 10. Motors Versus Serenity— 11. Untried Annuals— 12. The Glory that Is Nemesia— 13. Polyglot Gardening— 14. The Third Trial— 15. A Memory of Matting— 16. The Undesirables— 17. Gardening Clothes— 18. A Hazardous Hobby— 19. On Bridges— 20. Little Gardens— 21. The Joneses— 22. Imperiling Tombstones— 23. Drain Pipes as Decoration— 24. The First Annuals— 25. A Second Thought on First Flowering— 26. Collectors' Horizons— 27. Forcing Time— 28. The Five-Dollar Hole

LONG PIECE: The Jackdaw Instinct 53

MARCH *has Thirty-one Nights* 58

1. The Sinner that Repenteth— 2. Forgotten Gardens— 3. Singing After Meat— 4. Spring Temptation— 5. War on Wood Worms— 6. I Threaten Pigs— 7. A Grain of Salt— 8. Dr. Johnson Speaks His Mind— 9. Sand and Seed— 10. Soil for Transplants— 11. Keeping an Eye on the Miffs— 12. Lean Eaters— 13. Pharmaceutical Hospitality— 14. The Broccoli Legend— 15. Discoveries

under Glass— 16. Ecclesiastical— 17. Babel— 18. Before the Show— 19. Snow Lace— 20. Going Berserk with Impunity— 21. The Indicative Dump— 22. Niggardly Planting— 23. The King of Bashan's Bed— 24. Celestial Sedums— 25. A Sentiment on Little Pots— 26. Corn Solitude— 27. Garden Manners— 28. Unwinding the Mummies— 29. Sub-Surface Feeding— 30. God's Comedians— 31. Flash 14

LONG PIECE: The Column for Beauty 81

APRIL *has Thirty Nights* 86

1. Drillers— 2. The Little Herbal— 3. The Porcine Palace— 4. Wives and Delphiniums— 5. "Bring Out Your Dead!"— 6. Prickly Jousts— 7. Hic Jacet— 8. Curcubita— 9. Mediocrity in Flower Pots— 10. Absurd Grounds— 11. The Cause of an Acute Pain— 12. Sweet Peas— 13. Hunting the Magenta— 14. Planting Parsons— 15. Vase Seasons— 16. My Compliments to the Crabs— 17. Topiary— 18. Working Guests— 19. Father Elm and Mother Oak— 20. The Rise of the Border— 21. Closed for Birds— 22. Gladiolus Investments— 23. The Old Love— 24. Landscape Cows— 25. Hoch Der Dwarfs!— 26. Ancestral Pigs— 27. Little Acorns— 28. Rain Music— 29. Painters in Pantalettes— 30. Gardens of Imperfection

LONG PIECE: The Noises of Town 110

MAY *has Thirty-one Nights* 115

1. Soil Incense— 2. Ugly but Comfortable— 3. Blue and Yellow— 4. Smelly Carillons— 5. Noisy Borers—

6. Of Grape Hyacinths— 7. Gardening Postures— 8. Collecting Clematis— 9. Beethoven and Birch Beer— 10. The Meadow Fence— 11. Three Rules of Health— 12. The Cream of The O. P.'s— 13. Brighter and Better Texts— 14. Sudden Springs— 15. Consolation— 16. Varmints— 17. The Raphael of Flowers— 18. A Violet Garden— 19. Sanitation and Civilization— 20. The Louvre— 21. Columbine Flappers— 22. Calvin and the Swine— 23. The Weather and Dahlias— 24. Those High-Falutin' Names— 25. Strawberries— 26. A Quaint Hypocrisy— 27. Slave to Furniture— 28. Hugonis: Cave Man— 29. Gettin' Around to It— 30. De Mortuis— 31. Faded Ladies

LONG PIECE: Men as Trees Walking 142

JUNE *has Thirty Nights* 147

1. The Feast of Lanterns— 2. A Garden Shower— 3. Roses in the Heart— 4. The Alpinist Mind— 5. In Defense of the Rocking-Chair— 6. One Queen Speaks of Another— 7. The Prodigality of Pinks— 8. Compensating Defeats— 9. The Old Gentleman Shows His Medals— 10. Natives— 11. Pea Hedges— 12. Dependability and the Hardy Climbers— 13. Disciples of Gilbert White— 14. The Overlooked Gillenia— 15. Victorian Tonsorial— 16. Anger— 17. Sapphira and the Delphiniums— 18. A Birthday Sentiment— 19. The Versatility of Valerian— 20. Weather Trumperies— 21. A Wife's Thanksgiving— 22. Seasoned and Safe Roses— 23. A Hint for Lloyds— 24. The Brothers Baptisia— 25. Fertility— 26. If a Man Would Be a Titan— 27. Architecture and Vegetables— 28. Chrysanthemums Hold the Thirteenth Card— 29. Vain Promises— 30. Elegy for an Elm

LONG PIECE: The God of Kettles 172

JULY *has Thirty-one Nights* 176
1. The Vagaries of Nostrils— 2. Burning Bushes— 3. Book Rules and Summer Seeding— 4. Of Thee We Sing— 5. Plantain Lilies— 6. Beware These— 7. A Butterfly Garden— 8. A Solution for Wedding Presents— 9. Roots by the Mile— 10. The Thyme Bank— 11. A Color Trio— 12. Left-Overs— 13. Hemerocallis— 14. Forgotten Lovers— 15. Sales Resistance— 16. Men and Thistles— 17. Lean Souls— 18. Bells and Stars— 19. A Big Lily and a Little One— 20. Mossy Roofs— 21. The Gourmet's Hallmark— 22. Memorial Cimicifuga— 23. The July Let-Down— 24. Unenthusiastic Thoughts on Platycodon— 25. Sports for Dog-Days— 26. Cushioned Paths— 27. Serendipity— 28. Plants of Suburbiana— 29. Moses and the Crab Grass— 30. Cannas Can Be Good— 31. Banzai—the Japs!

LONG PIECE: "And So to Bed" 200

AUGUST *has Thirty-one Nights* 204
1. The Test— 2. Scissors for Visitors— 3. The Hole in the Ground— 4. A Panegyric on Tomatoes— 5. The Truth about Pig Weeds— 6. Eugenics for Iris— 7. The Penguins— 8. Modernism in Bouquets— 9. Mille Fleurs— 10. Five Arguments Against Shasta Daisies— 11. The Fiery Cardinal— 12. Doing Something about It— 13. Leperous Roofs— 14. Aphids— 15. The Pathologically Morbid— 16. As for Black Currant Jam— 17. Ridge Trees and Beer— 18. A Prima Donna Job— 19. Professor of Iris— 20. Zinnias and the Common Touch— 21. Self-Contained— 22. The Increase in

Narcissus— 23. The Scarlet Males— 24. Larkspur Should Be Blue— 25. But Annual Larkspur— 26. A Vinous Boneyard— 27. Madonna Companions— 28. The Spire Family— 29. Kitchen Colonial— 30. Death to Moles— 31. The Warning

LONG PIECE: Collecting Smoke 223

SEPTEMBER *has Thirty Nights* 227

1. This Year of Rain— 2. "Artistic Arrangements" and a Great Hatred— 3. Tagging Phlox— 4. The Dyspeptic's Text— 5. People in Boxes— 6. Single Asters— 7. For a Fall Border— 8. Turtleheads— 9. The Virgin's Bower— 10. Pillows of Fragrance— 11. A Pleasant Slavery— 12. Seven Little Enkianthi— 13. The Spectrum on the Floor— 14. Torch Lilies— 15. Dusk Dew— 16. Satisfaction in Obesity— 17. A Note on Gaillardia— 18. "Ridiculous Toyes"— 19. Eupatorium and Two Companions— 20. Boiled Greens— 21. The Balloon of Country Gossip— 22. No Good Cook Stacks Her Pots— 23. A Blue for Autumn— 24. Three Aristocrats— 25. Premature Frost— 26. The Cellar Test— 27. The Pups and the Peony Stick— 28. Chant for Sash— 29. Garden Giving— 30. The Completed Cycle

LONG PIECE: The Rise and Fall of Bells 247

OCTOBER *has Thirty-one Nights* 252

1. Verses for a Night Walk— 2. Black Narcissus— 3. Planting the Tides— 4. Rhus Toxicodendron— 5. Coquette— 6. The Strange Behavior of L. Sulphureum—

7. Strawberry Hill— 8. The Prevaricating Dentist— 9. Shrub Migration— 10. Winds and Tilth— 11. Eating Exhibitions— 12. Remarks on Hyacinths— 13. Hornet Hibernation— 14. Standard Heliotropes— 15. Black Frost— 16. Then Rain— 17. The Approach to Gardens— 18. Midget Gardens— 19. Reasons for Having a Microscope— 20. Flowers and Furniture— 21. Disappearing Artists— 22. Ferns in the Fall— 23. The Peregrination of Gardeners— 24. Persistent Bloomers— 25. Harvest— 26. Emerging Architecture— 27. New England Grows Young— 28. Christmas Roses— 29. The Escape— 30. Bluebirds and Mush— 31. Fall Freedom

LONG PIECE: Around the Old Melodeon 274

NOVEMBER *has Thirty Nights* 279

1. In Memoriam— 2. Night Return— 3. The Balance Sheet— 4. First Blooming— 5. Everlastings— 6. The Award for Sanity— 7. Quaint Possessions— 8. Sex Insulation— 9. Madonna of the Swine— 10. Snowberry— 11. A Good Riddance for Temptation— 12. Crumbs for Mice— 13. The New Orchard Generation— 14. An Orchard Garden— 15. Winds of November— 16. Manure as Diamonds— 17. Root Cellars— 18. November Cleaning— 19. Acknowledging Another Failure— 20. The Percentage of Success— 21. 3800 of Them— 22. First Snow— 23. Some Birds Roost Al Fresco— 24. Huddling Houses— 25. The Lovers of Flora— 26. Varnishing Day— 27. A Thanksgiving Window— 28. Vinegar Faces— 29. Dr. Titford Holds Forth— 30. Winter Mulch

LONG PIECE: The Quest of Tranquillity 298

DECEMBER *has Thirty-one Nights* 303

1. Intemperance in Gardening— 2. Gervase Markham Lends His Support— 3. Pioneer Women— 4. The Impermanence of Perennials— 5. Painting Meadows with Delight— 6. Runners— 7. The Smuggled Gem— 8. Yuccas— 9. Time-Toned Bricks— 10. The Useless Array— 11. House Plants and Pleasure— 12. The Great Disillusionment— 13. Pentstemon Frontiers— 14. Annual Mallows— 15. Obituary— 16. Ode for Pigs— 17. Early American— 18. Monkey Puzzles— 19. Transplanted Ladies— 20. Inside Summer Houses— 21. Imitation Snow— 22. Four Cards in Particular— 23. Imitation Snow Melts— 24. The Hectic Eve— 25. The Ass— 26. Five Things to Labor For— 27. Legend and Science— 28. Frosted Panes— 29. In Exile— 30. Procul Este Profani— 31. Finale

Introduction to the Modern Library Gardening Series

Michael Pollan

It took a woodchuck and a book to make me understand what's really at stake in the garden.

I'd come to gardening in the naïve belief it offered a fairly benign way to kill an afternoon, a refuge from the wider world, but even before the end of my first season I'd been forcibly relieved of my innocence. First came the rodent. A series of increasingly desperate measures to run a hungry woodchuck out of my vegetable patch escalated into a personal Vietnam (with me in the role of General Westmoreland, fully prepared to destroy the garden in order to save it), which promptly exploded the whole "garden-as-refuge" concept. The spectacle of my own rodenticidal rage suggested that more was involved in gardening than tending a few tomatoes and prettifying my yard. It put one into a relationship with nature that was anything but innocent.

But it wasn't until I cracked open Eleanor Perényi's *Green Thoughts,* a tart, smart, and beautifully written set of alphabetical essays (from "Annuals" to "Woman's Place") published in 1981, that I realized how much was really going on here, right under my nose. Perényi had found in the garden everything from sexual politics and class struggle to culinary fashion and, particularly relevant to my woodchuck problem, ecological insight. The garden, in other words, was better approached as an arena than a refuge, an idea I immediately seized on and have yet to let go of. Though I suspect neither party would especially appreciate the tribute, I can trace the discovery of my own vocation as a writer to the crossing, in 1984 or thereabouts, of that particular book with that particular rodent.

What Perényi had done was to introduce me to an unexpectedly rich, provocative, and frequently uproarious conversation that, metaphorically at least, takes place over the back fence that joins any two gardens in the world. Was there really such a thing as a green thumb? (Nonsense, said Perényi; why of course! countered Russell Page.) Was I within my rights to firebomb a woodchuck burrow? (Don't answer.) Must we concede the moral superiority of native species? And why is it magenta is so often maligned? (All too common, huffs Alice Morse Earle, before Louise Beebe Wilder leaps to its defense.) From book to book, across oceans and centuries, the horticultural backing-and-forthing unfolds with such urgency you'd be forgiven for thinking the fence of space and time were merely picket.

Right away I wanted in on the conversation, and, handed off from one writer to the next, soon made the acquaintance of a crowd of fine and fiercely opinionated talkers. There was Karel Čapek, a gimlet-eyed Czech who relished the human comedy he found in the garden, and Margery Fish, a gentle Englishwoman whose cottage garden in Somerset told the story of a marriage. Closer to home, there was Katharine White in Maine, reading her January harvest of seed catalogues as a species of literature; Charles Dudley Warner in Hartford, setting himself up as the Mark Twain of American horticulture; and Alice Morse Earle in Massachusetts bringing an almost Jamesian regard to the social swirl of her perennial border. (The peony, Earle wrote, "always looks like a well-dressed, well-shod, well-gloved girl of birth, breeding, and of equal good taste and good health; a girl who can swim and hike and play golf. . . .")

Most of these essayists were moonlighting in the garden, which usually meant they were fired with the enthusiasm of the amateur and the liberty of the writer cultivating a piece of ground some distance from literature's main thoroughfares. Their voices could be by turns personal and prescriptive, diffident and prickly, and, somehow, both self-deprecating and incontrovertible at the same time. Since these writers often came to the subject from elsewhere, they were particularly good at drawing unexpected lines of connection between what was going on in their gardens and the seemingly distant realms of politics, art, sex, class, even morality. I discovered that as soon as one got past the how-to volumes written by experts, and the illustrated coffee-table tomes of garden porn, the garden bookshelf brimmed with the sort of quirky, sui generis writing often produced by a good mind operating in a small space.

And so I read to garden, and gardened to read, counting myself lucky for having stumbled on a sideline with such a lively and lasting literature. For what other pastime has spawned so many fine books? Only fly-fishing comes even close. (Numismatics? Woodworking? Macrame? Come on!) Which is probably no accident: for gardening, like angling, engages us with the natural world, as actors rather than passive spectators. Both put us smack on the frontier between nature and culture, which is always an interesting place for a writer to stand. And both literary traditions pose practical and philosophical questions about how we might better go about rhyming our desires with nature's ways, questions that only grow more urgent with time.

The books I've chosen for this series are the classics that form the backbone of this tradition. What you won't find on this particular shelf are reference works and strictly how-to books; there's plenty of how-to here, but the emphasis is more along the lines of how-to-think-about-it than how-to-do-it. Even the oldest among them will be contemporary in the best sense, offering a still-vibrant voice in the back-fence conversation gardeners have been conducting at least since the time of Pliny. I'm not sure whether or not we should be surprised by this, but a great many of the issues that engaged Pliny are the same ones that centuries later would engage Alexander Pope and Vita Sackville-West, Gertrude Jekyll and Eleanor Perényi, Charles Dudley Warner and Karel Čapek, and will no doubt engage gardeners centuries hence. I'm thinking of the power of plants to change us in mind and body, the gratuitous beauty of a flower, the moral lessons of the pest, the ancient language of landscape design, and the endlessly engrossing ways that cultivating a garden attaches a body to the earth.

Introduction

Dominique Browning

I can no longer remember what clever soul introduced me to the works of Richardson Wright, but I probably didn't thank the person enough. I read *The Gardener's Bed-Book* as I began my job as editor in chief of *House & Garden,* and I was promptly smitten. This was the best sort of pillow talk—mercurial, passionate, irascible, sophisticated, outrageous, infuriating, vulnerable, funny, and sweet. The sort of pillow talk that sends you to sleep with a smile playing on your lips.

I proceeded to corner the market—indeed, for a while, I suspect, I was the entire market—on early editions of Wright's books; they became one of my favorite offerings to friends. Wright was prolific; he wrote twenty-eight books, and edited or contributed to nearly a dozen more. The bed-books are my favorites: *The Gardener's Bed-Book,* published in 1929, was followed by *The Bed-Book of Travel, Another Gardener's Bed-Book,* and *The Bed-Book of Eating and Drinking.* From these titles alone you can see what sort of fellow Wright was. Add to his gardening mania a sideline expertise in Russian history and politics (he began his career as a newspaperman, reporting from Siberia and Manchuria, and wrote three books about Russia—

four, if you count a collection of essays marking the centennial of the birth of a *nonexistent* Russian author, complete with bibliography) and a fascination with the margins of American history and culture, in particular with stories of oddballs, vagabonds, and vagrants (culminating in a book called *Grandfather Was Queer,* a history of eccentrics, and another called *Hawkers and Walkers,* a collection of pre–Civil War tales about preachers and strolling peddlers, foreshadowing the current academic fixation on history told through the commonplace). Wright was a gentleman of breeding and discernment. He was worldly, and at the same time he was devoted to the domestic arts. He believed in living well, and thinking large. They don't make too many like him.

Richardson Wright was the editor in chief of *House & Garden* for nearly thirty-five years, beginning in 1914 when he was twenty-eight years old—that alone was a noteworthy accomplishment in the magazine business. During his tenure, Wright wrote about flappers and Reno divorces; postwar affluence; Prohibition; a plant-quarantine law that kept many plants out of the United States; the economic collapse of the Great Depression; the stirrings of a suburban lifestyle; a romance with the Gentleman Farmer; World War II; Victory gardens.

The very idea of a bed-book is charming. Like a devotional, a book of prayers, or a book of Thoughts for a Day, such as the one Tolstoy put together of his favorite quotes, *The Gardener's Bed-Book* is meant to be read in bits, chronologically, with an entry supplied for each day of the year. Each day's meditation of a few paragraphs is followed by a sentence or two of practical advice; each month ends with a "Long Piece." Every reader will pick a favorite from these eleven pieces (no such entry for December). With May's essay, "Men as Trees Walking," I find Wright at his most passionately spiritual, but it would be hard to choose that piece over "And So to Bed," the July essay on learning to "enjoy the habits of living a little less efficiently."

Lest today's reader, bombarded with publications filled with "To Do, Today" lists, be put off—thinking Wright's must be the sort of advice that only obsessive personalities with a lot of money and servants appreciate (and give)—I assure you that his suggestions are typically of the airy, vague, and hope-releasing sort. I am the most sluggish sort of gardener, who would rather read about digging than dig, but Wright inspires, and never induces guilt. "Tomorrow see that your evergreens are freed from clinging snow." (Anyone can handle that.) "Sometime in the next three months prune your grapes." (And who doesn't have a grape arbor? Or three months to think about building one?) "The history of gardening makes fascinating reading. Start with the 1st Chapter of Genesis and work upward." (Not a bad idea at all.) "Adjust the cold frame sashes on a wintry morning to give everyone a breath of fresh air." (No cold frames? Get some fresh air yourself.) There is something soothing about any suggestion that begins with "Tomorrow."

Wright's tone throughout *The Gardener's Bed-Book* is warm, friendly, and unguarded; he writes as though he were chatting with an intimate; and though you are seduced by February, and feel you know him quite well by July, it is difficult, by December, to recall any specifics about his life. You find yourself so beguiled by the intricacy, and eccentricity, of his reflections that you hardly realize you have no idea who you are with or where you are. Only by my third or fourth reading was I coolheaded enough to notice that Wright grew up in "an old household" in Philadelphia, of Scottish-Irish and Quaker ancestors; his grandparents lived with his family. He is in his early forties when he writes the first bed-book, and is brooding a bit about middle age. He takes pleasure in his gin rickey—the "piously arid" be damned. He is married, and refers to his wife only as "She"; he seems wry, fond, loving, admiring, and grumpy about "Her." She is from Boston. There do not seem to be children about the place. Wright believes there are five things worth working for: "pleasure, power, money, learning, and God." These are all to be found in gardening. He is a man who loves old damask, old vellum, old bindings, old wine, and old brick walls. Every winter, he paints all his garden tools blue, "the blue of French flag-poles"; he has a gardener's aversion to lending them (the blue, perhaps, wards off evil requests). He cannot drive, does not want to learn, and heaps blessings on the inspector who tells him he will never be given a license, as he is a menace to other drivers. He is the sort of guy who goes berserk in grocery and household appliance stores; he finds elegant packaging and clever, useless gadgets irresistible. He treasures the "quaint possessions" he has, no matter how outmoded or misshapen or fussy they may seem to Her; such things are "necessary to those of us who are old sticks."

And Wright is funny. He leaves directions in his will that he is to be buried with his trowel in his hand, resting on his chest (the trowel presumably painted a celestial blue; who knows about the covetous glances of heavenly gardeners?)—the way soldiers were once buried with their swords, or kings with their scepters. He sends his brothers-in-law gift-wrapped boxes of shredded cow manure for Christmas, which sit under the tree until the stench shows his hand—and drives the family into a rage. He makes a centerpiece for the holiday dinner table of a basket filled with newborn puppies, so small they cannot squirm out; they have festive red bows with little bells tied around their necks, and they are nestled in mounds of warm, soft, snow-white flannel. The whole thing is hedged with holly, and silver candelabra are placed at either end of this strange Nativity scene.

The Wrights live in an old farmhouse in Silver Mine, Connecticut, a house that is constantly referred to as a work-in-progress, in need of rescue. It is hard to see what the house looks like, exactly, but what is *in* the house is described in ornate detail: one nutty collection after another. There is a room filled with maps and portraits of peddlers; another filled with flower pictures; another with barometers; another with bells from sleds and harnesses and collars and churches and temples. Wright has a horror of buzzers, and at dinner, he signals the end of a course with a small bell from the harness of a pony he rode across the Siberian steppes. The basement is filled with "shelves of preserves, the barrel of cider, the wine in its cask, the coal in its bin, the rat trap baited. Show me a man's cellar in Autumn and I'll tell you the sort of man he is." His root cellar in winter is stocked with apples, pears, onions, and cabbage, its "abundant effluvium" rising from the ample bins.

If the house is in dim shadow, it is virtually impossible to see the shape of Wright's garden. It seems to have covered several acres, at least. He has a barn somewhere on the grounds in which he keeps furniture and pigs; once he named a brood after his friends, but after they protested (the friends, not the pigs) he named them (the pigs, not the friends) after French perfumes—"Ashes of Desire; Qui-es-tu?" There is an orchard and fifty kinds of hardy climbing roses, and three gigantic elms. Wright took a train to work in town, and became miserable in the months of short days when he came home in the dark and could not see his garden.

Wright is an avowed horticulturalist, and cares more for individual plants than for garden design. He tells us his garden is "a hectic jumble." Horticulturalists may have shambolic beds, but, Wright says, perhaps defensively, their gardens have much more personality. And the gardeners have more fun. Wright does seem to know his plants. About tuberose, he says, "it appears to be the flower of forgotten lovers, lovers sufficiently forgotten to be safe." About doubling in flowers, like the ruffled asters, hollyhocks, and iris, which seems to have become the horticultural rage: "they have a tawdry air, like a stout woman plastered over with too many jewels." Nemesia brings out the ardent side; it is "a shy beauty . . . the sort of flower you love to touch."

He seems to have been busy all the time. Wright was, defiantly, a hands-in-dirt gardener. He had some help, but in the course of twelve months, it is him we see at work, coddling the seedlings; mixing crushed oyster shell into peat and sand; disbudding annuals; feeding the houseplants sheep manure; collecting wood for bean poles; sorting out the shriveled gladiola bulbs and dahlia tubers wintering in the basement; making labels for perennials; pinching green caterpillars off tomatoes and dropping them into cans of kerosene; saving ash from the fireplace for the asters; creating recipes for mulches. He knows about the important things in life: roots, beds, food.

He is writing at a time when "the most intelligent and zealous gardening in this country is now being done by women"; he is self-conscious, and slightly unnerved, at finding himself the lone male at garden club meetings and horticultural lectures. He is constantly deriding "the great mediocrity who play golf," but you sense that he would love to have some of those numskulls join him behind a wheelbarrow. Golfers aren't the only things that set him off. He is crotchety about American seed catalogues; they look like "children's primers." He complains about the dearth of sedum varieties available in this country—a mere nineteen from his best nurseryman, when five hundred exist. He would like to commit "justifiable homicide" on those gardeners who say, about everything in any other gardener's beds, "Oh, yes, I have that." People who buy special clothes for weeding and tilling earn withering disdain. He reserves a sly, cutting tone for the gentleman farmer who invests in a "landscape cow" to decorate his empty meadow. And Wright has a sharp eye—and sharp tongue—for social pretension, particularly when spotted in the membership lists of our most esteemed garden clubs. One of the wellsprings of delight in gardening, for him, is its democratic nature. Wright is dyspeptic, brooding, in the dead of winter; his mood lightens in spring; he is in a state of manic joy in June; mellow and weary in autumn; and as the holiday season unfurls, he is positively rhapsodic. It is clear, by December, that gardens have everything to do with matters of the soul, once you are done with matters of seed.

One of the pleasures of curling up with *The Gardener's Bed-Book* is imagining yourself into another sort of life, in another sort of time. Yes, and we may as well face it, it is startling, and upsetting, to hit the jarring reference to "Japs," or, once, to "Nigger Flowers," and even Wright seems to wince as he uses this once-common appellation for a plant. He is a man of his time and his class. And most of their prejudices. Such crude locutions aside—and may we be spared this damning look back when our time comes—Wright's world is mostly one of gentility, directness, and hope. It is a quieter and slower world, one that seems less complicated, if just as troubled, as our own. It is a world of bounty and beauty springing from the garden, and with those come a belief in grace, reached by the smallest of steps, grown from the tiniest of seeds. It is not a world beyond our reach.

The Gardener's Bed-Book begins with a meditation on marriage and the difficulties of reading in bed. Marriage is mentioned throughout the book, time and again; it is a subject Wright approaches with a glancing, biting wit. Yet you sense you are in the presence of a true romantic. She never goes into the garden, and for all we are told, She has nothing to do with its cultivation. He, devotedly, makes little offerings to Her from the garden; "it is my custom," he writes in June, "to bring Her the first flowers as they appear—the first Lady Tulips and Muscari and Crocus, the first Pansies and sprigs of Arabis and Creeping Phlox and Aubretia, the first Narcissus and so on through the seasons till the first of the Chrysanthemums." One day he brings Her the first of a golden, hybrid tea rose that he had years earlier helped name. She is entranced by its fragrant beauty, and as a way of thanking him, says, "I would rather have one Rose each day than all the other junk in your garden."

Her remark took my breath away. Although he and She may well have absorbed it into the daily marital give-and-take, I quickly averted my eyes from the page, feeling cut to the quick for Richardson Wright. Did She not appreciate how lucky She was, to have a fellow labor in the garden, and bring Her a flower at the end of the day? Did She think such husbands grow on trees?

He takes it with his usual unflappable poise. "And she was right . . ." he says. Spineless? Defeated? Or simply, always, a gentleman, and so superior, in his gracious deflection of the blow. How revealing, the murmured thoughts of bedtime. A garden book ought to be about all the gritty bits of life: sand and slugs and manure and mayhem, as much as about love and death. Just as a rose has its thorns, so will pillow talk have its cutting moments. This is what comes of taking to your bed such an open, unreserved, joyful, and interesting heart.

DOMINIQUE BROWNING is the editor in chief of *House & Garden,* and the author of *Around the House and in the Garden: A Memoir of Heartbreak, Healing, and Home Improvement.* Her new book, *Paths of Desire: The Passions of a Suburban Gardener,* is due out in 2004.

IN MEMORIAM

MATER DELECTISSIMA

SURGE, ILLUMARE, QUIA

VENIT LUMEN TUUM

FOREWORD

HOW TO READ IN BED AND STILL REMAIN HAPPILY MARRIED

Some years ago I made a serious investigation among people who had survived the first trying seven years of married life as to what brought on their first spat. Invariably they confessed to having struck this initial reef when one wanted to read in bed and the other wanted the light out.

The first six months the solicitous admonition runs, "Dear, you'll strain your eyes if you read any longer." The next six months it goes wearily, "Don't you think you ought to stop reading now?" The subsequent six, "Isn't it time to put out the light?" Finally, after the second year, that voice barks, "Put out that light!!!" And if, after this, some solution for reading in bed isn't found, the male of the species had better quietly begin saving up alimony.

Now the solution is simple. Read her (or him) to sleep first. The droning of your voice having proven completely soporific, then quietly pull out your own book from under the pillow. And, lest you should be suddenly caught and have to clamp the book shut and snap off the light, without finishing the train of thought, let your own book be in little pieces, small morsels that can be snatched surreptitiously, such as this Bed-Book.

RICHARDSON WRIGHT

Silver Mine
Connecticut
1 January 1929

THE GARDENER'S BED-BOOK

THE MONTH OF JANUARY

1. BLESSED BE GOD! Samuel Pepys (and an amusing and lecherous young man he was) opened the first page of his diary, saw to it that his quill was sharpened and wrote: "Blessed be God!" Having made this pious gesture, he started setting down the day-to-day occurrences of his life, his observations and his worries and the major and minor peccadilloes into which his amorous nature led him. How much poorer would the world be had he not done so!

The keeping of diaries is a form of vanity. That annals of our obscure doings should be preserved is a silly hope. Yet thousands of people have kept journals of just such obscurities, kept them year in and year out. Some say that in the rush of contemporary life this is impossible, that keeping a journal is the habit of a more leisurely age. I do not think so. Contemporary life is always hectic. Leisure is really known only to those whose days are crowded and fast-moving. The age has nothing to do with it. It all depends on the mind of the diarist. Affection, faith, learning, gentleness—these are the qualities of mind. It all depends on the sort of person you are. Slightly self-centered, and yet curious about life, not too old or too young, a little on the stout side, a lover of good things to eat and drink and of the beauty of women—one who enjoys tidbits of innocent gossip, one who forgives his enemies and is merciful to animals—such are the components of the ideal diarist.

Keeping a journal, besides being a forgivable vanity, is also an act of devotion. Lovers keep journals of their meetings, sailors of their adventures, soldiers of their battles, courtiers of their day at court, students of their discoveries—each man after his own heart.

To some of us, gardens and gardening are among the precious things of life. To us it means a great deal when the first Crocus drills through the icy soil, when the first Rose unfolds its silken petals, when there is rain or wind or sleet or hail. These matters that have to do with the things we love mean much to us, and we set down their occurring in little books at which no other eye will look.

Many years ago when first I started gardening seriously, I began also keeping a garden journal, and from that day to this my trafficking with green growing things has been recorded, together with whatever rural and domestic sentiments come to me.

Oddly enough, when I started writing in that first journal the opening words were those that Pepys used, and ever since (though I do not blush to own it) that phrase begins and ends the record of each gardening year. So—"Blessed be God!"

Resolve that, unless you can afford an extra gardener to watch it, you'll never let Plume Poppy, Bocconia Cordata, *loose in your garden.*

2. TREES OF LIFE. In many ways may a man seek immortality, and one of the pleasantest is to plant trees. This realization came to me the other day on a Long Island estate. The master of the house is a busy man, engrossed most of the time in international money affairs. Being endowed with sufficient of this world's goods, he is able to satisfy his whims. And although he is already known for kindnesses that will live after him, he was unable to find in them a guarantee of remembrance. So he decided to turn his estate into an arboretum. He began studying trees. From this study he went on to searching for rare and interesting species. And now gradually he is assembling a collection of which he can be proud. He is finding a peculiar satisfaction in the knowledge that long after he is gone, men and women will look upon the noble beauty of those trees, that their leafy arms will shelter children from the blistering heat of Summer, and for innumerable Autumns their red and russet mantles will delight the eye. His trees remind me of the trees the Apocalypse speaks of—the trees that grow beside the River of the Water of Life, whose leaves are for the healing of the nations.

Too much overhead watering ruins house plants. Instead, set the pots for an hour in a shallow pan of water.

3. LAYING DOWN AN ELM. Apropos of the previous arboreal sentiment, we might begin a custom of marking family anniversaries by setting out

trees. In England, when a son is born, the father of the house lays down an especially fine vintage of wine, and on the lad's reaching his majority, this is brought forth for the celebration. The piously arid of this country having forbidden us such innocently dissolute joy, why not set out a tree—lay down an Elm, with the fond hope that we'll still own the property when the lad reaches twenty-one and can sit under its shade to drink the beverages that a more enlightened future generation may then permit us?

Put up another feeding station for birds, but see that it is out of the reach of cats.

4. DOMESTICALITIES. In an old English diary that has come to light recently the author made a great point of setting down what he termed "domesticalities," observations on the everyday happenings of the household that brought a sense of well-being. We tried the idea the other night on a group of people: asked them what domesticalities they most enjoyed. Their answers focused on two strangely contrasted affairs. One was the pleasure of pulling off old wall papers and the other was the finality of hanging up a dish towel!

If you ever have taken over an old house and set about to renovate it, you will remember the peculiarly destructive joy that comes with tearing off old wall paper. It has the persistent attraction of a dish of salted nuts. You can't help picking at it! Some comes off with a roar in long strips, other stubborn bits must be soaked and scraped off patiently. There is a fierce iconoclastic sense of triumph that sweeps over one when the last scrap of old paper has disappeared and the walls stand naked and pockmarked.

The finality of the dish towel is something quite different. The various processes of washing and wiping having been gone through, the scouring of sink and kitchen table—then the dish towel is folded over its rack. Few things in this world give such a sense of finality. The artist's last brush stroke to the picture, the author's final polishing of the manuscript, the composer's completing notes to the score—these are endings that *are* endings. So is the final hanging up of the dish towel. Like a domestic goddess, the housewife then contemplates her labors, and seeing that they are good, may rest from them.

Between now and the first of March prune your grapes.

5. THE POSSESSIVE BLUE. I have a distinct aversion to lending garden tools, and lest there should be any doubt about it and any discussion, all the tools are painted a special color. Blue is my color—the blue of French flag-poles. In autumn, when garden work is over, the tools are gathered into the barn and subjected to a cleaning. In January they are given their coat of distinctive paint, and in spring, when we are ready to start work again, they are hauled forth—from the noble blue wheelbarrow to the humblest blue trowel—all wearing my color the way a jockey wears his master's.

Painted thus, few tools are lost during the working season—and few are borrowed.

Save wood ashes from open fires to work in around Asters.

6. AS FOR MAID SERVANTS. Dipping into some old books recently, I found two quaint references to maid servants. One was a law of the time of James I, wherein it was enacted that "no servant may toy with the maids under pain of fourpence." Not a staggering fine for such domestic trifling! The other was in a book of devotion written during the plague of London by Thomas Dekker, the dramatist, and called "Foure Birds of Noah's Arke." Some of the petitions are quite moving, for example, this prayer for a maid: whose beauty was rather for use than for parade: "Crown my Virgin-state with chaste and religious thoughts: and so temper my desires, that the wanton pleasures of the flesh may not drown in mee the heavenly treasures of the Spirit. . . So thou accounted mee fair, I care not how ugly I appeare to the world. And for that I am but poore, so blesse mee, that I may preserve my fame: for an honest reputation is to a maiden an ample dowry."

A nicotine spray will eliminate aphids from house plants. Wash the foliage occasionally.

7. A PLANT FOR SATELLITE CITIES. The Rubber Plant, known learnedly to nurserymen as *Ficus elastica,* will be with us so long as there are satellite cities, so long as there are Brooklyns and Camdens and Hobokens and St. Pauls. Once on

a time, in Boston, when accompanied by a plaster cast of Winged Victory, it marked the zenith of respectability. Today you can find it flourishing and cherished in the parlors and back summer porches of these satellite cities, and maiden ladies meticulously wash its shiny leaves with milk. Liberty Hyde Bailey estimates that upwards of 100,000 of these plants are sold each year, but he ventures on no estimate of the milk consumed for their bathing. An enterprising milk man might build up a thriving trade if he whispered it into the backdoors of these urban purlieus that his milk was especially suited for the Rubber Plant. For a matter of fact giving this lacteal diet is merely a work of supererogation. What the leaves should be washed with, when scale insects appear, is smelly sudsy fish oil soap, which, of course, isn't half so romantic as milk.

Tomorrow see that your evergreens are freed from clinging snow which might break them down.

8. FRAGRANCES. If you have recently come into the proud ownership of a pine-paneled room and wish your visitors not to forget it, dab Oil of Pine on the paneling before they arrive, and then watch them sniff. Though volatile, this Pine Oil will fling about the room the sweet fragrances of the forest for several hours, and your guests will be satisfactorily mystified.

In Versailles an artist of our acquaintance stained a paneled hallway with "Kitchen Bouquet" —that aromatic mixture of herbs all good cooks use in soup. The solution gave a soft brown tint to the wood and for many weeks afterward that corridor afforded the nostrils the sensation of walking in a herb garden—or bending over a bowl of *Petite Marmite.*

A good indoor job is painting old plant labels. Buy new ones now.

9. THE TRUTH AND ANTIQUARIANS. Living as we do in the palpitating center of New England's antique belt, I have been nursing a dream (which will probably never be realized) and that is to live long enough to meet a dealer in antiques who does not think—and say—that all other dealers in antiques are undependable and discredited. Apparently no good can ever come out of this Nazareth of antiquities. And I wonder why. Can it be (which Heaven forbid!) that these dealers sell freshly-made reproductions for veritable old pieces? Do they sit up nights concocting the romance and genealogy of this highboy and that chair, with which to impress and deceive gullible purchasers? Do they scour the hinterlands for old wood with which to make their ancient pieces?

Thus do wicked customs follow naturally on prior bad habits. As his grandfather was bent so is the antiquarian inclined. Scarcely had Connecticut given up making wooden nutmegs than she went into the antique business.

If tomorrow is sunny, tilt the cold frame sash slightly and let the plants have fresh air.

10. Prophets Without Honor. Among English gardeners there is a growing interest in raising flowers gathered from all corners of the British Empire. I've heard patriotic John Bulls speak of it as "Empire Gardening." A quaint thought, that, but one not calculated to take root here. First, we haven't the empire; and secondly, since our garden heritage is mainly British, it would never occur to us—save in the case of rabidly nationalistic souls—to make an All-American garden. It could be done, but not easily. For example: a Loving Reader last year wrote me asking where she could buy seed of the common American Field Daisy. For weeks I searched seed catalogues and combed the seedsmen and finally was obliged to direct this ardent soul to Henri Correvon in Geneva. M. Correvon has a great respect for our common American flowers. One of his choicest possessions, which he shows with great pride to all visitors, is a solitary specimen of Skunk Cabbage! Indeed, were I to start an All-American garden I would begin it in England, Germany and Switzerland. For the prophet without honor in his home town isn't a patch compared to the common American wild flower on its native heath.

Having almost recovered from Christmas bills, you are now ready for the temptations offered by the new catalogues.

11. No Wonder They Wilted. Solomon may have been puzzled by the way of a man with a maid and a snake on a rock, but what puzzles

me is the way of some women with flowers. With cut flowers especially.

The other night I chanced to be in a New York apartment and listened to the complaints of a young woman who despaired of keeping her flowers fresh. Some one had told her that when they began to wilt all she had to do was to drop an Aspirin tablet into each vase. Now this particular young woman is rather vague about *materia medica*. She forgot what kind of tablet she was told to use. So she dropped in the first kind that her hand lighted on in the medicine closet. And the flowers didn't revive.

Being of a curious mind, I asked, "Just what was it you put in the water?" She produced the bottle. It was medicine, but scarcely the right kind. She had used chocolate-coated cascara tablets!

Bring a few pans of bulbs indoors for forcing in a sunny window.

12. THE BEAM IN THINE EYE. There are two presumptions that may be forgiven. One is to stir another man's fire; the other is to pull the obvious weeds in another man's garden. And of these two, stirring the fire is least apt to cause resentment. Some visitors cannot resist the allure of toying with fire-tongs. These are usually people who have an excellent opinion of themselves as makers of fires. I accept their incendiary presumption with hospitable complaisance. But let a caller's eye catch the Pigweed amid the Phlox, let him

casually lean over and pluck it out, and I'm on the verge of saying, "What bad manners!" The mote that is in thy brother's eye, and which we are told we should leave strictly alone until we have first removed the beam from our own, is a mere trifle compared with the weed in a stranger's garden.

Now is the season for the winter spraying of fruit trees and shrubs that are prone to scale.

13. LA CHAISE PIERCE. Why is it that some people have such a horror of utilitarian things? Why do they think that because an object is primarily useful it must be hidden? The telephone, for example. It makes no pretences. It is a useful, necessary object. And yet we find it secreted in cabinets, in books, and clothed with the skirts of decadent dolls. This sort of thing belongs to Victorian days when nude statues were swathed with clothes. Even more offensive is the manner in which decorators are disguising an intimate and necessary plumbing fixture. How the shades of Louis Seize would weep to see to what base uses his lovely chairs are put! And yet Time has brought its revenge, for it was this monarch who first discovered that his lovely chairs could be put to such a base use. . . . I believe that, thus enthroned, he used to hold levees.

Tomorrow, to arouse your appetite for breakfast, make the rounds of your garden and lop off broken branches from trees.

14. BUXUS GETS INTO THE SOCIAL REGISTER. A new form of ostentation has appeared. Among certain classes, once on a time, the abundance and size of one's diamonds constituted a scale of social rating. That sort of display is now considered the very nadir of bad taste. Its place has been taken by—guess what? Boxwood. Good, old-fashioned *Buxus sempervirens,* the sort of Boxwood you see growing in great clumps by ancient houses.

About ten years ago landscape architects began realizing its beauty. Nurserymen scoured the countryside for specimens. Many a mortgage on the old home was lifted when decrepit owners parted with their Box bushes. And what a lovely thing a Box clump is—so gentle, so rounded, so sedate and contented, so very wise looking. Pass old Box, and it seems to impart a blessing to you.

Used judiciously, Box gives a garden an atmosphere no other plant can contribute; used indiscriminately, it becomes commonplace and vulgar. Today at luncheons you hear women boast of the number and size of their Box bushes and the Box hedges that cost their husbands a fortune. One almost wishes they would go back to diamonds.

Fruit stored in the root cellar should be examined now and the unsound discarded.

15. THOSE LITTLE SLITS. One type of window always fascinates me—those little half-windows below the eaves of Colonial houses. You

find them all through New York State and New England. Some are sternly simple and some have elaborate frames. In New York are windows partly covered with an edging of lattice, vaguely reminiscent of Mr. Chippendale's Chinese chairs, and up in Maine they even sport carved garlands that appear very frivolous and French in that stern and rock-bound State.

To my way of thinking, rooms with such tiny windows are no rooms at all. Of course some of the houses have full-size windows at the ends so that these upstairs rooms cannot be so badly ventilated and lighted. An older generation, which didn't set as much store by fresh night air as we, had its being in these rooms, and quite a healthy being it was. The children slept up there under the eaves—cold as Greenland in Winter and stifling hot in Summer. And they could sit down on the floor and peer through these slits upon the big world beyond.

Start a garden note book in which to jot down ideas found in your winter garden reading.

16. LILIPUTIAN LOVES. We Americans are very much impressed by size. This can be noted in many ways but in none is it more pronounced than in the garden. The biggest ear of Corn, the largest Carrot, the tallest Dahlia, awaken our admiration. This, perhaps, is all right for some people, but we decline to be classed with them. For us the small ear of Corn is preferable if it

is succulent, the small Peas if they are sweet, the tiny Carrot if it is tender, and as for flowers—we like them little and perfect. Better the diminutive beauty of a few Forget-me-nots and Primulas, the amusing colors of mignon Zinnias, the fragile grace of snowy Arabis and the little flowers of Thyme. If we were to bring a tribute from our garden to one of whom we were fond, would it be a gargantuan African Marigold and the biggest of the Roses? No, it would be those flowers that are little and perfect.

Hack out a frozen clump of Rhubarb and plant it in a box of earth in a warm cellar —thus enjoying your Pie Plant ahead of time.

17. THE HEIGHT OF FLORAL LUXURY. To pick one's own Nectarines in Winter off a glass house wall may be the dream of many a horticultural Maecenas, but the man I envied many a day was the lucky fellow in Porto Rico who went in for Orchid gardening. His place was on a heavily wooded slope that had been planted to jungle trees, with the reeling heads of Cocoanut Palms towering above. Poinsettias burned fiery holes in the undergrowth and Creeping Fig mantled the arbor pillars and Bougainvillea and Clerodendron draped its crossbars. Things that with us in New England were tiny plants grew to gargantuan size under the tropical rains and heat. And things we could never dream of owning grew abundantly here. For when this garden's

owner had a spare day, he went into the jungle to collect Orchids, and in many a tropical forest men stalked rare plants for him. On every tree, in hanging boxes, in shoals through the undergrowth he planted his Orchids. Scarcely a week but a new one would appear. And the pinnacle of his Orchid attainment was reached when he fastened on the tree close to his breakfast porch twelve orchids so selected that one would bloom each month. There would never be a day throughout the year when he could not drink his morning *café con leche* without the companionship of an Orchid. That is my idea of the height of floral luxury.

Since you never do have enough of them, make some more flats tomorrow.

18. GARROTING WIRES. Having just found a small Flowering Crabapple tree strangling itself, I learned the evil of tight tag wires. Copper is used on these tags because it lasts, but it also can cut like a knife: first the bark, then the cambium, then the heart of the stem itself. When trees and shrubs come from a nursery see that the wire on the name tag is loosened, and each year give it a glance. Had I done this, my garden would be richer by one *Malus floribundus.*

On bitterly cold nights draw the curtains behind the house plants in the plant window.

19. OF VIOLAS. Some flowers are like women who take their jewels out of the safe deposit box

only on rare and important occasions; others wear them all the time. If you want to see the jewels of some, you must be on hand at the right time. How much more gratifying are those that persist in flowering week after week and month after month! Such are the Violas. From the earliest days of Spring to the hot hours of July a patch of Violas flowered in my little rockery, clouds of yellow and pale blue and purple and the lavender and white tints of *V. papilio*. Never did they cease radiating beauty. Another year, and I shall have more of them. Cuttings will be rooted and seed sown, and next Spring the border edges will flash their colors in long ribbons, like a gay binding on a curtain! England and Scotland have long since appreciated the Viola. Why doesn't some enthusiastic specialist undertake to arouse interest in it here? Apart from Jersey Gem (which is all its name implies) and its larger cousin, Jersey Jewel, I can recall no new Violas during recent years which have come from America.

Having read your catalogues and spent imaginary millions, begin now to write down what you actually plan to buy.

20. BED AND BOARD. Is there a decay of privacy coming over the rural American home? Has the automobile turned many of our estimable country folk into potential innkeepers? Motoring up through New England last Fall scarcely a house we passed but flaunted the sign "Tourists Accommodated." Has the spare bedroom now

taken on a new lease of life? And will the front parlor, where no one was allowed, save for weddings and funerals, be flung open to every passing stranger?

All tree pruning should be finished before the end of this month.

21. HOW TO LOOK A SEED CATALOGUE IN THE EYE. There was once a very wise man, versed in such matters, who said (Scupoli was his name, Laurence Scupoli) that some temptations we should flee from as from the plague, and others that we should stand up and look squarely in the eye. Into the latter category fall those annual garden temptations, the seed catalogues.

After several seasons of gardening, most of us know them by heart; in fact, if some wise and enterprising seedsman should write a new kind of catalogue, he will make his everlasting fortune. We read the descriptions over and over again, the way children repeat "Peter Rabbit." We never seem to tire.

And each Spring, catalogue by catalogue, we order far more seed than we need or can use or even can afford. This is silly of us and wasteful. We buy alleged "novelties" that are no novelties at all; we load up on annuals and plunge in perennials, and when we are called to account for it by the economical member of the family, our excuses are lame indeed.

Last year I vowed I would be stern about it. I promised myself that I would stand up like a man, square my shoulders and stare that temptation of seed catalogues out of countenance. . . . Well, the catalogues arrived. I read them all. I braced my shoulders. I looked them squarely in the eye. Then I winked.

Both chicken manure and wood ashes should be stored in a dry place until you need them in the Spring. Don't mix them.

22. HOWITZERS. Isn't it about time we dispensed with the howitzers? Following the war, our Congressmen demonstrated ardent patriotism by distributing to their constituent towns sundry howitzers, trench mortars and decrepit anti-airplane guns. They scattered them about lavishly, the way they used to give flower seeds. In due course and with elaborate ceremony this artillery was installed in public squares. Then the town went about its business.

Today, as you pass through small towns and encounter these militaristic displays, you feel rather sorry for them, sorry for the towns. It seems such utter nonsense, such thoroughly bad taste, that the placid beauty, the calm, serene, every-day current of life should have to break against such ugly reminders. Their camouflage pierced with rust, their surroundings usually shabby and neglected, you realize now that their being placed there was a great mistake. Certainly the men who went through the horrors of the war do not care to be reminded of it, and to the rest of the people these grim and ugly decorations mean little or nothing. Either let us dispense with our howitzers or keep them and their surroundings in order.

About this season you should look over the Gladiolus bulbs and Dahlia tubers to see that none are attacked by mildew or are shriveling.

23. RUSHING LILIES. In the first flush of enthusiasm for Lilies many enthusiastic amateurs make the mistake of growing as many kinds as are available without regard for their requirements. And inevitably they meet defeat. The Lilies fail to prosper. Many of them succumb to disease. And the whole family is given a black eye.

This has always been the history of any flower suddenly accorded a popular reception. It has happened with the Rose and the Iris. We are apt to "rush" our flowers. Not until a study is made of the dependable kinds of Lilies for our varied climates can Lily specialization pass beyond the occasional gardens of highly-skilled amateurs and growers. The difficulty lies not so much with the Lily itself as with our ignorance of its needs, idiosyncrasies and weaknesses. However, there are enough sorts that have been tried and proved to satisfy the most ambitious gardener. It is better to grow these few well than to attempt a wide range of the miffy and difficult kinds.

Even this early, mulches may be put on lawns—tobacco stems, peat moss and commercial humus being the safest.

24. Single-Track Gardening. Gardening should really be done in blinders. Its distractions are tempting and persistent, and only by stern exercise of will do I ever finish one job without being lured off to another. I am setting annuals into the empty spaces of a border, for example. Midway between cold frame and border an unweeded Iris bed catches my eye. Down goes the flat of seedlings and, before I'm aware of it, I'm engrossed in the weed-choked Iris.

Since blinders are missing from my garden equipment I've had to make a list each working day of those things to be done that day. If the Iris remains unweeded, I merely look the other way when I pass. And being reproached for its untidiness, I seek refuge in that excuse which my gardener uses whenever I speak of neglected tasks —"Sir," says he, "I had no instructions."

Order fertilizers and tools this month and thus avoid the rush of garden bills later on.

25. Death Comes for the Gardener. I like the pagan custom of burying a man with the symbol of his profession in his hand—the sceptre for the king, the sword for the soldier, the chalice for the priest. Then why not the trowel for the gardener? It would be pleasant to think that on Judgment Day you could tell the gardeners apart from all the others by the trowels they carry!

I have left directions (and I hope they are obeyed) that I am to be buried with my trowel in my hand, that "Slim Jim" I bought years ago at Barr's in Covent Garden and which has been my inseparable companion ever since. And lest this will appear incongruous, perhaps they will dress me in my gardening clothes—the corduroys and the grayed undershirt. At least my neighbors will recognize me!

Rabbits that might gnaw the bark of trees can be tempted from their evil ways by scattering around fruit and vegetable parings.

26. COSTUMES FOR COFFINS. Continuing these grisly thoughts, I am reminded of the Scotch miser (is that tautology?) who died and whose penurious family thought it would be gross extravagance to dress him in his Sunday suit. The only other costume they could find was a domino which he had saved from his youth. And in the domino, ruff and all, he went to meet the angels.

All these seemly and unseemly thoughts have come about through a strange present the garden afforded for the dead. An old artist died, a gentle, sweet old man, who painted as long as he could hold the brushes in his hand. And when he died his palette was laid on his coffin, like a king's crown, and in the thumbhole was stuck greenery from the Euonymous and the Hemlocks—the only green available in these winter days.

Even in winter an untidy garden is an eyesore. Keep mulches of straw and leaves well held in place.

27. A NOTE ON OBESITY. It fell to my lot once to address a garden club that had never been known to smile. Like John Wesley, it had evidently vowed not to indulge "in any the least levity of behavior, or in laughter; no, not for a moment." The topic was Rock Gardening, and I spoke of that amiable recreation in terms of obesity—how that two dozen *Thymus serpyllum coccineus,* four *Cerastium tomentosum,* a batch of *Saponaria ocymoides* and a good assortment of *Dianthus, Primulas, Erodiums, Muehlenbeckia* and *Saxifrages* properly cared for from Spring to Autumn, could conspire to melt the most stubborn flesh. Indeed, by the time the talk was over, the club had almost resolved to melt to the extent of a smile.

Alas, I was never asked to speak to that club again, so I shall never know whether its members have learned to laugh—or have now grown to mere shadows of their former selves.

This is an excellent season for carrying on garden correspondence, especially with people a little less favored than you.

28. THE SECOND-STORY HABIT. In Philadelphia houses and thence southward is found a goodly custom that can be recommended to all those who plan to build a home. It is providing for an upstairs living-room. The living-room downstairs often becomes a public place, but upstairs, it takes on the atmosphere of a home sanctuary. It can be as informal as you please, but it should be first of all comfortable. Let it have

good books aplenty, an open fire, and a back stairs leading from it to the kitchen so that of nights you can patter down *en déshabillé* to raid the icebox.

Hang a Cabbage from the ceiling of the chicken house and make your hens take vicarious exercise.

29. HORTICULTURISTS' GARDENS. Just as the sex of a hippopotamus is of interest only to another hippopotamus, so the garden of a horticulturist is of interest only to another horticulturist. For, be it remembered, the "landscaped" garden, the garden planted to make pretty pictures irrespective of its plant material, is one thing, and the horticulturist's quite another. In the latter, the interest centers in the plants themselves. Mine, I'm afraid, belongs to this category. I have seen the owners of picture gardens leave this place with their noses tilted up to the empyrean and muttering, "My God! And he calls *that* a garden!" I have also seen horticulturists crouch in rapture before my one solitary plant of the rare *Daphne Ghiraldi*. Though they are usually hectic jumbles, the gardens of horticulturists possess more personality than those that are professionally landscaped, and are longer remembered. In clothing the professional custom tailor-made look is desirable; it is not always desirable in gardens.

The history of gardening makes fascinating reading. Start with the 1st Chapter of Genesis and work upward.

30. THE CONTEMPLATIVE GARDENER. Among the many advantages of gardening is that its tranquillities afford one a chance to contemplate. So much of it is merely working with the hands, whilst the mind can wander, like the wind, where it lists. Gardening with brains is, most of the time, a silly and useless affectation. Once the work gets under way, the heart is aroused, imagination takes wings and placid contemplation leads the way over yonder hill. Perhaps it is because of its contemplative qualities that gardening has been so slow to attain popularity in America. Here, as some wag has said, we contemplate only one of two things—we contemplate marriage or we contemplate divorce.

One of the ways to rid yourself of the temptation to grow Mushrooms in your cellar is to yield to it.

31. UNREGARDED FOLK. "He hath exalted the humble and the meek" is no mere pious *cliché* in gardening, for often the seedlings that give the least promise produce flowers of the most exquisite beauty. This happens again and again with raising Dahlias from seed, and with Pyrethrums it is axiomatic that the weaker seedlings bear the most interesting blooms, whereas the robust kinds bear flowers that are only passable. I have found this also true of Petunias.

These notes, being made for my own garden in Connecticut, are applicable especially to that region.

LONG PIECE

SCENTS OF DOMESTICITY

ONE day last Autumn, as I pushed back the front door of a Long Island farmhouse, there assailed my nostrils such a savory odor as to transport me thousands of miles away. A symphony of spices. From Arabia. From Ceylon. From the islands in the Indian Ocean and the islands in the Caribbean Sea. Ginger and Cinnamon, Mace and Citron, Orange peel and Nutmeg and Clove, all compounded into a domestic perfume of unbelievable sweetness. As I went deeper into the house, the savor gained strength. I trailed it through living-room, dining room and pantry into the kitchen. And there, on the altar of gastronomy—the stove—a cook was tending the incense of his culinary devotion. He was making Chili Sauce.

In this house, which has an ancient and interesting lineage, life is lived much as it was generations ago. It is self-contained. The truck garden, the berry patch and the orchard provide most of the food the owners need the year around. The domestic arts are preserved. Bread is actually baked at home. And, if you wish it, the housewife can mount the loom and weave you homespun for your clothes. Down in the cellar are cupboards loaded with all manner of preserves and good things to eat through the long winter months.

You feel an air of security about such a house and about such people. You feel that their eyes have waited upon the Lord and He has given them their meat in due season. The smell of the Chili

Sauce was only one indication of it. A dozen other sweet domestic odors assured you of its stability. You felt that the tradition of the housewifely arts had been carried on there for a long time.

Doctors and physiologists and men who dabble in such things state that we cannot remember odors. We remember only the associations these odors bring back from past experiences. The odor of newly-baked bread, for example, we cannot remember; but we can recall (and pity the man who can't) a mother or a sister taking the loaves from the oven and turning them out on a board on the kitchen table to cool. Bacon frying is an incense worthy of men and gods. To some it means a camp in the North Woods, to others the awakening household. Coffee is another—not the wishywashy stuff of restaurants but the lusty, full-flavored coffee of home that makes your eyes blink when you drink it.

There are some (and absurd people they are) who object to the smell of onions cooking. But onions have a piquant perfume all their own. They seem like prophecies of good things to come. In fact that whole gamut of pre-dinner odors is one which modern inventions are fast stealing from the home. Once on a time sweet savors were wafted up through the house, whetting the appetite. Today, with ventilating systems in use, we come upon our meals abruptly. A door is flung open and dinner is sprung on us without warning. No wonder we have to drink cocktails to create an appetite.

Except in large houses or where there are large

families, many domestic smells that enriched the past are completely absent. There was the store-room, for example, where food stuffs were kept in quantity—barrels of flour, coffee, tea, packages of raisins and boxes of spices. That room had a grocery-store smell, and blessed is the memory of the men and women who made it.

There was also the penetrating odor of the room up under the eaves where clothes were kept—the cedar chest or cedar closet. Some households had a camphor room. Now camphor is a distinct domestic perfume. Modern substitutes are poor imitations. And whereas camphor kept its fragrance until the end, disintegrating camphor balls today remind one, as they fade, of Cabbages and drains. A piece of camphor in a drawer, laid away among fine dress goods, will make the most jaded domestic nostril tingle with delight, for there is not alone the odor of the camphor itself, but the odor of the materials as well. Small children, when they fall asleep on their grandmother's bosom, know this odor of stiff satin and old lace that have been laid away in drawers full of dried Lavender.

Some years ago, Professor Saintsbury, an eminent English authority, wrote a quaint little volume called "Notes on a Cellar Book." It contained the record of all the wines he had owned and many he had drunk. To the arid Prohibitionist, the book would be anathema; so would the memories some of us have of old wine rooms. The room may have been in the cellar or in the attic, but wherever located, it had a musty, dusty air. Demijohns and syphons and casks and corks and bottles in racks ranged round the wall. The air was rich with the perfume of Port and Sherry, Madeira and Malmsey. Civilizations older and saner than ours have found it the better part of wisdom still to keep around the household these sweet fragrances of wine.

Not all domestic scents are gastronomic. There was an old smell that will remain with me to the last day: a library whose windows looked out on a quiet country town main street. It was lined with bookcases, and by the window stood a big flat top desk. The ancient gentleman who sat at that desk wore a stock and a swallow-tail coat long after they had become a memory to most old gentlemen. He read Robert Burns aloud when he wasn't expounding law. He also smoked what were called "grandfather's stinking stogies." Deep leather chairs were in that library, and in one corner a tall clock that ticked as though a little weary. Mention libraries, and the association brings up that old gentleman, those chairs, those leather-bound books, that clock, and above all, an incense compounded of stogies and old calf-skin. And the association sanctifies the odors.

THE MONTH OF FEBRUARY

1. SPARE THE ROD. By all the rules of the sophisticated, I should never have been a gardener: the first thrashing to be visited upon me was for trampling on a seed-bed my father had just planted. With childish contempt, I watched him plant it, and when he finished and was out of sight, I deliberately scuffed and kicked it into a desolation, nasty little brat that I was. Shortly thereafter the business-side of a hair brush was laid forcibly across my broadest dimension, and I retreated to a dark corner to curse seeds, seed-beds and horticulture in general. Had my father spared the rod, I never would have developed a fancy for gardening.

On frigid February nights evil men around these parts expose pans of hard cider to the elements.

2. A BOUQUET OF BARKS. If, on one of these days, when Spring seems very far behind, you are seized with a desire for living color, go forth into the garden and make you a bouquet of twigs. The Kerrias will offer their glossy green branchlets and the Willows their golden bark that quickens into yellow with Spring's approach. Dogwood twigs are scarlet, and the Viburnums wear a Quaker gray and the Red Osier a livery of purple-maroon. Another Cornus—C. *circinata* or *rugosa*

—found on woody hillsides will furnish mottled red and yellow. Bring these home and set them in a bowl under a light: you have color variation, differences in texture and formation on a day when all Nature seems drab. Recently I found just such a bouquet of barks in the hallway of a country house. It was bound with red ribbon and hung on the wall, and a gay touch it gave on that bleak February morning.

Tomorrow order garden stakes—plenty of them, in varied sizes—before the big Spring bills come in.

3. NOVELTIES. Whenever a new seed catalogue arrives I invariably turn to two sections—first to the novelties, then to the department of garden tools and supplies.

The supplies section has intrigued me for years because, ever since I have known seed catalogues, I have met one old friend, faithful and true throughout a generation—the gentleman in the derby hat and the chin whiskers who, for fully twenty-five years now, has been spreading a mat over a hotbed. Who was the original of this portrait? He must have been a contemporary of Gladstone or Queen Victoria's Albert. He should be immortalized with an ode. The telegraph has come and spread, the motor car has grown to a commonplace, radio is in every other home—but he does not change. He wears the same derby hat and the same early Victorian whiskers. He is our link with the irrevocable past of gardening, when men went forth in morning coats and derbies to spread mats over hotbeds.

The same sense of unchanging continuity is given by the novelties section. For years I have scanned that section for a real novelty and have found few indeed. The same picotee Zinnias, the same crested Cosmos, the same Antirrhinums, are offered year after year as novelties. We have been growing them faithfully for a decade now, we and the old gentleman in the derby hat.

Perhaps we can blame both of them on Quarantine 37. That enactment has many sins on its conscience, and it might stand a few more! Or we might even suggest that the men who make our seed catalogues shoulder some of the blame. Anyway, here we are in a progressive age being served up stuff that our fathers knew when we were children. We are told that they are novelties —and we don't bother to protest.

Pick up the catalogue of any English seedsman and see what novelties he offers. Look at the German and French and Swiss catalogues. Compared with them, the majority of our American catalogues are mere children's primers.

The various bush berries make good division hedges in a vegetable garden— Blackberries, Currants, Raspberries and Gooseberries.

4. TABLE CENTERS. It was a wedding anniversary and we needs must celebrate it by a dinner. To symbolize our domesticity, the center-piece

was composed of china cats—complaisant, fat and contented as two long-wedded folks should be. But a wag among the guests improved on it: he surreptitiously brought down from the Morning Room two Staffordshire dogs. Symbols of cat-and-dog life. Well, perhaps many a marriage existence is little better than that.

The best center-piece of all, however, was the Christmas table—that Christmas when our otherwise respectable wired-haired fox presented us with wire-haired Shetland ponies. Christmas came before her puppies were big enough to reveal their sire. They were cute, fluffy little balls. So around each neck went a red ribbon with a bell, and the whole litter was put in a big puppy basket padded with snow-like flannel and surrounded by a hedge of Holly. This we set in the middle of the table, with silver candelabra on each side. . . . None of the guests had ever seen a live puppy center-piece before and they simply refused to go home. I'm sure it couldn't have been the punch that made them linger.

This week start Sweet Peas indoors or in the greenhouse for early setting out. Keep them cool after the seed germinates.

5. A PROLEGOMENON TO GARDENING. We used to think that one was initiated into gardening by reading seed catalogues. That belief was based merely on a profound ignorance. The last and final rite, the trying baptism, the greatest of all prolegomenon, is to "get" Poison Ivy.

Some people are immune to this monstrous weed, and they laugh their weaker brothers to scorn. Country boys, they say, can even chew the leaves with impunity. But the rest of us must pass through the fire. Doctors seem to disagree on cures for it—some suggest washing with green soap and then bathing the welts with freshly-made spirits of nitre; others paint the welts with iodine, still others use the ordinary photographer's hypo solution. As a precaution, whenever we have been handling the pestiferous stuff, we run indoors and scrub hands and face vigorously with very hot common kitchen-sink soap-suds.

February is the month for spraying those trees and shrubs subject to San José scale.

6. TAKING IT FROM THE CHICKS. Being conscienceless where the garden is concerned, a friend of mine has recently been taking away from her chicks part of their ration of crushed oyster shells. This she mixes with peat and sand and a little loam, and makes up a potting soil that is ideal for many things. The peat holds the moisture, the sand gives drainage, the loam gives body to the combination and the oyster shells give lime to release the good properties of each. But it does more than that. Turn out the pot and around each particle of shell is wrapped a tiny rootlet. In the parlance of the boarding house, each root picks out its favorite piece of shell and puts out its feeding hooks to preëmpt it. I never saw better root growth than this soil mixture made. The

chicks will never miss the few handfuls of shell you steal from their food bin.

Tomorrow send in your seed order and thereby save the discount offered to early buyers.

7. THE FUCHSIAS OF YESTERDAY. Like collectors, good gardeners soon become specialists and select definite lines of plants to grow. I can imagine no finer sport than adopting for one's especial hobby the collecting and propagating of old varieties of a flower that have passed out of commerce. There are fashions in flowers just as there are fashions in clothes, and good things disappear from catalogues rarely to be seen again. Fifty to seventy-five years ago Fuchsias were raised in great abundance and wide variety. Then, like the bustle and the leg-of-mutton sleeve, they passed out of favor. Here and there in old-fashioned collections and gardens one may find them. Recent catalogues are of little help in these searches; one must go forth and peer over old, remote garden gates and into the flower windows of old-fashioned houses. Never attempt to pay money for such plants or slips from them—trade some of your newer things for a piece of the old. Swap a new Delphinium seedling for a cutting of an old Fuchsia.

And having sent in your seed order, eschew catalogues for a time.

8. SAITH A GROCER OF TROYES. Is the laziness of workmen a product of our modern civili-

zation? I thought so until recently, when we found that painters on our old house accomplished more in the two days we watched them than in the entire week when we were absent. And we were about to curse modern civilization when we encountered an old poem written in 1319 by a Grocer of Troyes. In one passage a tiler speaks as follows: "When I finally make up my mind to work, I take with me a young mate who knows nothing of the job, but I insist on his being paid the full wage of twelve deniers. When, at last, I get on the roof, I lay one tile in the time it should take to lay eight or ten. I ease off and sing a song, then take a siesta between two slopes of the roof. It is then time to knock off for dinner. After that, it is soon supper time, so we leave work for that day. Of course, with piece-work it is different; I can do as much in one day as in five days by the hour."

This is an excellent season to collect Pea bush and wood for Bean poles.

9. THE ULTIMATE REVENGE. There are many ways one can wreak revenge on a hostess for a dull week-end, but the strangest I know is that adopted by the Englishman who, being bored to death by the company and his hostess, on Monday morning turned the entire contents of the bathsalt jar into his tub and left for town immediately after breakfast. Well! Well! The English can be quaint!

Since Paper White Narcissi take only six weeks to flower in pebbles or peat, plant a new batch for Easter.

10. MOTORS VERSUS SERENITY. My neighbor in the Pink House at the foot of the hill complained recently that she no longer enjoyed the serenity of the countryside. Once the rural scene filled her soul with tranquillity; she reveled in its colorings, its stately progress from season to season, its soft bird and water music. This year she wasn't aware of these nuances. The reason? She has learned to drive a car. Today her eyes are glued on the road and she passes speedily from one spot to the other.

Some years ago the local inspector of aspirants for automobile licenses did me a great favor. I had been bullied, threatened, begged and shamed into trying to learn to drive a car. Finally the terrible day came and I presented myself for examination. When I had gone half a block the inspector took the wheel from me, growling, "Young man, you're a menace to the highway." With that utterance something died inside of me. I returned home crestfallen and ashamed. And never since have I attempted to drive a car. I haven't the slightest notion how to start or stop one, nor have I the least desire to learn how. I have escaped being a private chauffeur. After I am deposited on this hilltop, I stay here. . . . But if that unknown inspector ever appears in this garden, he can have the best flowers in it.

Tomorrow top dress or repot all plants, such as Palms and Rubber Plants, that have remained in their pots a long time.

11. UNTRIED ANNUALS. "So much to plant! So little planted!" This can be carved on the gravestone of a garden-lover.

Looking over the new catalogues, as they come in, I realize how signally I have failed on my resolution made years ago. This was eventually to grow all the annuals offered by English and American seed catalogues. How have I neglected Alonsoa and Amberboa, Bartonia, Cacalia and Calandrinia! And when will I find time to plant or space to grow Cynoglossum, Collinsia, Gilia, Echium, Eutoca, Jacoboea, Leptosyne, Torenia, Whitlavia and all those others that have never found a place in my garden! Perhaps some year I will simply resist the temptation to grow all my old favorites and devote a season catching up with that resolution. It would be a strange annual patch that year—like giving a party to people you didn't know!

Feed house plants some sheep manure and wash the foliage with an insecticide.

12. THE GLORY THAT IS NEMESIA. And yet each year it is a good idea to try one or two annuals that haven't been tried before and in that way widen the circle of one's flower friends. Among those to try is Nemesia, a humble little plant with a glory all its own. Some flowers show their beauty best at a distance—Tritomas and many of the Lilies, for example—others require close inspection. In fact, no flower is really understood until we have seen it both in the mass and individually; at a distance and in the hand. Indi-

vidual flowers of Nemesia reveal a shy beauty that can stand the closest inspection. It is the sort of flower you love to touch. Its color range has now been extended to include a good variety of tints and tones. In the mass—used as an edging—it rests on the ground like a delicate cloud.

Either in the cellar or under the benches of a greenhouse, Endive can easily be forced.

13. POLYGLOT GARDENING. This strange afternoon began when we hired into kitchen bondage a Jap. After his second day off he returned with a wife—a Finnish amazon who, as the weeks progressed, looked with kindling eyes on our Swedish gardener. Through this gardener she got to know the next door cook, who was German, and the nurse who was a Dane. We were waist-deep in Nordics and the Jap and I felt quite out of the picture. Then one day I brought home a Russian refugee, a half-starved scientist whom the Revolution had left stranded and who desired food, country air and sunshine, in return for which he would do a little gardening. Being a learned man, he spoke many tongues, including the Japanese. And the Jap cook, as I discovered, knew a little Russian.

These permutations and combinations of tongues appealed to me, and one afternoon I gathered the polyglots together for a big weeding fest. I gave the orders in English to the Swedish gardener, who passed them on in German to the

German cook, who communicated them in German to the Dane, who repeated them in Danish to the Finnish amazon, who thereupon said things in polyglot Japanese to her husband, who chattered them to the Russian. And the Russian after the manner of his kind, shrugged his shoulders and merely exclaimed: "Neichevo!" Thus the cycle of this polyglot gardening was completed, for "Neichevo" was the only word of Russian I understood.

One of the simplest ways of working off anger is to destroy tent caterpillar nests with a torch.

14. THE THIRD TRIAL. One day, one glorious summer day, walking in his garden with E. Augustus Bowles at Waltham Cross, I complained that there were many things I simply could not grow. "But have you tried them three times?" he asked. "Never give a plant up until you've tried it thrice. The first year you may have the worst possible weather in your gardening experience, and the plant will perish. The second time you doubtless will give it an exposure or a soil that is uncongenial. On the third trial, you'll succeed."

Tomorrow have the secateurs sharpened.

15. A MEMORY OF MATTING. Years and years ago, when Harriet Beecher Stowe was helping to edit a domestic magazine, she wrote a panegyric

on matting. Since that time many decades of bare feet have paddled over matting floors, many decades of nostrils have sniffed at its crisp, dry odor on dry days, which was like incense from the Orient, and many decades have been repelled by its overwhelming stench, which was like unto the odor of the inside of an old cabbage pot when days were damp. It served its purpose well and faithfully, but I'm wondering if people still use it. Somehow I never can disassociate matting from old-fashioned bedrooms with their immaculate washstands, those domestic high altars of a bygone age. Whenever I think of matting, I think also of slop jars.

Tomorrow see that the gardener cleans the lawn mower and repacks the gear boxes with vaseline or graphite.

16. THE UNDESIRABLES. In the Book of Chronicles is written the perfect remark about those people—and plants—who are a nuisance. Jehoran, King of Judah, having lived an evil life, is gathered to his fathers. Then the chronicler says, "And he departed without being desired."

While not many people affect us that way, some do, especially those callers who, having read the sickly sentiment about none coming too early and none staying too late, proceed to practice it. Some flowers affect us the same way. They act as if they have no homes. They sprawl all over the borders, grab more than their allotted share of room, spill their seeds on all sides or throw out roots in all directions. The next year their progeny become a menace. Physostegia is a plant of which we said last Fall that it departed without being desired. This year its descendants are back again. *Anthemis tinctoria* is another. If some of those lovely new Lupins acquired that habit, we might think differently of it. Just now we have dispatched a huge Evening Primrose that grabbed more space than its blooming justified. Its name has now been added to those which Won't Be Tried Again in this border.

If a warm day comes with rain, set the houseplants out of doors for a few hours.

17. GARDENING CLOTHES. You can tell a real dirt gardener by the clothes he wears. For a long time now my horticultural appearances have been commented on adversely by the Female of my family. She says I am not presentable—that those trousers are a disgrace, that the shirt should be buried, in short, that a man in my alleged position should never be seen in such clothes. What, I ask you, does She want? Does She expect me to garden in a derby hat, like the old gentleman in the back of the catalogues who spreads mats over cold-frames? Does She expect me to push a wheel-hoe dressed as though I were a movie hero? Does She think I can garden gloved as for a ride? No, the real gardener has no special clothes to work in; he invariably wears out old clothes. He never deliberately goes to a store and buys brand new

shirts and trousers and boots for this purpose. If he does, he isn't much of a gardener.

Some years ago, a friend of mine was caught with the urge of Spring to go out and dig. A city man this, very meticulous about his appearance. All his suits are made in London and his shirts built especially for him. When he walks down Fifth Avenue of a Sunday afternoon, he is a glass of fashion. He has never been known to commit a sartorial indiscretion. And yet this person was quite sincere when he told me that he wanted to come up on Saturdays and work in my garden. I told him to come ahead. Well, the following Saturday afternoon he appeared. He wore a pair of dirt-colored doeskin riding breeches, a flannel shirt as light as a feather, a special cap peaked fore and after, like Sherlock Holmes', to keep the sun off both his neck and his face, a pair of boots with fancy gadgets, and on his hands were gloves. I stood speechless before this apparition, I in my old blue serge pants with no knees, my old gray shirt and the run-down army boots.

"Well, I'm ready," he said.

"So I see," I answered. "But where did you get that rig?"

"I bought it especially for gardening at Brooks Brothers," he answered proudly.

The next Saturday I waited for him to come, but he never arrived, and never again did he mention gardening to me. A few weeks later he explained that he thought gardening a little too strenuous for him. He took up golf.

Cactus grown indoors needs water not more frequently than once a fortnight.

18. A HAZARDOUS HOBBY. Although I knew he wasn't a gardener, I had a suspicion that he found pleasure in some kind of country sport. We met at a dinner and compared notes. Yes, he had a farm—it was the rockiest farm in Connecticut, and Heaven would bear witness that he spoke the truth. Thither he went each week-end for exercise. "You have cows and such?" I ventured. "No," he answered, "I dynamite." It seems he spends hours drilling holes in these rocks. Then he sets the charge—and runs like blazes. Presumably that is how he gets his exercise.

Indulge yourself to the extent of a fine-nozzled rubber syringe for watering newly planted seed flats.

19. ON BRIDGES. When first we came to this Connecticut hill, there used to be a little old plank bridge at the foot, where the road crossed a brook. And there was always a plank loose, so that when any one drove over it, it went "Ker-plunk," and warned us that callers were approaching. In an efficient moment the road commissioner did away with it, and our warning is now gone. So also was our uncertainty in crossing it. Adventure was buried and a modern culvert is its tombstone.

There was a time when all bridges and foundations were looked upon with a suspicious eye, and to propitiate the spirits of them, sacrifices were made in their behalf. The gypsies, it is said, would sacrifice a baby by abandoning it on the bridge. In more civilized times they merely laid the child down and said this prayer: "Grant, O God, to this bridge, by thy power at both ends two Cypress branches, that they may be placed as a cradle for my baby. When sheep pass may they give him their udders. When rain falls may it bathe him. As many leaves as are shed, may they cover him. When the wind blows may it rock his cradle, a lullaby, my baby, a lullaby that my baby may sleep."

Crushed oyster shells, gravel and other drainage material for pots can now be laid in against the Spring work.

20. LITTLE GARDENS. When people complain that they really can't do thus-and-so in their gardens because they have only a little place, I'm obliged to suppress a smile. A little garden is the only sort of garden to have. The fine work of specialists in this country is being carried on in unbelievably small spaces. Excellent Iris hybrids come from a city backyard. One of the best and most varied collections of American wild flowers is contained in less than half an acre of suburban rocky soil. The small garden that one can attend himself gives more joy and is often more productive of really good plant results than a dozen or more far-flung acres.

It is said that when the ladies of the Garden Club descended on these parts, they yawned politely behind their hands at the big estates which had been laid out by professionals and maintained by an army of gardeners; but when they came to the little home-made and home-tended gardens, they went into ecstasies. My respect for the Garden Club has gone up several notches since we heard that.

You might consider, at this season, a more extensive and adequate watering system for your garden.

21. THE JONESES. There is a catty phrase in common use whereby people of contemptuous minds speak their opinion of their fellow men who wish to better themselves. Let that man improve his house, it is whispered of him that he is trying "to keep up with the Joneses." Let him discard his "suites" of furniture and gaudy curtains, his nasty rugs and tawdry lampshades, and he is "keeping up with the Joneses." Let him make a better garden, and he is trying to clear the hurdle the Joneses set by theirs. Indeed, it would seem that in some communities all progress is a social battle; men and women do not, of their own accord, attempt to better themselves and their surroundings. There needs must be a social bellwether to lead these dumb sheep!

Well, that's a grossly unjust way of looking at it. For what we do when we try to better ourselves and our surroundings is not to keep up with the Joneses, but to keep up with the stride of our dreams and ambitions. We pass through an evolution of taste as the years go on and our reading and observations grow more discerning. No one of us springs full-blown into the world equipped with perfect taste. The knowledge of beauty is a slow and painful acquisition. We must make a great many mistakes before our eyes and brain can choose exactly the right object for the right place. Many things we once thought beautiful and suitable will be discarded in the process so long as the curve of our dreams and ambitions keeps aspiring upward. This principle applies equally well to lampshades, chairs, architecture, books, pictures, music, clothes and the layout of gardens.

See a house and garden where the owner is constantly making changes for the better, where with each season a new improvement appears and the house and the grounds approach more and more to a finished picture—see such a place and you can be sure that its owner is a man worthy of his dreams. He is alive, keen, ambitious, constantly learning, constantly reaching upward.

Nothing is more indicative of a pronounced personality than this striving to better one's environment. The Joneses do not figure in the picture at all. The battle is not waged for social eminence; it is a battle waged to satisfy the insistent demands of what one's tastes and desires require of life.

That very wise philosopher, Emerson, set down this principle in his essay on "Domestic Life." He says: "A man's money should not follow the direction of his neighbor's money, but should represent to him the things he would willingest do with it. I am not one thing and my expenditure another. My expenditure is me. That our expenditure and our character are twain is the vice of society." Then further along he writes of a man, "his house ought to show his honest opinion of what makes his well-being when he rests among his kindred, and forgets all affectation, compliance and even exertion of will."

See that loose bark on fruit trees, where bugs might hide, is now scraped off.

22. IMPERILING TOMBSTONES. It is a striking paradox that New England, which boasts most loudly of its ancestry, has the habit of grossly neglecting its ancestors' tombstones. You can scarcely ride down a New England by-road but you pass one of these neglected graveyards, hidden in the tall grass, forgotten and unkempt. Well, some people in New England towns are like that too. They are tombstones—tombstones with good little angels carved on them, leaning tombstones that threaten to fall and crush you if you come too close to them.

Pots of paper, fibre or peat moss are useful for starting indoors such things as resent root disturbance.

23. DRAIN PIPES AS DECORATION. Observant Americans visiting England invariably comment on the fact that whereas American builders and architects artfully conceal the plumbing in the walls, the British expose their pipes to public gaze. This open plumbing openly arrived at, disfigures many a fine house in England: the drain pipe will run down the front façade and in well-appointed rooms, pipes crawl over the walls and ceiling. It is customary for the English plumber

not to begin work until the house is practically finished. He and his pipes are an architectural afterthought. Their exposure doesn't seem to offend the esthetic sense of the natives. Well, there's no use going to war about that.

If you are growing impatient for Spring to come, go South or to the Tropics and meet it there.

24. THE FIRST ANNUALS. Some flowers, like some people, make an unfortunate first impression, and it is unfair to judge them by it. Especially is this true of annuals. The first blooms may be lopsided, malformed and weak. Robert Burns calls such things an indication of the "apprentic'd hand." They are nothing to worry about, however. Be patient. Like the young bride with her first biscuits, annuals make these depressing first attempts. The same plant, as the season progresses, often develops perfect flowers.

Ground green bone fed chickens at this season encourages them to lay.

25. A SECOND THOUGHT ON FIRST FLOWERING. The child marriages of India aren't a patch on what happens to annuals in a bad season. Scarcely half grown, they burst into bloom, rush to complete their life cycle of flower and seed as though their time were short. Then having made this gigantic effort, their strength wanes and they fail. Their purpose accomplished, they die. Lest they reach their end too soon, it is often advisable to

disbud annuals until they have attained mature size. Whether it be Zinnias or French Marigolds or Scabiosa or Larkspur, it is better to forego early blooms and let the plant concentrate its efforts on growing. And not alone is this true of annuals: it is almost necessary with perennials—Tuberous Begonias, Delphiniums and even the wiry Coreopsis are better for not flowering the first year from seed.

Sawing wood, the sport of ex-kings, is a good preparation for the violent exercise of Spring gardening.

26. COLLECTORS' HORIZONS. The collecting hobby, as it is pursued through a course of years, becomes a series of narrowing horizons. At first the sky appears to be the limit and the collector acquires right and left. As his experience, taste and knowledge increase, his interests diminish in quantity and increase in quality, until he reaches that state where his interest centers on one group alone. Etchings may be his chosen field. He begins by collecting all kinds. As the years pass and his taste is sharpened, he may choose only the modern etchers. And in time these modernists may come down to one nationality, or one school, or even one man.

It might be possible to attain this final stage of collecting at one leap—to start from scratch and concentrate on one great artist or group of collectible objects; but then such a collector misses all the fun by the way, all the delectable experiences of swapping and acquiring. In this journey of narrowing horizons, there's a vast lot of delightful and memorable scenery.

See that potting soil bins are full and orders for fertilizers are placed now.

27. FORCING TIME. For Narcissi and Tulips, it is generally figured that six weeks are required to bring them into bloom indoors, six weeks from the time we fetch them from the pit where they were buried last Autumn in their pots and pans, to the time those pans are glorious with full-colored flowers. This is only the average, however, for some varieties take more or less time than others and no exact rule can be laid down. Because of this uncertainty, the nurserymen who help make our early Spring flower exhibitions a success have to raise many more plants than they exhibit in order to produce the few that hit the dates exactly. One nurseryman figured that in order to produce 100 Tulips in flower for a certain week, he had to prepare 300. Apparently there's more good luck than good marksmanship in this game.

Check up on the gardener to see if he has sharpened all edge tools.

28. THE FIVE-DOLLAR HOLE. A visitor from the Tropics watched me prepare the soil for a Bush Honeysuckle that was to be planted after frost. It was a blistering August day, yet I followed our usual procedure in preparing for trees and shrubs: the top spit of earth for a radius of three feet was removed and laid to one side; the subsoil to the

depth of two feet was dug out and wheeled away; then the top soil was thrown into the hole and good soil piled in from the compost heap and the pig yard and a couple of bushel baskets of peat moss, until it was heaped over the top. This is left to settle until the Autumn, when the bush is given its permanent home.

Contemplating all these labors, the man from the Tropics remarked that he would never work that hard for any plant. He came from a country where all the peon does is wriggle a toe to make a hole in the soil, drop the sugar cane and wriggle another toe to cover it.

Alas, the man from the Tropics has now gone from this place where there is worry about plants and planting (and whatever peace there is to find, may he have found it!) and the *Lonicera Mackii* flourishes and grows bigger every year.

As bird food is getting low, wire lumps of suet to trees and fill feeding stations.

LONG PIECE

THE JACKDAW INSTINCT

"THE Jackdaw of Rheims" was an ecclesiastical pilferer, you'll remember. He "prigged" the Lord Cardinal's ring for his nest. His crime evidently was heinous, for that lordly prelate cursed him thoroughly, "from the sole of his foot to the crown of his head." But when the ring was finally discovered in the nest and was restored once more to the finger of the Lord Cardinal, Jackdaw did such penance for his prank that the conclave canonized him "Jem Crow."

It's a pity, though, that the poor old bird had to be cursed for stealing something that would make his home more interesting. So few of us pilfer for that worthy purpose. We put on great airs and call ourselves "collectors," whereas we are merely jackdaws! Some are jackdaws of Rheims, and collect things of great value; others are just common, secular, lay jackdaws. Of the two we prefer to be the common sort. We never repent our folly and we'll never be canonized. We enjoy our pilferings. They make our nest lovelier to live in.

There was that day, having mounted the gangplank of an Italy-bound steamer, when we swore a mighty vow to each other. We agreed that we had congregated about us all the antiques and curio junk we could afford or the house could hold. We vowed then and there, as the steamer warped out from the pier, that this was to be only a sightseeing trip—under no circumstance were we to buy or otherwise acquire another antique or another curio! But such is the weakness of human jackdaws that scarcely had we set foot on Italian soil when the vow was forgotten and the promise shattered to a thousand pieces. At first we went about it secretly and alone—pretended to be setting forth for an art gallery when we really were headed for an antique shop. Then, when the bundles began to arrive, came the explanations and alibis. After that, being partners in crime, we went forth together, two American jackdaws, ready to prig a cardinal's ring or whatever else came within our reach.

Nor have we since had reason for regretting our weakness. The jackdaw can as soon change his habits as a leopard its spots. The collector born will collect to his dying day. And he will fill his house with the plunder and bore his friends to distraction telling when and how these pieces were acquired.

Apart from the fun we get in stalking antiques and curios, the justification for this form of sport lies in the manner one can use his quarry once he has brought it home. Let it become a part of the every-day surroundings of his house. Let it fill the rooms with the atmosphere of adventure and romance.

In this Connecticut farmhouse, resting under its three gigantic Elms, which I am pleased to look upon as Home, we have devised a way of making several little collections assume importance and distinction.

The Morning Room (so called because every one else in the neighborhood calls theirs a Living Room) holds the collection of flower pictures. Over the mantel hangs the portrait of a young lady—somewhat anemic—who tenderly holds a flower in her hands and contemplates space. Below her on the shelf stand two little glass domes covering baskets of dried flowers and bought from a near-by junk dealer for the intolerable sum of $1.50. Above the little sofa is a group—Japanese rice paper flowers, paper silhouette flowers from England and pin-pricked flower studies made by some patient soul in old France once on a day.

Near by hangs a colored flower etching, and above it in a shadow box, a bunch of flowers fashioned from human hair, a homely trophy run to earth in the antique purlieus of New Orleans. On another wall you find flowers embroidered in silk, in straw and some moulded in embossed wax. Beyond them range the bead flowers in little mirror frames, and over the desk—bought at the sacrifice of many luncheons!—a flower study in particolored brocades outlined with vellum. Further along you come to the tinsel flower pictures of early America and one of modern tinsel strings from Germany. The last wall holds two vases spilling over with flowers made of paper mosaic, pretty mementoes of the French 19th Century.

This little group—perhaps twenty-five pictures in all—represents several years of collecting. Today only flower prints go in that Morning Room. They give it marked individuality.

Back in the study is a composite from many collecting by-paths—old maps, for which I once had a weakness and still have—maps embroidered and cut out and those colorful charts made by the good John Speed. These mingle with old etchings of French gardens and, since I once perpetrated a book on that subject, with pictures, in various mediums, of peddlers. Here are two from France done partly in etching and partly in cloth with a watercolor background. Above them hangs a fine old brigand from Ireland, who peddled hardware. One of these days the maps will be moved to another room and the garden etchings to a third, leaving the peddlers to dominate the walls of that study.

In one of the bedrooms are dogs—French prints of fine ladies with all manner of curious canines and little wall what-nots with mirrored backs holding on their shelves a Staffordshire kennel of various breeds. Another bedroom boasts a little group of brass harness ornaments—martingales and bosses and bells. English regiments and hunt clubs once used distinctive designs for martingales, and collectors are always on the alert for them. Some of this group came from the Caledonian Market in London, others from Sicily, from Siberia, and from the hill-towns of Italy. They hang against a red criss-cross paper in a room that boasts scarlet curtains and a bedcover of the same brilliant hue. In this room also is the beginning of a collection of pigs, since I have acquired such a porcine complex.

Thus it is that two jackdaws have used their pilferings. Even with his Cardinal's ring the nest of the Jackdaw of Rheims was never so amusing as ours!

THE MONTH OF MARCH

1. THE SINNER THAT REPENTETH. One of these days, I shall found a society like the Big Brother Movement or the Association for the Care of Ex-Criminals. It will be an organization devoted to making welcome and encouraging men who have stopped playing golf and have taken up gardening. There may be joy in Heaven over one sinner that repenteth, but the very gates of the celestial regions must rock and resound when a man lays down the mashie to take up the spade.

Each week I hear of more of these repentant men. They act a little sheepish about their new hobby, and we should accord them kindly encouragement. Apart from a few outstanding male instances, the most intelligent and zealous gardening in this country is now being done by women. When a man first takes up gardening—relinquishes his old cronies of the links, and disappears from locker rooms—he is apt to feel self-conscious about it, the way any man feels self-conscious when he first enters a room full of women at a tea party. If he is made welcome, he may prove to be an excellent gardener, and will never go back to the old life. Perhaps the Garden Club of America or the Federated Garden Clubs might appoint an Anxious Seat Committee for the welcoming of golf-repentant husbands.

You can now begin to apply rock salt to the Asparagus bed.

2. FORGOTTEN GARDENS. It is customary to be sentimental and *triste* over a neglected, abandoned, unpeopled garden. So much human endeavor, we say, went into its making, so many dreams. Men and women and children were happy there once and knew its tranquillity and simple pleasures. Too bad that it is gone! And yet my reaction is often the opposite of this. Except you attend to its needs, there is no way of entailing a garden. Once human endeavor neglects a garden, it goes back by natural right into the countryside again. Deliberately abandoning it is like dying without having made a will and without heirs: the Commonwealth scoops the estate into the general pot for the public good. Nature steps in with her cohorts, and in a few short seasons that forgotten garden loses its identity in the vast treasury of meadow and forest, of bog and brook.

Tomorrow may be a good day for taking the winter boards off your Boxwood.

3. SINGING AFTER MEAT. In the 16th Century the customary after-dinner amusement was part singing. First you ate, then you sang. Dinner over, song books were passed among the guests at the table, and if you couldn't read a part at sight you were as much scorned as would be a guest today who could not play bridge. Picture, if you can, the guests at a smart dinner party today whiling away the evening with part songs! Thomas Morley, the madrigal writer, in 1597 tells how he went to a dinner and couldn't read his part.

His hostess and guests were shocked. "Some whispered to others, demanding how I was brought up." The next day he sought out a singing teacher so that he no longer need be ashamed of his bad company manners.

In the hotbed you can now sow the seeds of many vegetables—Tomatoes, Peppers, Egg-plant, Cabbages and such.

4. SPRING TEMPTATION. The way to rid one's self of some temptations is to yield to them. There is, for example, that temptation to plant seed too early. A warm day arrives and you rush out of doors panting with excitement. Spring has come! and all that sort of thing. The desire to sow some seed is irresistible. Your hands itch to tear open a seed packet. Do not attempt to resist it. Forget your Puritan and stiff-backed heritage. Become a weakling for a moment. But be careful what you sow.

With almost every seed order the seedsman makes a prodigal gesture—sends a complimentary packet of something. In my crass inexperience I used to think such seed very precious, and year after year I nursed it up to its floral mediocrity. Having done this several times, I began to suspect seedsmen bearing gifts. It is with such gifts that I now satisfy my irresistible temptation to plant out of doors before the Maples break into leaf.

All pruning of trees, shrubs and vines should be finished before the sap starts to rise.

5. WAR ON WOOD WORMS. That men make their livelihood shooting wormholes into furniture is a commonplace among queer trades, and with that rumor most of us rest content. Recently along has come a competitive volume devoted to an exhaustive study of worms in furniture and structural timber. This furniture beetle may be Xestobium or Anabium, the Greater or Lesser Death-Watch Beetle, and against it warfare can be successfully waged by simple means. June, it appears, is the month this bothersome pest chooses to go her rounds laying eggs, so June is the month to deal the *coup de grâce.* Put the furniture out on the lawn, says this authority (John Girdwood—an excellent name for a writer on this subject!), wash out the wormholes with turpentine and then fill them with beeswax. The worm-eaten wood, it appears, must be thoroughly saturated with the turpentine. The treatment is equally applicable to a chair leg or the roof of a cathedral. So far, so good. But the author has nothing to say on the destruction of the imaginary worms that make the tangible wormholes in many of our "antiques." Killing the worm is fair sport, but killing the wormhole-maker is first degree homicide.

Preparations for making a new lawn can be started this early; early grading brings early grass.

6. I THREATEN PIGS. The Porcine Complex is something that the high-domed philosophers of Vienna have still to elucidate. It is a particular

state of mind and a very definite urge, and it came upon me out of the blue without warning. At breakfast and apropos of nothing at all, I announced, "This year I think I'll have pigs." My explosion was followed by a silence. "Pigs," I repeated.

"I heard you," She said.

"Little pink pigs," I continued.

"Hogs, you mean, dirty, stinking hogs," She answered.

"Yes, hogs when they grow up." This chat and back-chat went on until we had reached our post-coffee cigarettes.

For days thereafter I scanned the pig columns in farm journals, had my ardor dampened by learning about hog cholera, had it quickened by reading of the profits accruing to those who raise pigs. Then with my jaw set firm, I ordered those pigs and having done so, made public acknowledgment of the fact. With the serenity of a summer's day, she merely replied, "And I have ordered chickens."

But She had never mentioned chickens! And therein lies a fundamental difference between the sexes: the male will cautiously and diplomatically announce what he intends doing—he likes to see where he is going to land before he leaps; but a woman will go ahead without warning and smile placidly when the deluge descends upon her. Even in the matter of pigs and chickens, women seem to have more moral courage than men.

Before growth of vines gets under way, paint wooden arbors and trellises.

7. A GRAIN OF SALT. Between the flower show and the garden is always a great gulf fixed. We go to a flower show, wax enthusiastic over a new variety of Rose or Chrysanthemum, order them for the garden—and then suffer disappointment. They never seem to grow so well for us rank amateurs as they do for the professional, and we wonder why. Well, the care of plants is the professional's business and with us it is only an avocation. Moreover, the professional grower, knowing that he is to meet competition from other growers, strains every nerve to attain perfection at shows. He disbuds his plants and grows for the single perfect or large bloom, whereas the average amateur grows for abundance of bloom. Souvenir de Claudius Pernet as seen in the florist's window or in his display at flower shows, is a horse of a different color from the Rose we struggle with in our gardens. It would be well for the American Rose Society to list those Roses that only professionals and well-equipped amateurs should grow. The same applies to Chrysanthemums. While the catalogues do warn us about the tenderness of certain kinds, we leave them unprotected over Winter, and mourn their loss when Spring comes. We also fail to disbud. The flowers we produce are usually woefully smaller than those we see at the exhibitions.

Why not issue, with each ticket to the flower show, a grain of salt that we enthusiastic amateurs can take at our discretion? Without it we'll soon become cynics.

Tomorrow you may be able to remove the mulch from the Strawberry bed.

8. Dr. Johnson Speaks His Mind. One day the great Dr. Johnson was looking at a large country house. Its vast expanse held his attention for a long time—its ranges of chimney pots and casement windows and ramifying wings. "What I admire in this," he finally remarked, "is the total disregard of expense."

That, if the truth be told, is the reason why so many of us like to look at just such houses or pictures of such large houses: we find a source of admiration in the owner's complete freedom from our own distressing habit of having to count the pennies. When we come to build that house of our dreams and furnish it and lay out the garden, most of us are frustrated by the narrow limits of our purse. We marvel that there are people who do not have to consider such mundane affairs, just as we marvel at men who do gigantic feats which our puny strength or courage do not allow to us. Wouldn't it be wonderful for just one day to enjoy the luxury of having a "total disregard of expense!"

The lawn should be raked clean of winter fallen twigs and excess mulch.

9. Sand and Seed. To procure good germination of seed, fill the flat or seeding pan with straight peat moss that has been saturated in water until its fibre is like a sponge that has been squeezed. This should be packed in tight. Over this spread sand to about one-quarter of an inch deep. Sow the seed. Cover with a sprinkling of sand, and set the flat in a shady place.

The peat moss has an acid reaction which is conducive to the germination of seed. It also will afford easy run for roots, so that an amazing root-system will form, and it will keep damp. Roots and rootlets penetrate the moss in search of food which must be in solution and there is a slight suggestion of food values in the damp moss.

The sand prevents an excess of moisture from collecting around the newly-sprung stems and seems to discourage the spores that cause damping off. An extra precaution, one that we use with very miffy seeds, is to mix with the sand some charcoal, little seeds of it that we buy for the baby chicks. The charcoal absorbs excess of dampness.

If tomorrow is a pleasant day, examine your fences and make the necessary repairs.

10. Soil for Transplants. When seedlings have reached the transplanting stage, then is the time to give them food. Prepare a potting soil of one-third peat moss, one-third loam and one-third sand, with a generous supply of bone meal. A scant dusting of lime may be intermixed before this, as the lime will counteract the acid reaction of the peat moss. However, if you are transplanting acid-loving plants, do not use the lime. Sometimes, when it is available, we also add soot, a pinch of flowers of sulphur and tobacco dust to this potting soil in the hopeful expectation that these three will pretty well combat any bugs or moulds that might attack the roots.

See that the compost heap is turned over this week and given a thorough mixing.

11. KEEPING AN EYE ON THE MIFFS. Expensive seed and the miffy sorts, once they have germinated and are ready for transplanting, can be set out in little pots. Sink these to their rims in the soil of the cold frame, thus assuring a maintenance of dampness. You can control soil in a pot much easier that you can control it in a bed. Besides, many of these miffy plants (Lupins are my special miffs) resent being moved and it gives them the least possible shock when they are slid out of a pot into their permanent home.

Winter washouts in the rock garden can be repaired any day now.

12. LEAN EATERS. It is a waste of time and energy to feed some plants too well. These Jack Spratts make quite a list, starting with Cheddar Pinks, *Dianthus caesius* and running through Butterfly Weed, *Asclepias tuberosa,* Bee Balm, *Monarda didyma,* the Showy Sedum, *Sedum spectabile* and the Yuccas. On the other hand I have never seen them resent a good meal, though they simply gorge themselves on it to no profit —throw up immense leaf growths with a minimum of flowering. A lean horse for a long race and a starved Butterfly Weed for abundant blossoms.

Examine perennials and shrubs planted last Fall and tramp down soil around the roots.

13. PHARMACEUTICAL HOSPITALITY. The other night we stayed in a country house guest room whose owner must have had a druggist for an

ancestor. On the bedside table were two little boxes. We always rattle little boxes to see what is in them, and this we did to these. In one were aspirin tablets, which are presumed to put you to sleep after too much coffee; in the other were soda mints, against the dinner of which you ate unwisely and too well. The hostess evidently had her doubts about her guests' digestion. Her thoughtfulness in this matter was so engagingly pharmaceutical!

However, in a magazine on the same night stand we discovered these friendly lines by Godfrey Elton, "For A Guest Room":

> Pull the curtains, bring the light,
> Dusk is drawing into night.
> Friend, the lamplit hours begin,
> Welcome to the house you're in.

These are days to spread lime on soil that needs it.

14. THE BROCCOLI LEGEND. A notion has gotten abroad that Broccoli, now quite popular, is a brand-new creation of the vegetable world, a veritable comet among succulent brassicas appearing suddenly on the garden horizon. Alas, that is a legend. It has been grown in this country for many generations. The *Yankee Farmer*, a rural journal published in Maine a century ago, contains advertisements of the seed, and it was grown commonly for generations before that.

Tomorrow, you can begin scattering on the border and vegetable garden the wood ashes you've been accumulating all Winter.

15. DISCOVERIES UNDER GLASS. In the Autumn we prepare one cold frame for those Spring flowers that will leap ahead into bloom under the warmth of the glass—a row or two of Pansies, some of the more delicately formed Narcissus, Wallflowers, a Primula or two and the little bulbs. Snugly banked with manure and matted, this frame begins to move when things outside are still at their beauty sleep. And though snow may have to be shoveled from it, I've yet to tilt that frame in March but it gave me some few blooms, blooms that are precious in those days because so scarce.

Start now to force Dahlia tubers from which to take cuttings later.

16. ECCLESIASTICAL. One of my particular dislikes is the type of house that is decorated with ecclesiastical furniture and vestments. Ladies of the stage and of the cinema seem given to this sort of thing. Let them find a blank space on their walls and they immediately cover it with a cope. Over chairs and tables are flung chasubles. Mantels are draped with altar frontals, stoles and maniples. A little of this may be all very well, but the excess of it is very bad taste. One luminary of the cinematic firmament on whom I once called served her high-balls in chalices.

Except from the point of taste there is no objection to using a few beautiful ecclesiastical vestments in decoration. They usually are made of exquisite fabrics—in fact, among ladies in Italy, France and Spain it is the custom to send their first communion, ball and marriage gowns to convents where they are made up into vestments and embroidered usually (so my Catholic authority informs me) by over-conscientious Flemish and German nuns. Before being used all these vestments are blessed. Then, after a time, if the convent or the church wishes to dispose of them, they can be secularized and sold. There is a special office appointed whereby these sacred objects are, as it were, "unblessed," before they go out into the world again.

Tomorrow being St. Patrick's day, celebrate it by planting Sweet Peas.

17. BABEL. There is no reason why the poor old tower of Babel should have to bear all the blame for the multitude of tongues when the gardener, in the course of a year, draws on enough of them to be the Father of Confusion—Latin, Greek, ancient Britain, Anglo-Saxon, Norman, Dutch, Swedish, Danish, Arabic and Persian. From Latin he takes Plantain, Rose and Saxifrage; from Greek, Coriander and Daffodil; from ancient Britain, Maple and Wormwood; from Anglo-Saxon, Hawthorn and Groundsel; from Swedish and Danish, the Rowan; from Dutch, Buckwheat and Snapdragon; from French, Mushroom; from Arabic the Barberry; from Persian, Lilac and Tulip. If we dug deep enough into the history of its common name, I daresay even our good old American Skunk Cabbage (which staggers, by the way, under the weighty botanical title of *Symplocarpus*

foetidus) would prove to have quite an international genealogy.

Rake off leaves from the mulching of borders and pile them on the compost heap.

18. BEFORE THE SHOW. Although it is a commonplace of gardening, I'm amazed at the people who are unaware that Spring-flowering shrubs and trees can be brought to bloom indoors in water. It's like peeking under a curtain before the show begins. Apparently lifeless twigs of Forsythia, Apples, Plums, Judas Trees, and such will break into leaf and blossom if kept in water in a warm room. About this season of the year we always carry cumbersome bundles of them into town and set them in a sunny window. The buds stand ready to uncurl, like a diver on the end of a spring-board, and in a week or ten days, they take their flowery plunge, casting a spray of cheerful blossoms over the room.

Cut out from climbing Roses the winter-killed wood, but mind the thorns.

19. SNOW LACE. It was worth waiting the whole winter for such a storm as came last night. A definite set of circumstances is required for it: a drab afternoon that starts drizzling before dusk. As night closes down the drizzle freezes on twig and branch. Then, during the night, comes powdering gentle snow without wind. The coating of ice glues the snow so that it piles up the tiniest twig into a fantastic heap. And if, by dawn, there is still

no wind stirring, set forth and make the rounds of garden and woodland. Such beauty the eye rarely beholds. The snow has left the sky clean washed and as blue as the Virgin's robe. Here Birch groves are bent into fountains, over yonder shrubs laid low like Russian dancers in rhythmic contortions. And over all, the white silence that is snow, seeping in upon you.

The beauty of an ice storm is the glittering beauty of diamonds and rubies, of sapphires, topaz and emeralds—an Amazon wearing all her jewels; the beauty of snow on ice is the beauty of old lace—a grand dame in billows of rose point and Valenciennes.

All hardy nursery stock can be moved as soon as the ground is free from frost.

20. GOING BERSERK WITH IMPUNITY. There are two kinds of stores that I dare any man to visit with a week's salary loose in his pocket: One is a first class grocery and the other is a shop that specializes in new and trick kitchen gadgets.

Go into a grocery, say, for an ordinary pound of coffee. Were you a sane and dutiful husband, you'd buy that coffee and clear out. But the gastronomic temptations are too great. Here is honey from Syria put up in a pretty pot. Yonder is Irish bacon, and, farther along, weird cheeses and uncommon fruits and all manner of strange and delectable foods put up in glass like jewels in cases. From one counter to another you pass, buying this and succumbing to that. Finally you stagger home under a load of parcels, a quantitary Father Christmas.

The same sort of thing happens when a man is left unwatched and unattended in a household equipment store. The child in him is fascinated by all the new things he sees—the trick lemon squeezer that will also beat eggs and cut cookies, the washing machines that purr and churn like speed-boats, the wide and fearsome set of knives, the steel that will not rust and the trouser hangers that are almost human. Let a man enter such a store for a package of picture wire, and he'll come out with enough equipment to start in as a cook or a carpenter. . . Which leads me to believe that men should buy the household equipment.

There is a notion that these matters appeal only to women. Well, they do appeal to the housewife's wise and sane view of household economy, but when a man is entrusted with such affairs, he usually goes berserk. There are so few occasions in the course of the normal married man's life when he can splurge with impunity. If he goes in for expensive bulbs and plants, his non-gardening wife will surely take offense. If he goes in for many and costly suits of clothes, she will accuse him—and rightly—of being vain. But let him loose in a household equipment store, and any extravagance he may commit will be forgiven.

These are dark and hard matters to understand, but every man has encountered them and has, after bitter experience, learned to accept them as among the mysteries of the marital life. Many a man has learned, too, that the path to forgiveness lies in the direction of a new ironing board and that all will be forgotten if he appears bearing the latest gadget to cut Grapefruit.

A good indoor job these days is to make permanent labels for your trees and shrubs.

21. THE INDICATIVE DUMP. Among the axioms of modern business is found the statement that a factory can be judged by its dump. Progress is marked by discarding out-of-date and inefficient machinery or by-products that were merely experiments made in reaching for higher standards of manufacturing. In the same manner you can judge a good gardener by what he flings—and willingly—on the compost heap; those Irises that turned out second rate, that Rose which failed to make the grade, those "novelties" that proved to be no novelties at all. It is the poorest sort of economy to give room, in either a factory or a garden, to junk.

Many annuals can be started indoors in a flat placed in a sunny cellar window.

22. NIGGARDLY PLANTING. The subject that at the moment annoyed this learned landscape architect was the habit pursued by many Americans of turning their gardens into unlovely arboretums and flower collections. Why not use fewer plants, said he. And to bolster up his point he cited the great gardens of Italy, which were composed entirely of only half a dozen or so kinds of trees, and shrubs, and flowers were few and rarely used. There was much to be said for his side, perhaps. The collecting habit soon becomes pronounced

when one takes an individual interest in his garden. Imagine being satisfied, though, with great masses of one kind of Lilac when there are available all the lovely hybrids of Lemoine? Conceive a garden with just one kind of Peony, when the creations of Kelway, Dessert, Lemoine, Miellez, Richardson, Hollis, Brand, Pieas and Shayler are to be had? Or a walk of merely one Iris when the subtle variations of Sturtevant, Farr, Dykes, Cayeux, Yeld, Perry, and Vilmorin are purchasable for a small sum? Perhaps a Rose garden of only Radiance would satisfy some, but I dare any one to resist the beauties that have come to us from Paul and Pernet-Ducher, from Dickson and Pierson, Hill, McGredy, Cook, Lovett, Van Fleet and Howard and Smith. Without these, gardens would be niggardly indeed.

The answer to this disgruntled landscapist lies in the fact that when the great Italian gardens were being laid out, flowers were not classed among the ornamental material suitable for garden-making. Most of them were grown for their medicinal virtues, and were relegated to the kitchen and herb garden.

As soon as freezing nights have passed, see that the water for the garden hydrants is turned on.

23. THE KING OF BASHAN'S BED. One must be very patient with a man cursed with the name of Og. Fit ground for a healthy matricide that. The original old Og painfully Ogged down the centuries until the cross-word puzzle rescued him

from oblivion. "Of the remnant of the race of giants," he was said to be, and "behold, his bedstead was a bedstead of iron, nine cubits long, four cubits broad." That is, 13½ feet long and 6 wide. In the parlance of today, Og's iron bed was *some* bed. Perhaps it compensated for the shortness of his name.

One of these days, when we make over the barn into a guest house, I am going to see that it is equipped with Og's beds, for among our friends we have many that are remnants of the race of giants. While they are indoors they must move cautiously lest they bang their heads upon our low ceilings; it is only fair that we give them Og-size accommodation for the night.

If you can't consume all the eggs the hens are now laying, put down the surplus in water-glass.

24. CELESTIAL SEDUMS. Of the tribe of Sedums, so far as I can find out, there are sealed five hundred. A vast family of lowly plants, out of which most of us are satisfied if we know only a few—the golden-flowered Stonecrop, *Sedum acre,* with blooms like twinkling stars; and *S. album,* with white blossoms that are as stars on a frosty night; *S. maximum,* with its purple foliage and salmon-pinkish flowers; the rampant *S. sarmentosum,* elbowing his way hither and yon; *S. Sieboldi,* of the changeable foliage; and *S. stoloniferum.* These most of us know since rock gardening and the planting of garden pavements have become a habit among American gardeners.

To these acquaintances we should add *S. spectabile,* with the flat planes of pink flowers, coming in late Summer and early Fall. A lover of dry soil, this fellow. . . . But what a meagre handful this is! All we can muster is a slim corporal's guard out of a great army. My pet American nurseryman lists only nineteen kinds and my favorite English dealer offers only forty-three.

In that horticultural reincarnation which I hope is coming to me, I shall put down as among the first things to do: "Grow all the five hundred known Sedums!" But let's hope my angelic assistants won't mix the tags of my celestial Sedums, for all you've got to do with most of these little succulents is to snap off a bit and drop it in the soil, and it roots forthwith.

Offer a prize to the member of the family who finds the first Violet.

25. A SENTIMENT ON LITTLE POTS. Whenever I see inconsequential people living in a large house and wandering around their large garden (in which they never lift a finger) I am reminded of those plants that lay down on their job of flowering when they have too much pot and too much root room. Amaryllis will act that way. Put the fleshy bulbs into big pots, and they simply stand still; move them into smaller pots where their roots have to scrape around for food and they throw beautiful stalks. Coddling is a habit with sentimental gardeners. Most coddled plants up and die the moment you turn your back on them. Treat them casually after you have once given

them their bare necessities, and they somehow manage to make a good account of themselves. Discipline and restriction are counsels of perfection for men and plants alike. Perhaps in some future Utopia the inconsequential people who now live in large houses will be obliged to live in small ones. They may then cease being inconsequential.

As soon as Delphinium shoots appear above ground, pop some Bordeaux mixture on them.

26. CORN SOLITUDE. Beyond our house the road is tucked under the elbow of a sprawling hill, and on the hilltop lives a farmer. Most of the winter months the bad roads would seem to isolate him. He has no telephone and no desire for a radio, and the car he drives is one of Mr. Ford's maiden efforts. Dropping in one day, I asked, "Fred, don't you ever get lonely up here?"

"Not in Winter or Spring," he answered. "Then I can see across the valley to Jim Betts. It's easy to see him moving around his place in Winter, and in Spring when I'm plowing I can see him plowing too. He kinda keeps me company." Then he stopped and thought for a moment. "But gosh, ain't it lonely when the Corn gets high!"

Tomorrow indulge yourself to a new pair of heavy gardening shoes.

27. GARDEN MANNERS. The person I could cheerfully slay (and probably will some day) is the visitor who, on passing up and down the border and among the rare seedlings in my mini-

ature nursery, answers, with a lofty air, to the name of each unusual plant, "Oh, yes, I have that." The fisherman is a proverbial prevaricator, and one who doesn't stretch the truth seems a poor fisherman. To the golfer and the hunter are allowed their legitimate margins of exaggeration. Custom has never given this license of fibbing to gardeners, however. We are supposed, we gardeners, to be a truthful race, but a terrible lot of the sistern and brethren have backslidden.

It should be written in the Book of Garden Manners that well-brought-up gardeners never say, "Oh, yes, I have that." I trust it is, for I would be saved from the habit of muttering into my moustache, "Cheerful liar." Which, also, is bad manners.

Don't fork or spade soil until it is dry enough for the clods to crumble when they fall.

28. UNWINDING THE MUMMIES. Toward the end of March there come warm days that are deceiving. Our natural impulse is to rush out and rake the mulch off borders and uncover the Roses. It takes courage to withstand the temptation, but those who are as ice to its desire have their reward. These are dangerous days; the thawing and freezing of the soil uproot plants and bring desolation. Far better to let it stay frozen. Garden mummies must be unwound gradually: take off only the boards and boughs that hold down the mulch, and count that labor enough for the day. The next week, lift some of the mulch, and the

following week, complete the job and turn back the soil that you heaped last November around your Roses.

To prevent damping off see that the frames containing seedlings are given a daily airing.

29. SUB-SURFACE FEEDING. I explained this to a Scotch gardener, and he vowed it was a good work. Each Spring, when the frost has opened the ground we feed the roots of all trees and shrubs. Take a crowbar and, around the perimeter made by the tree's outmost branches, drive it down to the depth of a foot or more. Make these holes a foot apart. If the bush or tree be big and its spread expansive, bore holes in concentric rings a foot apart until you come to within about a foot from the trunk. Then fill the holes with bone meal or shredded cow manure or, better still, a mixture of one-third Muriate of Potash, one-third Nitrate of Soda and one-third Thompson's Phosphate. Mix this at least twenty-four hours before using. If it is being spread on the surface, keep it eighteen inches to two feet away from the trunk of the tree or shrub. It is more effective underground, however.

The purpose of this sub-surface fertilization is to feed the roots. Spring rains make a sweet liquor of the fertilizer, which is carried down to the little rootlets by which a plant assimilates its nourishment. Were it merely scattered around the soil or dug into the top layer of earth, the roots would reach up to it. This system keeps them down where there is constant moisture. The effect on the trees and shrubs is magical.

When ordering seeds, try some new flower or vegetable you've never grown before.

30. GOD'S COMEDIANS. My gardener, for whose judgment I have ample respect, stated the other day that, in his opinion, chickens were God's comedians. You can't see this in a casual glance, however; you have to watch them a long time, said he. The more I watch chickens, the more I think they are God's perfect dumb-bells, granted that the Divine Wisdom would so forget Itself as to create a dumb-bell. Two nesting boxes are in the chicken house. Are they ever both used? Never. If one is occupied, the other hens will stand around patiently until that hen gets out, completely ignoring the box that is empty.

The top covering of the Rose bed can now be taken off.

31. FLASH 14. The six hundred and seventeenth time that I lost my heart was when I encountered a stove. I had visons of a country stove of the sort many men could sit around, and, in the Rabelaisian manner of yokels, spit upon. The local stove dealer spoke familiarly of his wares by their names. He offered a Jim Dandy, a Flirt or a Flash 14. Something about that last name piqued my curiosity. The combination of name and number was mysterious. So Flash 14 was bought into bondage and duly installed. It had a girth like an Oak; its feet sprawled out nobly to the four

points of the compass, and its head was crowned with such a pinnacle of cast-iron fretwork as to make its designer immortal. For many a long Winter's day and night Flash 14 and I have been companions, close and warm companions. I have fed her rapacious craw and toasted my palms at her ruddy flanks and defied the storms outside because she was with me. And yet it was not for all these estimable virtues that I loved her. Estimable virtues rarely are loved. It was for her name, the utterly incongruous title that she wore across her blinking forehead and which set her apart from all the other stoves in the world.

When the Maples begin to leaf and you can plant outdoors once more, thank God that you've lived to enjoy another Spring.

LONG PIECE

THE COLUMN FOR BEAUTY

ACCOUNTANTS are exact and matter-of-fact men. Their minds run in orderly columns. Items either go up and down a column or across a row of them. Everything must have its place and be in it. Totals that balance are their delight. They know no despair save when totals fail to balance or they encounter an item for which no column exists. Vague abstractions are anathema to them. If they must be set down, they are rated under sublimely mediocre headings.

Knowing these things to be so, I went to an accountant with this question: "In making up a list of expenditures, into what column do you put Beauty?"

Now Beauty is one of those fatally abstract notions we all toy with. Philosophers have striven vainly to pin it down with a definition. Poets and artists flutter about its shadow. The average mortal finds it concretely expressed in a thousand ways. But it will not be defined nor pinned down. Its shadow passes quickly. We reach out to touch it, and it has gone.

Because of its evasive character, the accountant was stumped. He knew as an axiom that Beauty pays, hence it is an asset. He also knew that it may not be obtained without effort and a price, hence it must be classed as an expense. I could see him mentally running up and down his columns and striding them crosswise. Finally, realizing that an answer must be given, he assumed his most serious pose and said, "Beauty should be put down to capital expenditure."

Capital expenditure, as it was then explained, is a basic necessary expense, but you must never make that necessary expense unless you figure the interest you would have received had you not spent the money. So you must pay for Beauty first as an investment, then as a loss. Consequently, when you are considering an expenditure for this vague abstraction, Beauty, you must never forget that it will constantly extract its price from your purse. If you are tempted, then, to surround yourself with beautiful things, you must figure both these costs. Yes, so this accountant agreed, you must compare the price of the Rose bush with the enjoyment you receive from the Rose, then, if the latter outweighs the former, you are justified in making your expenditure.

"Then how do you figure enjoyment?" I pressed. "And pride of ownership and . . ." Seeing that I was a dunce at figures he went back to his books. And I knew, and was happy in knowing, that for many, indeed for most of the things that make life richer, there are no columns and there never can be.

There is told a story of an Arab who had a famous garden and who, on being obliged to move away from that section of the country, offered to sell it to a friend. Being a good business man, the friend set about making an appraisal of it, and eventually he brought his figures to the owner. All the items were set down—the cost of the grading and the masonry, the water pipes and the pool, the cost of the walls and the arbor and the trees and shrubs and vines and flowers. After studying it awhile the Arab said, "This is no appraisal, my friend. You have not appraised the perfume of my Orange groves, nor the glories of my Iris, nor the exquisite aroma of my Spice Trees. You have not appraised the song of the birds that make their home in my garden. You've said nothing of the tinkle of water from my fountain. The material things you have priced are merely the framework for the beauty that gives it life and character . . . But alas, these things you never can appraise. Their value will depend entirely on your capacity for enjoying them."

In so many ways can Beauty surround us that a man may soon beggar himself in acquiring them. And yet the "capital expenditure" for that chair which has a beauty of line raised above the dull commonplace herd of chairs, those curtains, that interesting wall paper, that deep-pile carpet, that rug laboriously and wonderfully created on the loom—may we not say that such "capital expenditures" are justified so long as we have the capacity for enjoying the Beauty that is in them? The well-planted garden, the well-designed house, the etching on the wall, the linen and crystal and silver on the table, the books on the shelves, all must be bought ever remembering that their value to us far out-weighs their costs. Indeed, many of us who cannot afford to own them, will deliberately sacrifice things others consider essential in order to surround ourselves with their beauty.

The more we enjoy those things that are beautiful, the more we realize that the very best part of life finds no column in the material registers of accountancy. There is no place for the song of birds or the music of water or the sunlight flooding a lovely room. There is no place for the grand sweep of a roof-line or the noble strength of a chimney. Man has not yet devised a budget wherein such things can be calculated. The seven senses refuse to stay put in a column. There are no account books for the heart.

Shakespeare asked, "Where is fancy bred? Or in the heart or in the head? How begot, how nourished?"

Tempted by some "capital expenditure" in Beauty, we soon learn the answer—we begin valuing it by the head; then, as the desire for it increases, its material price grows less and less.

We succumb. And taking it home rejoicing, our steps keep merry pace with the rhythm of that catechism of those who live full lives:

"Where was I first taught to enjoy Beauty? In my heart!"

THE MONTH OF APRIL

1. DRILLERS. Among the marvels of this season (and may many years of gardening never dim their wonder) is the way bulbous plants drill their way boldly and profusely through the crevices of the frozen soil. Try it for yourself—try driving a crowbar through the ground when frost still grips it; then imagine the insistent, tireless force, the energy and chemical heat that raise these green points to the wan light of the early Spring sun. The early Tulips, stout little fellows that they are, appear capable of this kind of job, but the thin-stemmed Clusiana—truly a Lady Tulip—isn't bothered by it at all and the multitude of small things that spatter the shadowy places under shrubs—the Scillas, the Snowdrops, the Grape Hyacinths and Chinodoxas—drill through this frost-stoned soil apparently without effort.

Tomorrow order those Dahlias that you saw at last Autumn's show.

2. THE LITTLE HERBAL. The day that had begun cloudy, closed down with rain. Most people were home at dinner and those outdoors went scurrying along head down. For a Naples street on a rainy night is an inhospitable place, nor man nor beast wants to be there. We, too, trudged along hotelward, thinking of dry clothes and a good supper, when suddenly our eyes were caught

by a lighted shop window. Another antique shop! Come along! We had been in dozens of antique shops that day with scarcely a purchase. But this was particularly dirty and disorderly, and in we went.

Half an hour later, we came out bearing a treasure and blissfully happy, even if the rain did lash our faces. For in the dingy purlieus of that shop we found a tiny herbal—"Erbalario o Distinta delle Erbe." Some loving soul, back in the Year of Grace 1737, had made an herbal of her own garden—cut from an older book the wood block prints of all the flowers that she grew, colored them, arranged them alphabetically, made an index, and then bound the leaves in stout vellum. This wee personal herbal measures only five inches by four, but what a treasure, and how uncanny a place and time to find it—a dismal Naples back street on a rainy night!

Bush Roses can be pruned now after the hilling of earth has been pushed flat.

3. THE PORCINE PALACE. Among the multitude of my rustic experiences the building of the pig house will remain epic. It stands out above my many endeavors like a mountain peak above valleys. For weeks I had saved a design for it, clipped from a farm journal. There came a false Spring day in March—a warm Sunday that brought the valley folk out of doors. From the miasmic, dusty depths of the barn were hauled the accumulated packing cases of many years' shipments. With these and some old timbers, the gardener and I

began rearing this noble structure. The sound of our hammering brought the family out, then neighbors appeared, attracted by this unseemly Sabbath noise. They sat around in concentric rings casting jibes at us, making Rabelaisian suggestions, but never for a moment did we cease. First the floors, then the sidewall timbers and finally the ridge pole, its skeleton arose. This we carefully clothed with boards from the packing boxes, until that house, built like an acute angle, reared its head up to the empyrean.

It is difficult to describe the grim satisfaction that came over me as I nailed that last board in place amid the ribald jeers of my neighbors. Nor can I picture the pride with which I turned to them and, leaning upon the flank of this porcine palace, made a manly gesture. But scarcely had I thus communicated my sentiments when something cracked. Something fundamental gave away. Beneath my weight the whole house collapsed and I was thrown into its débris. A terrific shout from the audience, and I was sitting where the pigs should have sat, crestfallen on my hams, amid a chaos of broken boards. . . . And may it be counted to me for grace that I did not swear.

Melons germinated in sod in the hotbed can now be set out under small forcing frames.

4. WIVES AND DELPHINIUMS. A good Delphinium, like a good wife, has a price above rubies, but neither of them is to be had for the mere wishing, and neither is productive if ailing all the

time. About this season of year I inspect the places where the Delphiniums were planted last Fall and gradually take away the ashes that were heaped around to ward off slugs, to whom Larkspur sprouts are as caviar and chocolate roll and Bourbon whiskey. Then begins a dosage against root rot and blight—the lime and tobacco spray, with Bordeaux dug around the crowns. One of these days I'm going to set out my seedlings in soil that has been given sulphur and soot, and see what that does to the root bugs. No plant can be healthier than its roots and the sickly Delphinium had better be banished to the limbo of the compost heap and its place taken, after the soil has been sterilized with a solution of Semesan, by a fresh young seedling. But long before this point the simile of the wife has been forgotten.

See that you have plenty of Dahlia stakes and Bean poles on hand.

5. "BRING OUT YOUR DEAD!" At about this season of the year, the gardener becomes a stretcher-bearer. The Battle of the Winter over, he sallies forth across the frost-trenched garden to dig up his dead and count his casualties. Of those dozens of Rose bushes he planted last Autumn in fond hope of a sure Spring resurrection, how many remain? Of those Crocuses and Tulips he committed to the earth, dreaming of a gorgeous Spring display, how many have the moles and field-mice left? Of all those speculatively hardy things—those Chrysanthemums and Tritomas, those Brooms nursed carefully all last year and

then left out-of-doors—of these how many have the soil-ripping frosts and the intense cold permitted to survive?

To the hardened gardener of many years' experience, this is all part of the day's work, just as in warfare, burying the dead and picking up the wounded is a job that has to be gone through with however unpleasant it may be. There comes a day in early April when it is safe to venture abroad, when the barrage of cold lifts and we begin to uncover the beds and unwind the Box bushes and brittle conifers from their swaddling gunnysacks and tilt back the glass of the cold frames. Gingerly we lift off the winter mulch with a fork—the leaves and hay and the boughs and boards that held it in place.

At this point you may tell a hardened gardener from a beginner. For a beginner is a meticulous soul. Like a new bride with a brand new house that she keeps uncomfortably clean, the beginning gardener will clear off every vestige of mulch down to the naked soil; whereas one longer practised in the game leaves the bottom layer on to rot into good leafmold and protect those tender white shoots that appear early.

You may also know the practised gardener by the fact that he has no illusions about the casualties of winter. He goes along his borders, as once on a day in the plague times of London, the drivers of the death-carts used to pass, shouting, "Bring out your dead!" He knows that he will have some casualties. The beginning gardener has a notion that, by the kindly favoritism of Nature, his garden will be skipped. Wouldn't it be pleasant if, like the Hebrews of old, we could mark the lintels of our gardens so that the Angel of Winter Death would pass them over! Alas, that age of miracles is gone! To amateur and practised gardener alike, Spring reveals her casualties.

And further, you may know the type of gardener by the way he takes these casualties. There is no use crying over spilt milk or weeping over dead plants. Bring out paper and pencil and list your dead. Send off to the nurseryman for more. The garden ranks must be filled up. The procession of the Spring is going forward—it must not show ugly gaps.

And having done that, forget it. For there is too much talk and bother about Winter killings. It may be the bugbear of beginners, but to those long in the game, it is proof of their gardening fortitude, the evidence of that calm, philosophic attitude which comes from long association with fickle, eccentric Nature.

Before sowing seed in drills see that the drills are parallel, using for this mathematical surety either a string or board.

6. PRICKLY JOUSTS. I am writing with hands that might have been in a cat fight on a back fence, whereas they have been in even a more scratchy encounter on a back wall. In spite of thick leather linesmen's gloves and the most gingerly approach to thorns, my early Spring battle with climbing Roses leaves me a scarred veteran. It is one of the pleasures I reserve for myself, this trimming out of winter-killed wood. The first

week in April is the time for it in our latitude. The job of pruning finished, the tangles of barbed vine are piled on the vegetable garden and burned. Then I retire to the house to lick my wounds.

That is the April pruning. In early August we prune again to cut out the old wood that has flowered. On this encounter even more of me gets torn, for thorns penetrate a shirt sleeve with the ease of a hot knife through butter. Since I have a mask and goggles for spraying, why not a chain armor shirt for riding in the prickly jousts of this Queen of Flowers?

The bud spray for fruit trees should be given twice at about this season.

7. HIC JACET. When we mentioned buying that orchard on the hill, my neighbor hesitated. It was a precious place to her, it seemed. As she sat on her side porch complaisantly rocking those Summer days, she could look out through the shadows of the Apple trees, and the empty reaches became peopled to her. In the long years she had lived here (some of them desperately lonely years) her companions had been cats and dogs and birds, and one by one, as they passed, she laid them away under the shadow of those old Apples where in Springtime their graves were covered with the snow-sheet of fallen blossoms. Though eventually she did surrender it, I never go into that little orchard without thinking of the Great Frederick and his lovely Summer home, "San Souci," at Potsdam, and the spot at the end of the terrace

where his favorite dogs lie buried, each under his little stone.

When Sweet Peas are up four inches, begin filling the trench.

8. CURCUBITA. May I never become so serious and precious a gardener that I neglect to grow Gourds. Varied of shape and amusing, these Cucurbita, as the learned gentry call them, come in about thirty forms, in tints of green, yellow, orange and brown, so that all you have to do is to pay your money and take your pick. Visitors always acclaim them with delight, children cry for them and scarcely a one but goes home with his share of the harvest. We plant them behind a high rear fence, loop the vines over the top and onto the roof of a Summer house, and when Black Frost turns the vine itself to a mere string, here are festooned golden Oranges and sulphur Lemons, Turk's-caps and eggs, Pears and strange Apples, like decorations on a Christmas tree. Later we hang them indoors to make a Harvest Home window and heap them up for table decorations. Indeed, they lend themselves to many an amusing purpose before they take up their ultimate work in the depths of the stocking bag.

Potatoes can be set out any time now to get a good start before hot weather.

9. MEDIOCRITY IN FLOWER POTS. Year after year and generation after generation American gardeners go on using the same form of flower pot. A few of them dip into Italy and France,

see the infinite and beautiful forms the common flower pot takes in those countries, wonder vaguely why we don't have them in America—and then come home and do nothing about it. Here we are, a great creative and commercial nation, and in such a common, ordinary affair as a flower pot, we never rise above the dead level of a utilitarian mediocrity.

A fortune awaits the man with the temerity and capital to break away from the accustomed forms of flower pots. He should also be awarded the gold medals of the horticultural societies of this country.

You may know that Spring has come when the first "peepers" begin to make their infernal squallings at nights.

10. ABSURD GROUNDS. We Americans are notorious the world over for forming societies. Let some bright soul give birth to his one bright idea, and forthwith he must form a society to bring it to accomplishment. Yet in this way many excellent things have been attained, and not the least of them the popularizing of gardening. The garden club idea has now reached every type and size of community. It is affording new personal and civic interests to people who hitherto lacked them. The ladies, of course, lead in this worthy endeavor, and their golf-playing husbands tolerate the descent of the local club upon their homes with a condescending and amused air. Eventually we may have garden clubs for men only—one or two already exist. But I doubt the wisdom of

attempting them. They probably would only furnish Reno with a new ground for divorce. Incompatability of gardening temperaments may sound a little far-fetched but, then, most grounds for divorce are far-fetched. Perhaps we might found a society for proving the absurdity of grounds for divorce.

Even this early you can make the first of your fortnightly plantings of Gladiolus corms.

11. THE CAUSE OF AN ACUTE PAIN. And while I am on this subject of garden clubs, let me venture a bit of advice. Too many of them are merely social organizations. Too many of their meetings degenerate into tea parties. Now tea is an excellent institution and not for the world would I raise my voice against it, but sometimes it does devastate gardening interest. So also does the silly idea that one's social standing in a community decides one's eligibility for the local garden club. Gardening is a divine form of democracy that has naught to do with one's forebears or the kind of car one drives or the clothes one wears. Wherever I find a garden club boasting that its members were chosen from the local social register alone, the pain in my neck becomes acute.

A universal and generous distribution of bone meal is the first step in successful Spring gardening.

12. SWEET PEAS. Although in more favored climates St. Patrick's Day is the official time for planting Sweet Peas out-of-doors, we usually

postpone this rite until April. The real forehanded gardener, of course, plants them the previous Autumn, or, if he has a greenhouse to start them in, they should be well under way by this time. But whether started indoors or out, in Autumn or in Spring, there is no use attempting Sweet Peas unless two necessities are provided: a trench deeply dug and well enriched for them to grow in, and first-class seed. And of these two I'm beginning to believe that the seed is more important.

Young plants of Cabbage, Cauliflower and Lettuce, sufficiently hardened off, can now be set out.

13. HUNTING THE MAGENTA. The good old sport of hunting the fox pales into vagueness beside the modern game of hunting the magenta. It all began with some esthetic soul proclaiming (in the 90's I suspect) that red in gardens was just barely tolerable but magenta was the unforgivable sin. Ever since then the female of the species among gardeners have ridden down this poor old magenta and never ceased for a moment until they've come in at the death. Let a stray Aster, so forget its forebears as to go magenta, and out it is snatched. Let a Phlox dare lift its magenta head in the border, and a hue and cry is raised. To horse! To horse! And before you realize it, this miscreant Phlox is hurled into the oblivion of the compost heap.

They say that hounds are no real good for fox hunting until they've had a taste of blood. Do these esthetic ladies, I wonder, subject their new trowels to an initiatory first taste of magenta?

If you are planting in new soil, test it for acid or alkaline reaction and treat accordingly.

14. PLANTING PARSONS. In England the country parson becomes either the local archeologist and historian or a gardener. And were it not for those planting parsons, English gardening would be much poorer today. Among the clerics, who carried on the heritage of those monks who drained the fens and made them give their increase, are men to whom we will be eternally indebted—dear old Dean Hole, P. H. Pemberton, F. Page-Roberts and Foster Melliar, all giant Rosarians; Joseph Jacobs of Tulip and Crocus fame; W. Wilkes, who gave us the Shirley Poppies and Foxgloves named after his parish; Henry Ewbank who contributed to our lore of the Oncocyclus Irises.

Somehow our American country parsons don't seem to be stirred by horticultural ambitions. Only a few of them have made any marked efforts along these lines. The others, well, the others seem to be busy trying to give the impression of hail-fellow-well-met and taking an occasional crack at golf, just to prove that they're 'human." Pish-posh and bah! How I loathe these aggressive, "good fellow" parsons!

Plant thick and thin quick is the rule for vegetables and flowers in rows. Start thinning when quite young.

15. VASE SEASONS. The progress of our garden seasons is marked by the vases we use. This time of year only the smallest are brought forth for the first little flowers—the pewter porringer for the Pansies from the cold frame, the base of a sperm oil hand lamp for a Crocus or two, or sprigs of Creeping Phlox and Arabis. When the Daffies come in, the vases get taller, and by the time of Delphinium and Phlox and Turk's-cap Lilies and Gladiolus, they grow wide-throated, monstrous and tall. Then, as these pass, and White Frost is succeeded by the killing Black Frost, we go back to the little vases again, for the few blooms of Verbena and Stock that are spared, with one or two leggy vases saved out for Chrysanthemums.

Tomorrow and ten days later spray Currant bushes for the green worm that devastates them.

16. MY COMPLIMENTS TO THE CRABS. The Flowering Crabapples are a family whose praises should be sounded on clarinets and trombones, on gongs and xylophones and big bass drums. Twenty varieties are disposed at various places around this little hillside property, ranging from the dwarf Sargeant Crab to the more commonplace *Malus floribunda* which, being my first acquisition from this family, found a place at the head of the lawn by the road, where it enjoys the background of a tall Forsythia and Lilac group to cast its lovely pink and white flowers against. Here Grape Hyacinths gather about its feet. In

the orchard, where others stand, their falling petals mingle with a carpet of Daffies.

The generous manner of the Flowering Crabs will repay such little care as they require—the spraying and feeding and cultivating—for not alone does each kind write its own Spring poem on the April and May skies, but it plays an abundant Autumnal return engagement of tinted leafage and of colorful fruit in which the birds delight.

Lima Bean poles should be put in place before the seed is sown.

17. TOPIARY. Among the styles of garden decoration that happily have passed out of favor is topiary work. Innocent and inoffensive Box, Yew and Arborvitae were clipped to represent animals and various inanimate objects. One still encounters them occasionally around English cottages, and in German gardens. This "abandonment of Nature" for the "offspring of fancy" as the famous English landscapist, John Papworth, called it, was begun by the Romans, who in designing their gardens made them the antithesis of the informality of Nature. The Italians, French and Germans followed the Roman and "the Dutch with equal zeal, applied a similar practice to the singular circumstances of their country." It took no time for the taste for topiary work to cross the Channel, and at the beginning of the last century the English garden that lacked its grotesquely clipped Evergreens was considered no garden at

all. Then the reaction against them set in with the rise of "Capability" Brown and his naturalistic school of garden design. By 1825 topiary work was being called "the disgrace of modern times."

Evergreens may be safely moved and planted in early Spring.

18. WORKING GUESTS. About this season of the year guests begin putting in their appearance. A warmish day in town, and these urban romanticists start to recite the jingle about coming down to Kew in Lilac time, and showing an unwonted curiosity about the progress of this place of ours in the country. We usually are able to stave them off for a while, since early Spring and late Autumn we reserve for ourselves. But by the end of April there's no dodging their hints.

Once, in my innocence, I had visions of these guests lending a hand in the garden: when we invited them we made a point of saying that we lived informally and be sure to bring old clothes. Well, that was in my innocence, I say, and my innocence is long past. Looking back over a decade of these supposedly working guests, I can recall only one who did a lick of work, and that was a girl. May her name go down to remembrance! She worked like a Trojan and then asked for more. She knew weeds from flowers. The secatures were safe in her hands. However, she only came once.

Since then, when we are pinioned by these direct hints of Spring-haunted city friends, we tell them that we live rather formally and *do* bring clothes for parties.

Chicken manure, harbored over the winter and now mixed with sand, can be raked into beds and borders.

19. FATHER ELM AND MOTHER OAK. Once on a day, when such things could be done in safety, I ventured a tramping tour from Amsterdam to Paris. My companion was a little Englishman who preferred, in our dispatches, to be known as "Firefly." Likewise a natty fox terrier to whom "Jack" was enough of a name. What the sentiments of Jack happened to be I could not tell, but "Firefly" assumed the most extraordinary attitudes toward forests and big trees: he always doffed his cap when he passed them. This reverence was strange to his otherwise unsentimental English ways and when I pinned him down about it, he answered like a poet: "Merely respect for age, my dear fellow. I have a great respect for age. Especially aged and noble trees."

It was the Druid in the lad. For once on a time—and many primitives still do—people believed that the human race sprang from a tree. Yggdrasil, the tree of the Universe, symbolized the life-giving forces of Nature. An Ash, its fruit was said to be the seed of stars. Others thought the source of mankind an Oak. The Eddas of the Scandinavians, the Aeneid, the Odyssey and even Genesis itself, the ancient scriptures and paintings of Egypt and Assyria, all have their Tree of Life and the Hindoos have their legendary trees of which the fruit brings immortality.

> Brother to the Ash am I and cousin to the
> Cedar.
> Son of Father Elm and Mother Oak!

Begin to train climbing Roses in the way they should go.

20. THE RISE OF THE BORDER. In these April weeks and on through May and into June we watch the yearly phenomenon of the Long Border rising to its full stature. After the Winter mulch has been removed, for a few days we can tramp its length and breadth without hindrance. From then on, gradually and steadily, its entire area arises. Higher and higher, through Tulip leaf and Iris blade and Peony frond, through Phlox clump and Baptisia spray, by Larkspur head and Columbine. A mighty host of men arising to their feet. Like a mob of Moslems, head-down on their prayer rugs facing Mecca when the Muezzin of Spring calls. Prayer over, they lift their heads and scramble to their feet and go about their business.

Tomorrow the garden furniture can be set in its accustomed outdoor positions.

21. CLOSED FOR BIRDS. The first Spring we came here birds began nesting under the eaves of the front porch and in the foliage of the Honeysuckle and Wistaria and Roses that clamber over its balustrade. Spring after Spring they have returned;

renovated the nests or built new ones, laid their eggs, hatched their broods and kept up a chatty social life under our bedroom windows. At that season callers must enter the house by the back door, for a rope is stretched across the bottom of the porch steps and the way is barred by a sign that reads "Closed for Birds."

Cannas can now be divided and potted up for rooting before being planted out-of-doors.

22. GLADIOLUS INVESTMENTS. Like picking up money in the street is the increase of the Gladiolus. And one of these early April days the boxes of dried corms are hauled forth and spread on the barn floor. I sit amid the heaps and count my gold. Scarcely a corm gives less than two of its kind, with a multitude of cormlets gathered about it for good measure. And each year, with this increase and a few additional novelties thrown in, the Gladiolus patch grows bigger. Each week, from mid-April on to July, a new line is planted, and all through the border they are scattered with a liberal hand. For this bulb is a seasoned, gilt-edged investment. It pays not only generous dividends of flowering, but every year offers innumerable rights to new issues of abundant corms. Would that my banker could accept it for collateral!

Clear away all high grass from fences and buildings and thus reduce danger from grass fires.

23. THE OLD LOVE. The mason who has been laying up a wall for us announced that when he reached eighty he was going to quit work. As he still had quite a distance of wall to build and as his eightieth birthday was only a week off, he must work fast. A strange wall that—a drunken sort of wall, straight here and crooked there. The old man's eyesight isn't as good as it used to be. Nor is his hearing; he is stone deaf. We had to write messages on bits of paper, and then he had to search around for his specs and, like as not, he couldn't read the messages correctly. Besides, he was headstrong; he had been laying up walls long before we were born, and you can't tell a man with all that experience that his wall is crooked.

One day, he was seized with romance. In the midst of work he stopped to tell us that sixty years ago, when he was buying horses for Grant's army, he met a girl. Oh, such a girl! And there he stood, in that August sunlight, wondering what had become of her. He didn't come to work the next day, nor the next. A week later he returned. He wore a new cap. He had a collar and a tie, and he carried himself as one upon whom a woman has looked with favor. She no longer lived where she used to, he reported, but he had found her grandniece, and from that clue traced her up to Vermont. What an Autumn romance! After questioning him on bits of paper he finally acknowledged that she was unwed; that he had proposed, but that having already survived two husbands, she wanted a little time to think it over. So he came back to work while she was thinking, back to the stone wall that is straight in some places and crooked in others.

Well, finally, his old love answered him. She had thought it over and had decided that two husbands were about enough. The old man took it hard for a time, then he turned to work as a surcease from his grief. The stone wall was his salvation.

Weed all borders thoroughly, as a weed caught in time saves nine.

24. LANDSCAPE COWS. Among the landscape architects are some who have now attained the dizzy zenith of their art. Not content with landscaping an estate, they suggest that the proper rural notes be added, and the landscape cow has come into being. Of course, some of these country place owners don't want a cow, don't need a cow, but since the Maestro says so, they bow their heads to better judgment. For what is a meadow without a cow? How absurd does a clump of old apple trees appear unless a cow is resting in their shadow contentedly chewing the cud and viewing the landscape with placid eyes? Nevertheless, though their owners are convinced that a cow is necessary to the picture, that their places will simply never be furnished until they acquire a cow, they are on the horns of many a dilemma: shall it be a black and white Holstein or a fawn Jersey or a Guernsey? These are momentous questions to decide.

We once knew an artist who gained a reputation and made a fair livelihood from his painting of sheep in meadows, and we naturally thought that he owned quite a flock. Not so! This canny artist had one solitary, respectable, old sheep. It was tethered in the meadow below the studio window. He would paint it grazing, stroll off and smoke a cigarette, come back and paint it in its new position. By the end of the week, he had an entire flock on canvas.

Perhaps these new landscape meadows can be so planted that one lone Jersey will give visitors the impression of a herd and its owner will gain kudos thereby. How economical! How truly rural!

Plant another line of Gladiolus in the cutting garden and slip some into the border.

25. HOCH DER DWARFS! There's a pleasing gnomelike, squat, well-fed quality about the dwarf Iris that is flowering now. Crouching down to inspect their chubby heads as they bloom in my rock path and in the diminutive Alpine garden, I can think of nothing else save those German families that cluster around the tables in the Hofbrau Haus in Munich, those shining-faced, robust and ruddy people contentedly eating their Radishes and drinking their beer. And my enjoyment of this Pumila beauty is tinctured with solemn curses on the head of Mr. Volstead and his arid kind who have left us only the Radish. The words of my mouth may be smoother than butter, but there is war in my heart. Had I good Munich beer at hand, I would saunter up and down this rock path shouting, "Canary bird, Prosit!" . . . "Your good health, Citrea!" . . . "A long life

to you, Grand Mogul!" . . . "Petite Anne, salute!" . . . "Villereal, bottoms up to you!" . . .

Should it rain tomorrow, make some slat covers for the frames to be used after the glass is stored away.

26. ANCESTRAL PIGS. I had said they would be pretty little pink pigs, and so they were, as pink as babies and with the manners of grown-ups. They immediately took a fancy to their Porcine Palace, set about housekeeping and were regular at meals. Those who had mocked at my poor carpentry in building the pig house, now came to marvel at their beauty. We gave them (the pigs, I mean) peat to tread upon and fed them succulent things from the table and the garden. Their coming opened a new chapter in my life. Here I had lived all these years and never had a pig! And yet our sympathy and understanding was immediate and mutual. Perchance my enthusiasm for them was a throw-back from a prior generation; perhaps that Irish grandfather, of whom there was so much boasting, had been closer to the soil and the creatures of his native heath than the family would care to admit.

Montbretia, Galtonia and such Summer-blooming bulbs may now be safely planted.

27. LITTLE ACORNS. If you begin gardening late in life or are one of those fortunate fellows who can afford to create immediate effects, then this suggestion is not for you. But if you elect to grow

old along with your trees and shrubs, each year invest a few dollars in plant material that is small. Nurse it along for a year or so and then give it a permanent place on your grounds. You may even have the patience to start some of these shrubs from seed. Of the many things that delight my eyes on August mornings, in nothing do I take such complete satisfaction as in two Rose of Sharon bushes. Eight years ago a Loving Reader sent me, from Mount Vernon, seed of Althea that came, so he said, from Martha Washington's garden. I planted it with visions of having historical Hollyhocks, but when the true leaves appeared, my dream faded. These weren't going to be Hollyhocks! However, we grew them along and today I can sit under the shadow of those bushes.

To dirt gardeners a year more or less means very little. If we don't live to see that sapling grow into a big tree or that flowering shrub toss its sweetness on the Spring air, there are others who will. Meantime we have enjoyed watching it prosper under our hands.

It is about time to bring forth the screen doors from their winter hibernation.

28. Rain Music. Rain by day is a melancholy dirge, discouraging, disheartening and drab; rain by night is a lyric, it has a sweet and appealing timbre that can lull the uneasiest sleeper into placid dreams. Even the tattoo of day rain on a tin roof has a tranquil quality not possessed by that which falls by night. So have those gusty night showers that beat on closed windows. But

rain in fury, whether by day or night, is a hideous cacophony, and Heaven spare us from it. Hissing and roaring its wrath, it castigates the earth with cords of whips that snap and crack as though the sky had gone berserk in a saturnalia of flagellation.

When the first planting of Carrots, Beets and Spinach show above ground, make another.

29. PAINTERS IN PANTALETTES. In a London shop, one sunny June morning, I unearthed the record of a quaint endeavor. It was a pile of flower pictures, painted with meticulous care and exact botanical knowledge, on sheets of vellum. A hundred years ago, when flower-painting was held to be among the requirements for a well-bred young lady, the head mistress of a famous school had made these paintings as examples for her pupils. An accomplished artist, she set a high hurdle for her girls to leap. And how they must have groaned and sighed with despair, these dear little Victorian misses, over attaining the unaccomplishable! A glance at my framed examples of the Rose and the Clematis, and I can see these young ladies in their lace-trimmed pantalettes and candlestick curls struggling with their paints and pencils. Well, if the battles of England have been first won on the cricket creases of Eton, isn't it fair to believe that the glory of her womanhood was raised in this gentle endeavor of painting lifelike flowers?

Michaelmas Daisies may still be divided for blooming this Autumn.

30. GARDENS OF IMPERFECTION. I have often thought that were I starting the garden over again I would undertake its planting in a much more intelligent way: plant only the best varieties in each group—the best Lilacs and Mock-oranges, only those Irises and Peonies that have been given a rating of 80 points and over by their respective societies, only such Roses as the intelligentsia of the American Rose Society recommend. Yes, I would know better—but I would be missing a lot of fun. For progress in gardening, as in collecting and in business and in the most of life, does not advance in one unbroken front; here it progresses, yonder it falls back. Our failures contribute as much to the evolution of taste and the sharpening of intelligence as do our successes. There is no such thing as a garden of perfection. We should love a garden as much for its uncouth wilderness sides and its crass errors as we love our friends for their petty weaknesses.

Begin eating out of doors as soon as the weather permits.

LONG PIECE

THE NOISES OF TOWN

WE WERE working side by side, this countryman and I, he in one row and I in another. The spring air was soft and full of bird music. A slight haze wreathed the farther hills, and in the valley the Elms and Maples were untwisting their leaves. After the manner of gardeners, we spoke only occasionally and disjointedly about this and that—

he of things he did when a boy and I of things that had happened in town. And so the day would have passed, up one row and down another, peacefully, uninterrupted, had not there suddenly broken into the silence a persistent staccato sound.

"Guess that new owner is plowing by tractor," said he, indicating with a soil-dirty thumb a house farther down the ridge whence the noise came. "Yes, I'm sure it's a tractor." Having made that assertion he went to work again, although, to rest his back now and then he straightened up and made sage remarks on tractors.

Two days later he came around and said, rather sheepishly, "You know that noise the other day? Well, at first I was pretty sure it came from a tractor. Then the more I listened to it, I began to have my doubts. Well, it wasn't a tractor. No, sir. That noise came from one of these new-fangled concrete drills. Never heard it before. Funny to hear it up here. They're using it on that house down the ridge, punching holes in the cement to make new windows." He seemed to feel better now that he had gotten that new noise straightened out.

And that is one great difference—that knowledge of noises—between the man of the lonely farmland and the man from town. The town man lives through a whole range of noises that rural folks never hear. And blessed are the ears that are not subjected to them! Lucky are the men and women who do not have to pass their days and nights in the hellish uproar that accompanies life in cities!

The steam shovel and the compressed air drill

are two symbols of material progress. Swift and gargantuan tools, they tear down and build up at an amazing rate. They are the vital instruments in the metabolism of the modern city—this American city which is forever ripping up streets and razing buildings. Without them the work would progress slowly indeed. But we have to pay an appalling price for their efficiency.

Physicians have segregated the diseases of dirt. In a few more years we will find them classifying the diseases that come from noise—nerves subconsciously frayed out by the constant pulsation of traffic, the ripping and tearing of drills and the prodigious panting of steam shovels; ears dimmed to more delicate perceptions by the roaring of elevated trains and the rush of subways.

Some there be who would count this concatenation as music; in fact musicians of the modernist school deliberately try to simulate it in their compositions. We are supposed, if we lay claims to being modern, to like this kind of noise, to find beauty in it and stimulation. It is supposed to symbolize progress.

The countryman, on the other hand, knows a different sort of progress and lives through a different category of noises. Very few of them are unpleasant; very few are nerve-wracking. Most of them are subtle and require a trained ear to appreciate their beauty. The whole range of bird calls, for example; the rush of water over a dam in the first days of spring and the trickle of water over a stony brook-bed in midsummer; the low of cows; the homely grunt and whine of pigs; the contented cluck of hens; the assertive and pompous boasting of roosters; the awkward cry of guinea-fowl; the gobbling of turkeys; the bleat of sheep. They know the soft rustle that follows the wind blowing over a grain field and the sweep of it through tree tops; they know the soughing of the Winter wind through Pines, and the crunch of a tree limb rubbing against a house. They know the patter of rain on a tin roof, which is like the roll of drums; the creak of a loose shutter at night and the conversation of crickets and peepers and the hoot of the owl. They know, too, the gee-haws of a man calling to his horses as he plows, the clatter of a reaper, the hum of a thresher. A few of their noises strike terror—the clap of thunder, the dismal whine of a fire siren or the distant clang of a fire bell—but these are noises not regularly heard.

To one whose life is sweetened by such country sounds, it was only natural that he should think this new noise to be a tractor. Indeed, the progress on which the city world prides itself today is not without just such touches of pathos. It is inevitable, perhaps, that as the old order changeth, there shall be left in its wake little back-eddies where humanity drifts a bit aimlessly, wondering what it is all about. You find such folks in rural regions, puzzled, hesitating people of an earlier day—grayed men and women whom the main stream of progress has passed by. Ears that once could infallibly identify the clack of a distant hay-rake falter now before the drone of a gasoline tractor; eyes that knew each passing bird wing lose their sureness when the air mail goes overhead. And they cannot quite understand it, these old folks.

Happy and blessed above others are they who cannot understand these things, for life has kept them unspotted from a world that, in the end, doesn't seem to make much difference anyhow. . . . It were better to know the call of the wild dove than the shrieks of an elevated train; it were better not to recognize a compressed-air drill when one hears it.

THE MONTH OF MAY

1. Soil Incense. As the smell of hot leather to the huntsman, as the reek of a husband's old pipes to a widow, so is the incense of newly-turned soil to a gardener in Spring. After a Winter of city reeks and the dismal stench of muddy roads in the gum-boot days of March and early April, go forth into your vegetable garden as a devotee into a church. Discard all the clothes the temperature and your proximity to neighbors will allow. Have the feet well booted. Drive the fork straight down till its tines disappear. Lift the clod. Clout it. And around you arises the incense of the soil, which is better than all the perfumes of the East.

Were I a millionaire, and could I afford a host of gardeners, I would never permit them to perform this initial rite for me. For strange as it may seem, this benison of the nostrils can come only in its fullest beauty to those who turn the soil themselves. Merely walking across a newly-plowed meadow or a newly-spaded garden patch brings only a weak suggestion of that earth perfume. Its enjoyment is inextricably commingled with the rhythm of the body's swinging, the play of muscles, the lash of the sun on the arms and back and neck, the clutch of the fingers, the delight of the eye as the brown earth is turned to the sun, the delight of the skin in its gross sweat.

Take care, in your early cultivation, not to disturb the roots of Platycodon.

2. UGLY BUT COMFORTABLE. There's a town not so far away that I enjoy riding through because it has had a respectable past, and it lives on in that past with great dignity. Its houses all look ugly but comfortable. Again and again as I pass old-fashioned houses, I find myself uttering those words—"ugly but comfortable." Many of the houses built in the 1890's were without architectural form, and yet they are mighty comfortable to live in. And, so far as I can discover, two kinds of people live in them—those who know they are ugly, and are unhappy about it; and those who don't seem to sense the ugliness, and are wedded to their comfort.

Now and then, the unhappy ones burst forth from their discontent and hire an architect to modernize their monstrosity. Not always is the result successful. They remind me of vain old women who have had their faces "lifted." If it is the only house you have—and the only face—perhaps it is wiser to be contented with it.

Start mowing the lawn now while the grass is fairly short.

3. BLUE AND YELLOW. A spring combination of which I rarely tire is a massed planting of Rev. H. Ewbank Darwin Tulips with an under-planting of the Munstead strain of Polyanthus Primroses. Thus you have large heliotrope heads rising above the crinkled foliage and yellow and white Polyanthus blooms. In a shadowy corner, a corner

where the Polyanthus may remain undisturbed, this combination has a repressed glow.

Or the combination may be reversed by using the fragrant, slim golden yellow Tulip, Mrs. Moon, the sulphur yellow Moonlight and the canary of Inglescombe Yellow in mingling drifts above a tiny marine-scape of Myosotis Royal Blue—that intense blue of tropical waters.

A third blue and yellow combination that delighted us one Spring was the yellow-orange of Siberian Wallflower supporting drifts of the bright violet William Copeland Tulip, and the bright purplish violet of Tulip Mrs. Potter-Palmer. This, in full sunlight, has a dazzling quality mingled with subtleties—like pulling out a loud diapason on an organ and having it echoed by a pianissimo reed stop.

Manure water poured around Spring-blooming perennials will often produce larger flowers.

4. SMELLY CARILLONS. At this season visitors invariably stop before a strange clump or two in the border and remark, "I ought to know that." Somewhere, dimly in the past, they have encountered this flower. Or their mothers and grandmothers knew it. (Can't we inherit memories? I'm sure we do.) The "that" is always the taller Fritillarias. Among the first to push their knobby heads through the cold soil, they shoot up far above the other things in the borders, and hang out veritable carillons of colorful bells—the orange of the Crown Imperials and Aurora, the

red of Crown-on-Crown and the orange red Big Ben of *Maxima rubra.* Alas, some of these flowers can boast no sweet fragrance—quite the opposite in fact—and they had consequently better be viewed from a distance. The Crown Imperial has a pronounced foxy odor; to some nostrils it is disagreeably reminiscent of over-roasted coffee—a quality by which these plants protect themselves from browsing animals. However, I like them, and when I found my Society for the Repopularizing of Forgotten Things, these smelly taller Fritillarias will be included among them.

By this week all ground covers—Pansies and such—for Darwin Tulips should be planted.

5. NOISY BORERS. In an ancient copy of a Boston paper, printed before the Gay 90's, there was once published the following advertisement:

"Two Antique Chairs for Sale. Heirlooms in vogue in 1776. One contains wood-borer; gnawing plainly heard."

For years now we have been searching for a criterion by which to judge antiques. Learned persons and eminent specialists have talked profoundly on this and that. The slimy trail of the faker has been pointed out to us so that we now know it on sight. But never before has the ultimate judgment, the final criterion, the last word on what makes an antique antique, been vouchsafed us until we encountered this advertisement. Hereafter we shall listen intently for the gnawing of the wood-borer.

Now that the open season for American antiques has arrived, now that the countryside will shortly be blossoming with countless articles and pieces of furniture that were "heirlooms in vogue in 1776," let us pass on to our patriotic fellow-collectors this bit of wisdom: listen for the gnawing!

Frankly, we've never heard it. Nor have we heard a jabberwock calling to its mate in the stilthy wood. But that does not prove that these creatures do not exist. The wood-borer is very real. He is the torment of all collectors. Learned monographs have been written by experts who would track him to his lair and destroy him and his abundant progeny. Verily the wood-borer in antiques is a menace.

But not all of us can live our entire existence doing evil; sometimes in spite of ourselves, we attain virtue. Thus it is with the wood-borer. For years he has worked his way through ancient woods stalked by irate owners armed with acids, oil and gas. His name has been anathema. Suddenly around his head appears the aureole of good deeds. By their wood-borers shall ye know the veritable antique!

A word of precaution, however. Let your antique first ring with the gnawing of its borers. This will be enough to assure you that it has age. After this, investigate its structures carefully, and if it is well eaten by borers, if the sound of this gnawing fairly deafens the ear, insist that your antique dealer give you with each piece an accident policy.

The other day we were entertaining a person

of quality on whom we wished to make an impression. For her especial benefit we dragged from its safe corner an antique chair that was antique beyond any shadow of doubt, for its patine was pocked with wormholes. This person seated herself gently in the chair—and the next moment she was sprawling on the floor. The worms had eaten the supporting wood completely. Only by the grace of a beneficent Providence did she escape injury. And it took several moments to restore her dignity and coiffure.

So it is possible for an antique to be too antique. The careful collector should listen to the gnawing with an ear attuned to the subtler shades of tone, the way an impresario listens to a singer. A bass gnaw may mean grave danger; a tenor may be safe; a contralto safer; but a soprano safest of all.

Corn, Lima Beans, Tomatoes and Peppers may now be planted out.

6. Of Grape Hyacinths. Apart from the Crocus, the smaller bulbs of Spring have never appealed to me half so much as the Grape Hyacinths. Perhaps because these two have always succeeded with me, and we naturally have an affection for flowers that take a liking to us. Were I rich or utterly incompetent of caring for my own finances, I should plunge in these delightful Muscari—mingling the more expensive white with shoal after shoal of Heavenly Blue. I would drift them under Forsythia and beneath the sprawling branches of the dwarf Sargent's Crab-apple, and

let them trickle generously out to the open sunlight of a sloping lawn.

In using commercial fertilizers take care not to scatter it on the foliage.

7. GARDENING POSTURES. Did the arid and fanatic anti-Evolutionists of Mississippi, Tennessee and Arkansas ever study the favorite gardening postures, they would cease questioning our simian ancestry. There are the stoopers and the squatters and the sitters and those who flop. There are those who hoe upright and those who push a hoe as though it were a perambulator. There are weeders who hunch along a row as if doubled up with cramps and there are those (myself among them) whom the *Bon Dieu* has endowed with a firm foundation and who use it to advantage. The sitting gardener may not appear active but his posture by no means limits the scope of his work. However, having traveled quite a distance from my monkey progenitors, I find it difficult to assume and hold two desirable garden postures: Could I sit on my heels hour after hour in the manner of the Pink-bottomed baboon, the picking of Currants would be a joysome task; could I cling by one paw and a tail to the bough of a tree, how simple would winter pruning of the orchard become!

Start slaying aphids with nicotine solution. Roses especially need this protection.

8. COLLECTING CLEMATIS. If you have the type of place to grow them and the patience to put

up with their idiosyncrasies, there's nothing more fascinating than collecting Clematis. And if you start in these Years of Grace and Freedom, you'll begin your hunt by growing blasphemous at the Federal Horticultural Board whose quarantine forbids entry to plants from abroad save under a strict survey. For you pick up the catalogue of Jackman at Woking—descendants of the man who made so many Clematis hybrids—read of 250 variations, and gnash your teeth. Not more than a dozen of them are available here, but with these dozen make a beginning. Add the various native types, and you are well on your way. The bushy kinds of *Clematis recta* and C. *Davidiana* of the fragrant blue flowers, can find a home in the shrubbery border; the others go on trellises and along walls and fences.

Lime-lovers, these, with a habit of wanting their feet cool and damp. Before planting, excavate a hole 2′ x 2′ and fill it with a rich mixture of loam and bone meal and rotted manure and lime. Before planting, cut off the top of the vine so that only one or two sets of eyes remain, and bury these fairly deep in the soil. This is done to prevent the spread of an obscure Clematis pest that often devastates the family. Along in late September is the time to set the plants in place. If you have a low-growing shrub to shield their feet against next year's sun, the better they will be.

Continue planting succession crops of vegetables as soon as the first crop appears above ground.

9. BEETHOVEN AND BIRCH BEER. Among the least of God's mercies (and 'twere better they be obliterated from the face of the earth) are those roadside refreshment booths that line our highways. Our roads have become huge and endless gastronomic gullets. We either fill ourselves or fill our motors. The Romans, it appears, had them, too. A *diversorium* was a roadside inn—you diverted from your way to reach it; a small eating house was a *caupona* and a little shelter for eating and drinking, a *popina*. How much prettier "*popina*" is than "hot dog stand"! Surely the Roman were never so ugly as ours. May a tornado take them—save one, and perhaps it will be spared for its devotion to beauty.

We came into it hot and tired after a long cross-country drive. The booth was deserted except for a large and elderly woman who sat in one corner before a radio. We asked for ginger ale but she merely reached for the nearest bottle, flipped off its cork and handed it to us. "I can't be bothered to get up and get you ginger ale. They're gona play Beethoven." And we sat there sipping an especially detestable brew of birch beer while the rich wine of the Egmont Overture laved over us.

Tomorrow indulge your winged friends to the extent of a bird bath, and see that it is kept filled.

10. THE MEADOW FENCE. The meadow had lain fallow for many a year, and the last man who put plow to it had long since slept with his fathers.

Its unkempt air was shocking. Having filled my head with rural ambitions after a winter of reading farm journals, I determined to do something about it. So the turf was turned under in the Spring and Soy Beans planted, and these in turn folded under to make room for Rye, each crop accompanied by enough fertilizers to pay a king's ransom. Finally when the soil was in good tilth the second year, in went grass. Then arose the problem of the fence.

The country rule for fences is horse high, bull strong and hog tight. And all of these virtues does that fence possess: a four-bar English hurdle set up in sections under the blows of a wooden mallet after the holes had been made with a crowbar. There followed weeks of painting it white, at which neighbors shook their heads, so I explained that I came from Pennsylvania where even the stone walls are painted white. Then in the Autumn we set out thirty Paul's Scarlet Climber and between them, plants of the Virgin's Bower. When the hay is cut in June it reveals a white fence spattered with sprays of crimson, and in late August little clouds of fragrant Clematis are resting there.

Stake Peonies before the buds begin to swell and for larger bloom take off small side buds.

11. THREE RULES OF HEALTH. One of the ancient natives has just confided to me a pearl of his ripe wisdom. Through eighty years of hard work,

hard cider, strong tobacco and simple food, he has observed only three rules of health, viz:

Feet warm
Head cool
Bowels open

Dahlia and Canna tubers may now safely be planted. Prepare their holes beforehand.

12. THE CREAM OF THE O. P.'S. Until you have grown Lula A. Neeley, Jeanne Mawson, Trilby, Lord Lambourne and King George, you'll never know what an Oriental Poppy can be. And having grown them, you'll give all the rest to your less sophisticated garden friends, yea, every such delicacy as the apricot Mrs. Perry and E. A. Bowles and the salmon of Enfield Beauty. Lord Lambourne and King George, I first saw blooming in the garden of the late W. R. Dykes at Nodding Hill near Woking, and a fine, windswept day it was. Their petals are deeply laciniated to the quality of lace. Lula A. Neeley (how I hate that name Lula!) is, with Lord Lambourne, an orange scarlet, but King George has even a brighter hue. Trilby bears vibrant red flowers and Jeanne Mawson coral-pink. Give them the companionship of white Iris—White Queen or White Knight—with some of those soft lilac Dream Darwin Tulips not too far away. And if, after that, your meticulous friends deride you, saying they dislike red in borders, especially Oriental Poppy red, turn the conversation to the weather. I can also see these lifting their heads before a clump of Anchusa or flinging them carelessly in the neighborhood of

those white single Peonies L'Innocence, Le Jour and the perfumed La Fiancée.

Tomorrow sow an extra batch of annual seeds in an open bed.

13. BRIGHTER AND BETTER TEXTS. Having just dozed through a long and dreary sermon that gingerly skirted the edges of infant damnation, I am come home to see if there aren't some brighter texts that these country parsons might choose. For example, what couldn't they do to the following:

"They shall have linen bonnets upon their heads and shall have linen breeches upon their loins." Ezekiel, 44:18.

"Nay, but we will abide in the street all night." Which is the saucy reply Lot gave the angels in Genesis, 19:2.

"And the Lord showed me four carpenters." Zechariah, in his first chapter and twentieth verse, was the fortunate soul. Would that the Lord had shown us four carpenters when we were trying to remodel our barn!

"The horseleech hath two daughters, crying, Give! Give!" Proverbs, 30:15.

"And when the Pharisee saw it, he marveled that he had not first washed before dinner." An excellent suggestion for dirty small boys, from St. Luke, 11:38.

"Curse not the rich in thy bedchamber." Ecclesiastes, 10:18. But why only in the bedchamber?

For a congregation of sighing, obese ladies: "But Jeshurun waxed fat and kicked: Thou art waxen fat, thou art grown thick, thou art covered with fatness." Deuteronomy, 32:15.

"Drink no water." Which 1st Kings, 13:22 graciously furnishes as the slogan for the Association Opposed to Prohibition.

"And a wench went and told them." This happens in 2nd Samuel, 17:17, and has happened many times since.

"Go not empty unto thy mother-in-law." An excellent bit of advice for bridegrooms, culled from the 3rd chapter and 18th verse of Ruth.

"A man shall not discover his father's skirt," a bit of ripe wisdom dropped into the 22nd chapter of Deuteronomy at the 30th verse.

And lastly, were I a country parson and had to keep a congregation awake, I would give them a good dairy talk from the 10th chapter and 10th verse of Job: "Hast thou not poured me out as milk and curdled me like cheese?"

Newly planted trees and shrubs will benefit by a grass or peat moss mulch laid against the Summer sun.

14. SUDDEN SPRINGS. In Munich I bought a handbook of Alpine flora and began counting the days until we should reach the upland meadows of Pontresina that spread beneath the sapphire skies like huge Oriental rugs. At last the day came, and the train began its cross-country and upward climb that brought us into this Alpine bowl. It was the end of May and I thought the next morning to tread those flowery carpets, book in hand. But the next day snow fell and for a solid week it

piled a blanket over everything. All we could do was go to the post office and come back again. Then suddenly the sky cleared. The sun's rays hosed down the paths and meadows, and through the slush myriads of flowers lifted up their heads. It was a sudden Spring. With one warm day we had leaped into the flowery heart of it.

As this was strange to one accustomed to the gradual Spring of Connecticut, I happened to tell of it one night, but my story paled into insignificance beside the yarn of a sudden Spring in Texas. Friends who were calling that night had motored across the continent. In a little Texas village they were obliged to stay over for repairs. It was in that part of Texas where rain falls only once every three or four years. And that night the rain came. The next morning the flat barren prairie was green. By night the plants had shot up and flower buds appeared. The next day the plain was a carpet of flowers. Here millions of seeds had lain dormant for years, merely waiting the resurrection of rain. As soon as it came—within forty-eight hours—they hastened to complete their life cycle of blossoming and setting seed that would drop and await another three years until rain came again.

Even now it is not too late to plant a few more Roses. Buy these in pots.

15. CONSOLATION. On these Spring days when I must forsake the glory of the garden and journey to town to sit at a desk where people come asking foolish questions and the telephone constantly

jangles in my ear, I think of what that excellent politician, George Saville, First Marquis of Halifax, wrote his brother, "Notwithstanding my passion for the town, I dream of the country as men do of small beer when they are in a fever." It was this same Restoration epigrammatist who wrote, "Men make it such a Point of Honour to be fit for Business, that they forget to examine whether Business is fit for a Man of Sense."

Sow Celery seed now and set out the plants when four inches high.

16. VARMINTS. At this season of the year, the air in the vegetable garden begins to assume a bluish tinge. Muttered imprecations, staggering oaths, fine old bucolic cuss-words, the by-hecks, by-gollies, the witness of Heaven called down. You set a row of Cabbage plants, and the blankety-blank cut worms lay them flat. Put tar paper collars around the new batch to foil the cut worms, and rabbits appear from nowhere to complete another destruction. Crows drop down from the skies, plant their feet in a Corn hill and breakfast off the newly-sprouted shoots.

Of course, the logical gardener will say, "Why don't you take precautions? You know perfectly well, etc., etc." All that is true; we do know perfectly well that such varmints must be foiled and routed, but sometimes we forget. Sometimes we nurse the vain hope that the angel of cut worms and crows and rabbits will pass over our humble little vegetable patch this year. Most times, though, we are wearied by the poisonous side of gardening.

We are really not cast for the rôle of the Borgias. It is distasteful to go forth each day with a plant in one hand and Paris green in the other. Our idea of Heaven is a garden where bugs and varmints never penetrate, where the sprayer and the dust gun are unknown and even visiting dogs, who lead astray our own border-shy wire-haired fox terrier, are kept "without the gates."

As soon as the flats are cleared of annuals, begin sowing perennials.

17. THE RAPHAEL OF FLOWERS. The ninth commandment is completely and thoroughly smashed every time I find some one owning a flower book illustrated by Redoute. This worthy and enviable artist flourished between the years 1759 and 1840. He came of a line of artists—his father, Charles Joseph Redoute, and brother, Henry Joseph, both being of that profession—but Pierre Joseph Redoute will be remembered the longest. He commenced drawing flowers in his brother's studio and his fame for them soon spread. In 1805 the Empress Josephine appointed him one of her court painters and in 1822 he became Professor of the Iconography of Plants in the Royal Gardens. That he invented a new method of reproducing water colors, and that a genus of Malvaceas was named for him, and that his birth-town, St. Hubert, erected a fountain in his memory—these are tame legacies compared with his two great books on Roses and Lilacs that won him the name of "The Raphael of Flowers." He is

buried in Pere Lachaise Cemetery. Perhaps, if one of these days I look up his grave and lay on it a wreath, my luck may change—perhaps I may thereby gain merit enough to own one of his books.

In cutting Iris remember to leave some foliage for future growth.

18. A VIOLET GARDEN. One of my dreams (I shall attain it ere long) is to make a Violet Garden, wherein will be assembled in sweet accord and each in its own little pocket of tasteful soil, the variations of Violets that our countryside affords. The sweet white *V. blanda;* the taller *V. canadensis;* the Dog Violets, *V. conspersa* and *silvestris;* set in a moist corner; *V. cucullata,* our common wild type; the yellow *V. lutea* from Europe together with the *odorata,* the common sweet English Violet. To these would be added, some blue and some white *V. palmata;* and, where the sun bakes warm, the Bird's-foot, *V. pedata,* and *pedata bicolor.* Finally the yellow native *pubescens* and that sturdy native *septentrionalis,* so liberal with its bloom. If between these groups were planted little drifts of the dwarf Narcissus—*Triandrus Albus, Cyclamineus nanus, Bulbocodium citrinus* and *Bulbocodium conspicuus* and such other small denizens as *Hyacinthus azureus, Muscari, Tulipa primulina* and *T. dasystemon*—then this Violet Garden would make Spring still more unforgettable.

Weed-killing solutions may now be carefully spread on walks and drives.

19. SANITATION AND CIVILIZATION. One of the most brilliant eras the world has ever known was the Elizabethan Age, brilliant for its accomplishments, for the impulsive energy and vivid desire of its men, for the enormous whims, infatuations and vanities of its women; brilliant for the vast areas its endeavors touched and for the lasting heritage of thought, action and inspiration it bequeathed succeeding generations. And yet this age had very little conception of privacy and comfort. Even less did the generations that preceded it.

It may seem strange that the times which gave us Shakespeare, Raleigh, Sidney, Drake, Johnson, Marlowe and their fellows should know so little about the things we consider essential to our being. The mistake may be ours.

Vast quantities of Americans—intelligent, educated and reasonably well-bred people—have a habit of judging a country's civilization by its plumbing fixtures. They go to Continental countries, they go on world-encircling tours, they spend Winters in those delightful islands of the Caribbean. Presumably, they have an enjoyable time; but if they make any criticism of these countries, it invariably is based on sanitation.

It would be interesting some time to set down comparative tables of the accomplishments of each age and country and tabulate beside them their plumbing arrangements.

Tomorrow you may begin to stake Delphiniums, Gladioli and other perennials.

20. THE LOUVRE. The foregoing sentiment reminds me that one of my country neighbors boasts

a gallery of rare masters. Her house is equipped with a bathroom, toilet and all such newfangled short-cuts to comfort, but she steadfastly refuses to use them, preferring the more primitive accommodations of the Gothic ticket booth in the backyard. "What was good enough for Grand-dad is good enough for me." That's her sentiment. But she has stepped a little beyond Grand-dad's stern and Puritanic ways. Friends in their travelings have sent her post cards from many lands which she has tacked on its walls—a glimpse of lovely old Rothenberg, the Sistine Madonna, the Grand Canyon, Botticelli's Spring, the Baby Parade at Asbury Park, Max Sennett's Bathing Girls, Buda by moonlight, Whistler's Mother, the Blue Boy, ladies in bloomers riding down the Main Street of Honesdale, Pa., Michelangelo's David, the Tip Top Inn at Belcher's Lake with an arrow pointing to "our room," the gastronomic canvases of Franz, Snyders, Von Wytreth and Jan Fyt, Roosevelt charging up San Juan Hill, Feeding the Pigeons in Saint Mark's Plaza and such. To enter this gallery is a rare treat for those who love travel and the old masters. Whenever I'm in that neighborhood I like to drop in just for a glimpse of my favorite canvases. To us, this accommodation is known privily as the Louvre.

Tender annual vines can now be set out
and their leading strings tied up.

21. COLUMBINE FLAPPERS. In spite of their propensity for root rot, their devastating allure to root lice and their comparatively short lives,

Spring would not be Spring at all without long-spurred Columbines. The dowdy, squat and unkillable purple *vulgaris* clumps are only a bad memory once one has grown these taller, larger, long-spurred kinds. By tall I mean four feet at least and I've had them nearer five. And in subtle tints and tones of mauve, blue, yellow, pink and silver. The red and yellow kinds are amusing: they always remind me of the Fire Cracker Plant we used to have as youngsters. The pure yellow of *A. chrysantha* behind the tranquil blue majesty of Iris *Pallida dalmatica* has rejoiced our eyes several Springs. I'm trying Chrysantha (and hope for a tit-bit of subtleties) with the delicate lilac tint of Iris Aurora.

Aquilegia seem to me the perfect companion flower for Iris, even more so than Peonies. The one has a dignity and stiff beauty—like an Amazon type of woman—the other has an airy, looser, carefree and wayward grace—a tousled-haired flapper, her cropped curls blown askew in the Spring breezes.

Before putting away the cold frame sash see that all panes are fastened in tight.

22. CALVIN AND THE SWINE. I happened to be contemplating the pigs when a voice remarked, "Mighty lucky, them hawgs!" And I turned to see a caller from near-by. Now it happens that this caller was weaned on undiluted Calvinism. He is constantly teetering on the dizzy brink of eternal punishment—actual fire and brimstone and torturing thirst throughout untold ages. He has none

of the bland optimism of the shallow and unbelieving; he holds that he is among those destined from the beginning of time to suffer throughout the remainder of it. As he stood brooding there over that pigsty it seemed as if he were gazing down into vast gulfs of sin and eternal reprobation. "Yes, mighty lucky, them hawgs," he repeated.

"They ought to be," I answered, "they get plenty to eat and drink and clean bedding once a week."

"No, it ain't that," his voice came up from the depths of his Calvinistic despair. "They don't have to worry about goin' to Hell."

Move all tubbed plants outdoors, give them a little fresh top soil and liquid manure.

23. THE WEATHER AND DAHLIAS. The Dahlia hobbyist will doubtless rush his tubers into the ground as soon as the frosts have gone, but we prefer to take our time. The week of Memorial Day sees the run of Spring work pretty well in hand and we can then turn our attention to Dahlias. After all, the Dahlia is a tropical plant and needs warm sun for abundant growth—warm sun and water. Given these two, together with a cupful of bone meal to each plant and a stake to lean upon, and the average Dahlia will flourish. However, let the season be too wet or too dry, and there's no depending on what it will do. I've seen a wet, overcast June and July force them into puny blossom far ahead of time. An excess of

moisture makes for sappy growth. The baking heat of the sun is quite as necessary as the moisture, despite the fact that the Dahlia is 90% water.

By this time the wheel-hoe should be given its first mulching exercise in the vegetable garden.

24. THOSE HIGH-FALUTIN' NAMES. The novice among gardeners is often annoyed by the way his more accomplished brothers insist on using botanical names for flowers, trees and shrubs. He—often it is she—remarks that the good, old-fashioned names should be used, and not these high-falutin' and teeth-cracking titles. John Ruskin, good old John, clung to the same sentiment. For a matter of fact, botanical Latin is the Esperanto of gardeners and the so-called common name has such infinite variations that they change with every locality. Some years ago students of this subject went about the various shires of England setting down these common names. Their findings were bewildering. For *Viola tricolor,* they record thirty-seven; for the Digitalis, seventy-one; for Centaurea, fifty-five. And so on through a long line of familiar flowers of garden and meadow and roadside.

Tomorrow you should begin to enjoy your fill of Oriental Poppies. Help them along with a little manure water.

25. STRAWBERRIES. Let other gourmets sing the praise of Asparagus and other and less prosy composers write odes to the slithery Rhubarb. The

burden of my encomium rests around the ruddy, toothsome flanks of the Strawberry.

We keep two beds going—the old and the new. After the second year of bearing, the runners of the old are rooted in pots of compressed peat moss and then the whole bed is forked up and the plants, with their bugs and diseases, are consumed in fire. After this the loam is forked, a liberal spattering of bone meal given and then Crimson Clover sown. By late August the Clover is high enough to spade under for a manuring crop. Then the new plants, which meantime are growing along in the little pots, are set in rows. December, and the patch nestles beneath its bedding of Rye straw held down from the obstreperous Winter wind with chicken wire. By May, straw is well tucked under the plants and the flowering stems laid on it. Then commences disbudding for big fruit—removing all but one or two flowers on a stem. Then also begins the hunt for slugs, damn them! And finally, when color begins to appear in the swelling berries, the patch is canopied with a net that foils the slyest endeavors of the most persistent robin. After these simple exercises, all you need do is to provide the cream and sugar.

Now that they are in bloom is the time to decide which Irises you will keep and which discard.

26. A QUAINT HYPOCRISY. Like a boxer warding off the blows of his opponent, the respectable housewife rushes to verbal arms at the slightest suspicion of her hospitality. Since Prohibition has

driven drinking into the home, it is a rare country house (and I speak advisedly, having been in hundreds of them in many states in all sections of the country during the past five years) where the liquid hospitality is limited or begrudged or totally absent. Nevertheless, let it be said of a guest—male or female—that he shows evidence of having had just "one drop of the best as is," and the hostess rushes to the defense shouting, "Well, he didn't get it here!" Such are our quaint hypocrisies.

Tuck a straw blanket under the Strawberries and put up a net to discourage ravenous birds.

27. SLAVE TO FURNITURE. Several years ago there died in England a nobleman who left behind him an extraordinary will, in which he stated that all his life long he had been "a slave to his furniture." Death, it seemed, offered a pleasant release from this overpowering bondage.

The picture this man's life presents is rather pitiful. You can see him, on coming into his title, inheriting a vast quantity of possessions—country places and perhaps a place in town—filled with furniture and knick-knacks of previous generations, the accumulations of these pieces making a vast and bewildering conglomeration. To them were doubtless added his ancestors' and his own taste for collecting antiques and curios. Little wonder this particular nobleman groaned under the shackles of his possessions.

The heathen Chinese, to whom we send missionaries, worships his ancestors, a habit the missionaries hope to correct. We, on the other hand, are much more idolatrous and material, because we worship our ancestors' possessions. The custom of collecting and treasuring antiques is, in a manner of speaking, nothing more than the cultivated, genteel and popular Christian style of ancestor worship.

Now that it is warm, the tender Water Lilies can be set into the pool.

28. HUGONIS: CAVE MAN. Late May, and the Roses are still awaiting the touch of June's sun to force their buds. One wildling spurts ahead, a wildling out of China—*Rosa Hugonis.* Like a runner reaching the final tape, it stretches out its flowery arms and wins the race in a shower of gold. Having watched his triumph several Mays, I was seized with what seemed a splendid idea: to make a Hugonis hedge, a yellow wall, and so I took to studying the habits of this treasure. Like many another beauty before it and since, *Rosa Hugonis* is stubborn. When it grows tall, its base is leggy, and if you shear its top and sides to shape it into a hedge, you sacrifice a lot of the bloom. And every now and then, for no apparently accountable reason, part of it gives up the ghost. It seems to say, "See here, I'm a wildling. I'm a cave man. Don't try to tame me! Don't fuss around me with your darned old shears! Leave me alone!" I've often felt that way when a meticulous She told me the sort of clothes I should wear. *Rosa Hugonis* and I understand each other, so I'll never attempt to make him into a hedge plant, but let him grow each

side the top of a cross-path step, with early purple Iris clumped about him.

Plant a few more hills of Corn but watch the avaricious Crows who pull up the sprouted kernels.

29. GETTIN' AROUND TO IT. The unscientific and slovenly farmer, when you mention using modern methods or suggest improvements on his place, invariably answers, "Yes, I was gonna do that, but I ain't never got around to it." This business of "gettin' around to it" also marks the difference between the successful and the slovenly gardener. He either has, or has not, that extra ounce of ambition and energy which makes for progress.

The average country place retains its value and much of its charm only so long as its owner insists on "gettin' around to it." Good gardens are to be had only at the price of persistent maintenance—grass well cut, edges trimmed, weeds eliminated, tall things staked and bugs combated. To excuse yourself on the ground that you "ain't never got around to it" is to acknowledge failure.

Tomorrow invite your neighbors to help themselves to your flowers for Decoration Day.

30. DE MORTUIS. We met the old fellow trudging along the road bearing a home-made wreath of flowers, and since this was Memorial Day we knew where he was headed. So the car slowed down and he crawled into the back seat. It is natural to sup-

pose that all men over eighty must have fought in the Civil War, and we made remarks to that effect, but they brought no patriotic response. This old veteran spurned the bait, and when we came to the cemetery we found out why. He clambered out, went to a distant corner of this little plot and carefully laid his wreath between two graves. The tombstones revealed his story. He had survived two wives and had buried them side by side, but, being of a Yankee, economical turn of mind, he considered one wreath was enough for the two. Nor did he linger very long to mourn, so we naturally surmised that he was indeed a veteran—a veteran of two wars and many battles long ago.

White Peonies, the blue of Iris and the red of Oriental Poppies make a vivid combination for a soldier's grave.

31. FADED LADIES. Toward the end of May the Tulips, their bloom faded and bedraggled, stand in the borders like groups of passé ladies—nice, respectable ladies who have just enough to live on and so go to Italy to spend their declining days. You meet them in galleries and cathedrals intent on studying an art that is almost as forgotten as their own erstwhile beauty. One by one, Destiny closes their chapters and a newer and lustier generation takes their place. So these Tulips: one by one we lift them to make space for annuals that will be flowering in a few weeks.

Don't work so hard in your Spring gardening that you haven't the time or strength to enjoy your Spring garden.

LONG PIECE

MEN AS TREES WALKING

A BLIND beggar was sunning himself in a quiet spot of the Bethsaida Road. Now and again some one scuffled by, or a donkey train passed on its way to market. From where he sat he could hear the hum and chatter of the town. Suddenly he felt himself surrounded. He stretched his hand for alms, but, instead of giving alms, some one said, "Come along, old fellow," and they led him into the town. There they halted, while the men about him began urging, "Touch him!" (Poor sport this, to make fun of a beggar.) A stranger did touch him—took him by the arm and led him out to the peace of the fields again. When they halted he felt a hand pressed over his eyes and heard a voice saying, "Do you see anything?" (See anything? How could he? He had been blind from birth.) "Do you see anything?" the voice repeated. A film of light crept across the blind man's eyes. Gradually things about him began to take shape. "Yes! Yes!" he cried, moving his hands weakly through the impalpable air, "I see men as trees walking!"

An amazing first impression, that. Here was a man who had never seen a tree or a man. He had felt of trees' rough bark, had passed his hands over their smooth leaves, had breathed the perfume of their flowering, had enjoyed their fruit and in the hot noondays had known their cool shade. But of their leafy and towering heights, of their graceful shapes, he was ignorant. And yet the first impression his new-born sight gave him was that the men around him were as trees walking. In his mind, there existed a definite relation between trees and people. He saw men as trees walking because men were like trees.

In uttering those words he gave us a penetrating classification of people. Apply it, and see how amazingly true it is. We understand people better once we have found their tree.

Many people are like trees that grow close together—like the White Birches of our northern woods and the Bamboos of the Tropics—gregarious, dependent one on the other, lacking individuality. Crowding makes them slim. They struggle against each other, reaching up for sunlight and air. This battle for existence takes its toll—through the clump you see the withered trunks of those for whom the battle was too strong; elbowed out of life. . . . Many people in crowded cities are like that, and not a few of those who live in suburbs, where social competition comes fast and thick.

There are the sprawling trees that know the wickedness of winds, and having combated them for generations, have learned the wisdom of bending before them. Such you find on gale-swept sea coasts and on open mountain slopes. The Cypresses of Monterey and the procumbent conifers of the upper Rockies and other mountain ranges are equally in this class. Tough-fibered and gnarled, they live to great ages because they are able to accommodate themselves to overwhelming odds. . . . There are people, too, like that, people who come through great vicissitudes, outwardly warped and often sinister appearing, but wiry, vigorous, dependable, long-lived.

Contrasted with these are the trees and people who refuse to bend before the wind, who stand up untouched despite it. Invariably these trees are deep-rooted and firmly buttressed. Consider the penetrating anchorage of the Red Cedar's tap root, the great White Oak and the Beech reaching underground, the tentacles of the Elm, the buttresses of the Ceiba, the Banyan and the Redwood, the closely-woven mat of the Rubber Tree that sprawls for a great distance on all sides, the soil-preëmpting roots of the Eucalyptus. Meticulous gardeners complain that they can never grow flowers or grass under such trees because their roots drain the soil of all its nourishment. People who are akin to such trees do the same. Find a man who has the outstanding personality of an Elm or a Banyan or a Redwood, and he tolerates no lesser competition. Towering over all, lordly in shape and mien, he is not only captain of his own soul but master of all near by. Wind and torrential rain hold no terrors for him. He fears only lightning from the skies and the decrepitude and decay that old age brings.

Many are the trees and men who exist and are planted only for the fruit they give. They are tended and fed and pruned that they may produce bigger and better crops. The Apple, the Pear, the Cherry of the Temperate Zone, the Date Palms and the Cocoanuts of the Tropics, such are the workers of the world. Such, too, are the men and women who devote themselves solely to business. They care for their health so that they can do more work; they discipline their lives so that their work may be more productive. We are apt to judge them merely by their fruits, forgetting that such trees have their yearly hour of glory and beauty upon which the fruit depends. Scant blossoming means a scant crop. If the beauty of the flower is not there abundantly, the fruit will never follow.

There are also the slim upright trees, such as the Poplars, and some of the Cedars and the Cypresses and the pendant, weeping trees that appear in many arboreal families. These we associate more with women than with men. Their grace is a feminine grace, their fiber supple. Whether it be the dark Cypresses of an Italian hillside, or the Weeping Willow along a brook bank in a peaceful meadow, or the pendant flowering Cherries planted on close-cropped lawns or the rangy lines of Lombardy Poplars—these all are feminine trees. Some are useful and long-lived, some merely beautiful and short of duration. They serve to delight the eye with yielding grace.

Whereas the Oaks and the Elms of the world are noble and estimable people, it remains for one great family to supply its geniuses. Of all the tree groups none assumes so many forms as the Palm. The Cocoanut Palm, its frowsy head reeling in the wind like a tipsy poet's, may be brother to the Traveler's Palm, exactly mathematical and architectural of shape, but few would believe them to be kin. The Date Palm and the Sago may be sisters under their barks, but few would guess it.

"I see men as trees walking." So spoke the blind man of the Bethsaida Road. In that glimpse he saw more than most of us.

THE MONTH OF JUNE

1. THE FEAST OF LANTERNS. Of the many flowers that have an airy grace, Heucheras may be ranked high indeed. Along in June their wiry stalks stretch unpromisingly into the air. Then, of a sunny morning, you come out to find them hung with bells—blood-red and pink and white, according to variety. Gazing at their fragile beauty, I am reminded of a fête in Japan when, darkness coming on, a little hill town burst into a thousand lanterns, and men and boys went about the streets bearing long poles from which half a dozen lanterns winked and twinkled in the soft night air. So that week in June when the Heucheras are in blossom we have come to speak of as the Feast of Lanterns.

Should the season be dry, keep watering trees and shrubs that were moved this Spring.

2. A GARDEN SHOWER. Did you ever hear of a Garden Shower? Palpitating brides, so the custom goes, are subjected to "showers"—kitchen showers, linen showers and such, when their friends and relatives, conscious of their domestic needs, descend upon them with pots and pans and sheets and towels with which to begin housekeeping. These "showers" usually happen before the wedding. After that, life becomes almost uneventful.

Why not start a new custom and give the bride a garden? Let her get settled in her new house and then descend upon her—friends, neighbors and relatives, each bearing plants? Before she knows it her garden will be started.

I heard of one such bride recently who had had a Garden Shower, and so abundant was it that she and her husband consumed a whole week setting out the plants. This exertion reduced her husband fully ten pounds, she alleged, a reduction which golf would never have accomplished.

Tomorrow get up early enough to cut flowers for the house before the sun strikes them.

3. ROSES IN THE HEART. Perhaps no one before him, or since, uttered or shall utter a more truthful and touching *dictum* on the Queen of Flowers than the Very Rev. S. Reynolds Hole when he wrote "A Book of Roses." Since few people know it beyond the opening sentence, let me quote it in full:

"He who would have beautiful Roses in his garden must have beautiful Roses *in his heart*. He must love them well and always. To win, he must woo, as Jacob wooed Laban's daughter, though drought and frost consume. He must have not only the glowing admiration, the enthusiasm, and the passion, but the tenderness, the thoughtfulness, the reverence, the watchfulness of love. With no ephemeral caprice, like the fair young knight's, who loves and who rides away when his sudden fire is gone from the cold white ashes, the cavalier of the Rose has *semper fidelis* upon his crest and shield. He is loyal and devoted ever, in storm-fraught or in sunny days; not only the first upon a summer's morning to gaze admiringly on glowing charms, but the first, when leaves fall and winds are chill, to protect against cruel frost. As with smitten bachelor or steadfast mate the lady of his love is lovely ever, so to the true Rose-grower must the Rose-tree be always a thing of beauty. To others, when its flowers have faded, it may be worthless as a hedgerow thorn: to him, in every phase, it is precious. I am no more the Rose, it says, but cherish me, for we have dwelt together; and the glory which has been and the glory which shall be never fade from *his heart.*"

Melons, Cucumbers and Squash vines should be pegged down in the way they should go.

4. THE ALPINIST MIND. Having scrambled over the jagged rocks of many alpine-loving friends and ruined many a pair of shoes thereby, I have come to the conclusion that the rock gardener is a type of mind set apart from others. It is an enthusiasm and an all-absorbing avocation, as distinct as fox hunting, contract bridge or playing the market, and if you haven't the sort of mind and heart that can be given to such matters, there's no use sashaying around the fringe of them. You can't simply dabble your toes in these pleasant pools: you must plunge in up to the neck. And you must be sure of your pool.

One day I made the mistake of loaning a good

friend one of Henri Correvon's books. He was a normal person, this friend, with a slight leaning toward the garden. Scarcely had he finished the book than he developed a marked weakness for rocks. He began hauling them. He searched his woods for them. He spent weeks rolling them into a heap, hired teams and gangs to move great monoliths, and by the end of Summer had transformed a lovely forest glade into what he thought to be a rock garden. But it wasn't a rock garden: it was a pile of rocks. The business of planting it came as an after-thought. No amount of expensive Saxifrages will ever transform that heap of boulders into a rock garden. This man dived into the wrong pool.

The way to get into rock gardening is sedulously to avoid being a geologist and to devote one's self for a long time to a study of alpine plants. And if, after learning of all their strange ways and idiosyncrasies and uppish requirements, you still have the courage to become a real alpinist, then you are a gardener raised above the dead level of the rest of us.

By this time the leaves of Narcissi planted in grass are dried and the grass can be cut.

5. IN DEFENSE OF THE ROCKING-CHAIR. Whenever I see a country front porch furnished with rocking-chairs, I have an admiration for the people who live there. For in this age of alleged taste, the rocking-chair has to be enjoyed secretly. A few—a very few people—dislike it because they really dislike rocking; the rest of us mutter some

excuse about its ugliness but, in the secrecy of our own rooms, fly to its comfortable and soothing agitation. Decorators hold it to be anathema. Let a client meekly ask for a rocking-chair in the library, and the wrath of the Heavens descends. Rocking-chairs simply aren't done.

This prejudice must have some reason. And I'm venturing that the reason is based on three facts, namely—the rocking-chair has no perceptible and decent heritage; it is, in the main, a homely piece of furniture; and it is American.

Most of our furniture pieces have traditions; you can trace them in books the way you trace a family tree; authorities write preciously about them. You can't do that about the rocking-chair. Search the histories of furniture, and such a thing as a rocking-chair is rarely mentioned. It is merely a "crazy American" concession to comfort.

Yet though it be homely as sin, the rocker serves a real purpose. It does its homely job well. It is like a homely scrubwoman who scrubs well. If you ever found a handsome scrubwoman you'd immediately be tempted to make her a waitress or a parlor maid, in which positions she'd be unhappy and useless. Let her do what she can do well. So with the rocking-chair. It is rarely a thing of beauty—but it is a joy forever. It just happens to be one of those things that never was intended to be, and never conceivably could be, beautiful.

Prune all Spring-flowering shrubs now; to do so in Autumn will sacrifice next year's bloom.

6. ONE QUEEN SPEAKS OF ANOTHER. It is my custom, and I trust I shall never neglect it, to bring Her the first flowers as they appear—the first Lady Tulips and Muscari and Crocus, the first Pansies and sprigs of Arabis and Creeping Phlox and Aubretia, the first Narcissus and so on through the seasons till the first of the Chrysanthemums. On a day in June I brought Her the first uncurled bud of a Ville de Paris, the hybrid tea Rose I had helped name in the Bagatelle Concours des Roses two years before. She gazed upon its golden beauty, drank in its rich fragrance, which is like unto the perfume of a Magnolia, and remarked, "I would rather have one Rose each day than all the other junk in your garden." And she was right, for no flower can whisper like the Rose—"of peace, and truth, and friendliness unquell'd."

Begin now to pinch off Tomato plants to not more than four main stems.

7. THE PRODIGALITY OF PINKS. Some flowers, when they bloom, come in such abundance that we are apt to accept them casually. The Pinks are prodigal. How magnificently they spend themselves in their days of flowering! When I find myself taking such flowers as a matter of course, I go out and pluck a little bouquet of one blossom of each variety, and set it on my desk where I can study the flowers in detail as I write. The chubby little mats of fragrant Cheddars, the fringed blossoms of Sand Pinks, the stiff profusion of *Dianthus neglectus,* the crimson of Maiden Pink, *D. deltoides* above its narrow leaves, the small,

sulphur-colored, scant bloom of *D. Knapii*, the white of Sand Pink, *D. arenarius*, the delicately poised *D. sylvestris*—each of these rock garden denizens is a distinct personality in a vast family. Later come the annual Chinese with a dazzling array of colors, from a snow white to a white-edged maroon that is almost black. The ordinary grass Pinks, *D. plumarius*, in white and pink and dark red, fill the area near the desk with the old scent of cloves. Each year I am tempted by more of their colors and each year dip deeper into the family names of the Alwoodi creations. With many have I failed. For all my fond hopes and nursing, I never did bring *D. furcatus* to decent flowering, and *D. pyrennae*, *D. mouspessulanus* and *D. subcaulescens* decided not even to germinate. However, of those that have survived my neglect, there are enough to warrant a long season of admiration.

Brown beetles on Peonies, Roses and such, can be picked by hand and exultantly dropped into a can of kerosene.

8. Compensating Defeats. Though it may appear the height of cynicism, I always assume an air of satisfaction when other gardeners acknowledge failure. Not that I would crow over their defeats, but it is consoling to realize that I am not the only one who fails dismally. Recently when a great horticultural don gravely stated that he had given up trying to raise those gorgeous English hybrid Lupins, I felt better. Many times have I tried them and many times failed to bring

them past the seedling stage. Or some of the trick Iris. Or some of those grand hybrid Clematis. Not to mention whole ranges of Primulas. My garden misery loves company at such times. But would that I had something more difficult or more sophisticated to offer as evidence of my horticultural prowess than a batch of healthy Zinnias! Would that I could compensate my failures with a sky-scraping *Lilium giganteum* or a big bed of Eremerus or a dazzling shoal of the violet *Meconopsis grandis* or the blue beauty that is *Gentiana Farreri!*

By the time early Peas are ripe for eating you should stop cutting Asparagus.

9. THE OLD GENTLEMAN SHOWS HIS MEDALS. It was the first Concours des Roses held since the war and consequently there were many awards to make. Having judged the Roses at the Bagatelle and named the honors, we all returned to the Café Pre Catalan where the City of Paris set before us a welcome array of fine dishes and excellent wines. With this array most of us were content, but one man there was who hid behind a great stack of flat boxes. All I could see of him was a pate scantily fringed with hair and the great sweep of his moustaches. A life's work, those moustaches. They made me think of Texan long-horned cattle. And I wondered how this genius ever got in and out his tiny greenhouse, for they told me he did all his hybridizing and creating of priceless Roses in a glass-house no bigger than my vest-pocket study. Finally the last of the dishes were cleared away

and the last of the glasses drained, and, in the manner of the French, each Titan of the Rose World leaped to his feet, unbidden by the toastmaster, and sputtered his greetings. One alone cowered in silence—the man of the moustaches, hiding behind his pile of boxes. Some one eventually called his name. There arose a great clamor for him. He came slowly from behind the boxes. A smile extended his moustaches till they were level with his ears. One by one, and without comment, he opened the boxes. Seven of them, and each contained a gold medal.

For the man of the moustaches was the late M. Pernet-Ducher, creator of Mrs. Aaron Ward, of Souvenir de Claudius Pernet and Ville de Paris.

Annuals can be pinched back to induce busy growth. Many transplanted perennials should be given the same treatment.

10. NATIVES. One of the first delights you have on going to the country to live is coming in contact with the native son. And the older and queerer the native is, the more the delight. For there is something about the canny innocence of the born countryman that compensates for his inefficiency, his slowness, his prejudices. Make him your friend, and he is loyal to the death; ignore him and his attitude is dangerous.

Employing a native gives one the same friendly feeling that one has toward a walking stick cut from one of his own trees. The feeling is difficult to describe; it is a sort of kinship. It is the sort of feeling a man has when, having wandered far away from his home, he finally returns to it. Perhaps, after all, we who live in cities, are members of lost tribes, strayed away from our native heath. And when we come back to it, the native, who never left, treats us just as he treats one of his own kin who goes off to the city to live and then comes back: suspicion mingles with curiosity, prejudice with pride.

As hot weather begins, mulch Sweet Peas and see that they never lack for water.

11. PEA HEDGES. Man may make ever so many inventions and many a goodly custom become corrupted thereby, but I doubt if any invention of wire or string or slats or what-not will usurp the place of brush for garden Peas. There is the pleasant business of gathering it from the roadside bushes in March, of jamming it in place between the rows of newly sprouted seed, of weaving its soft twigs into a wattled wall. Then follows the directing of the first tendrils in the way they should go and finally the pride of growth when the twig fence is a hedge and the pods begin to swell. Somehow I simply can't take the same interest in garden Peas when they are grown on a length of chicken wire.

Perennials in flats should now be given the protection of a slatted or cheesecloth-covered frame.

12. DEPENDABILITY AND THE HARDY CLIMBERS. Winter-killing, that bane and dread of those who are devoted to hybrid tea Roses, is often a

heavy strain on our affections. Though the rules for winter protection are followed to the letter each Autumn, the Spring finds us facing a long list of casualties. And in that Spring day when I count my losses among hybrid teas, I must confess that I turn apostate. I feel like jilting these fair ladies, and I look toward hardy climbers with a kindling and affectionate eye. About fifty kinds have found a home on the place, and not a one of them gives us the slightest trouble over winter. If Silver Moon or Paul's Scarlet or Dr. Van Fleet or the three Lovett sisters or American Pillar or any of the others should fail to survive a winter, it would come to me as a distinct shock. It would be like having a trusted friend suddenly go bad, or, (which is a greater tragedy) having one of my national heroes fall lower than a man of middle class.

Roses should be given weekly doses of manure water from now till the end of July.

13. DISCIPLES OF GILBERT WHITE. "The Natural History of Selborne," which all who love the country should constantly read, set a whole race of amateur naturalists poking under bushes and digging into the earth to observe the wondrous ways of bees and bugs, birds, butterflies, stones and running water. And that new race, in turn, bred its writers, the prince among them being J. L. Knapp, who just a hundred years ago wrote his "Journal of a Naturalist." It was widely read and then promptly forgotten. You can pick up copies

for a quarter. The one I read in bed of nights cost even less. Dipping into its calm pools of thought and observation, I'm wondering if we aren't due for another race of Gilbert Whites and J. L. Knapps. Those who love a garden can't devote all their interest to its familiar phenomena. Leap the wall and plunge into the meadow! Explore the wild land and the depths of woods! Look to the birds! Study the rocks! Watch water! And having observed them, let us also reflect upon them. Accumulating mere facts about the natural world soon wearies, but who can weary of its music and poetry and vivid romance?

Arsenate of lead either dusted or sprayed on in solution is the customary specific for leaf-chewing bugs.

14. THE OVERLOOKED GILLENIA. The habit of going through plant catalogues and checking off the things I hope some day to try brought Gillenia to my garden. For years I had read its name and made a mental promise to give it a trial. So many of these things that pique my curiosity—things nurserymen grow adjectival about—find their way to the compost heap after the first season! But Gillenia managed to escape banishment. I was stubborn about it, and as those mere twigs developed into floppy, informal little bushes, my hopes rose. The third June brought my award. A delicate airy mist lay above them one morning. People asked, "What's that?" We plucked the white, loose, starry flowers and gave them Columbines for vase companions. We put them with Sweet Peas.

With that first blossoming, Gillenia won its permanent home. They say it thrives better in a damp spot, but my plants are in full sun and dry, although the soil is deeply trenched. *Gillenia stipulacea* is the Indian-physic or American Ipecac and *G. trifoliata,* the kind we grow, is Bowman's Root. Sometimes you find these two listed under the name of Proteranthus. The garden possibilities of Gillenia are many. It deserves not to be overlooked.

This month, Apples, Pears, Peaches and other tree fruit should be thinned.

15. VICTORIAN TONSORIAL. Every now and then comes the rumor that a revival of Victorianism in furnishing is at hand. To a few precious decorators, the smell of the cosy corner and the musty air of an overstuffed room brings the same thrill as once fire bells did to fire horses. And I suppose we will be expected, if we are to keep up with the current of taste, to jettison the Early American or French Provincial or comfortable conglomerate furnishings that make our country homes so pleasant, and break out into wax flowers under glass domes, stuffed birds, antimacassars and Turkish nooks. May Heaven throw dust in the eyes of these disturbers! Next we will have to grow beards. . . . What was it the mid-Victorian miss wrote in her diary? "As I entered the ballroom I was faced by a row of curly brown beards—a really beautiful sight!"

Begin staking Gladioli and such perennials as are apt to be broken by the wind.

16. ANGER. Three things throw me into a towering rage. One is the self-conscious, arty, "artistic arrangement" found at many a flower show. The second is any garden article that quotes "My garden is a lovesome thing, God wot." The third is the garden book that repeats the thread-worn yarn about the gardening wife who, on being asked what she wanted for her birthday, requested a load of manure. However much my plants might be dying for manure, I'd consider such a present as justifiable grounds for homicide. One Christmas I did send each of my brothers-in-law (and each possessed a garden) a large bag of shredded cow manure. It was delivered boxed and the boxes solemnly placed under the Christmas tree. Did I earn their eternal gratitude? Did they think me a fine and thoughtful fellow? *They did not!* And were I to quote the indecencies they hurled at my head, this book would be hanged at yard-arm by the censor.

Keep extra flats of annuals in reserve to follow as successors to Spring bulbs, and short-lived other annuals.

17. SAPPHIRA AND THE DELPHINIUMS. If Ananias and Sapphira were stricken dead for merely concealing profits and lying about it, what punishment, I'm wondering, will be meted those gardeners who look you square in the face and blandly state that their Delphiniums never have blight. Californians aver they've never heard of it. Nor have they ever heard of earthquakes and floods. Here in New England we must spray and dust

from the first moment the shoot appears above ground until frost cuts down the last; and even then some of the blight eludes us. That's the sporting chance you take. If you can raise a batch of good Delphiniums—say with an average of three to three and a half feet of flowers to the stalk—and have fairly healthy foliage on them, then you're a man, my son. Better, though, to treat them as biennials: sow the fresh seed from the first blooming, set out the seedlings in Autumn (and that I've found far better for Delphiniums than Spring setting), take your virile growth, let them give you a second blooming, and then send them to perdition *via* the fire. Trouble and bother? You take that much trouble with Canterbury Bells, Siberian Wallflower, Foxglove and a host of others.

A fortnightly planting of annual Baby's Breath will supply continuous succession of bloom.

18. A BIRTHDAY SENTIMENT. This being my birthday, I am reminded of the remark of a French philosopher to the effect that by the time a man attains fifty he is either a drunkard or a gardener. There are still several years to pass before fifty is reached and I'm gardening furiously. But this shall not prevent me opening my best bottle for dinner tonight. Like the yokels of Gay's poem, "in ale and kisses I shall forget my cares."

Keep an eye for slugs in the Strawberry patch—they usually hide under the straw.

19. THE VERSATILITY OF VALERIAN. It is discouraging at times to read the cold, scientific facts about one's garden friends. Valerian, for example, *Valerian officinalis*, All-Heal or Cat's Valerian or Garden Heliotrope, whatever you may wish to call it. In Hampton's "Flower Scent," I find that the rich odor it gives off is really the effluvium of valeric acid, which is a strong component of perspiration. And its roots in drying, according to Step's "Herbs of Healing," develop the smell of newly-tanned leather. Now we know the worst. And yet for countless generations these dried roots were prescribed for everything from cramps to epilepsy, and even today a tincture of them is given for hysteria, nervous disorders and palpitation of the heart. How gratifying to find that a plant which is so versatile as to have architectural beauty and wear graceful flowers on its head can also be bitterly utilitarian! Hereafter when I pass it in the border I shall think of a beautiful woman who is also an excellent cook.

After every rain see that the soil is lightly cultivated to form a dust mulch.

20. WEATHER TRUMPERIES. When Dr. Johnson advised Boswell to keep a diary, he counseled him "to omit registers of the weather and like trumpery." It was clear that, as a gardener, the great doctor was a good dictionary writer. He probably didn't know Yarrow from Daisy, Burdock from Herb Bennet. Had he shown an inclination toward horticulture, he would have entertained a pronounced sympathy for weather

registers. I can imagine him stumping into my study and growling, "What! Three barometers? Pish-Posh!" For three there are. One is a modern, business-like affair with a dial as complicated as a time-table. Another is a column of mercury that many a generation of weather-wise owners have watched night and morning for, scratched beside its thermometer, are such "trumperies" as the fact that the temperature was such and such in Paris in June 1753 and that it fell to so-and-so in St. Petersburg. These two columns—the mercury and the red fluid of the thermometer—are mounted on a panel gay with sprays of Tulips and Roses and Pinks and delightfully perforated by wood borers. The third barometer is an old Dutch weather-glass that arrived the other day from London. It is a glass flask with a high spout in which the water rises when stormy weather is due and from which it fairly boils when the day is hot. Among the pleasurable amenities of our rural existence is a daily inspection of these barometers. Between the three of them, and Dr. Johnson to the contrary, we somehow manage to learn what weather lies ahead.

Peonies and Roses last longer for decoration when cut in the bud and allowed to open slowly in a cool place.

21. A WIFE'S THANKSGIVING. Having never been a golfer or a sailor or a huntsman, I'm not posted on what the wives of such sportsmen have to tolerate, but, having quietly compared notes with other gardening husbands, I'm afraid we're

no better than the rest. So, one of these days I shall have lettered for Her, to hang over Her bed, the thanksgiving set down in her diary by the Viscountess Mordaunt almost three hundred years ago—"I bles my God for giving me patient to ber with my Husband when he is in his passionat Humer."

As Tulip leaves begin to wither, lift the bulbs and allow them to ripen in a corner of the garden. Fill the evacuated space with annuals.

22. SEASONED AND SAFE ROSES. If I were a genuine, sincere and rabid Rosarian (and could afford to satisfy my whims) I would order Rose nurserymen to send me every new hybrid that comes their way. And what an utter fool I'd be! There is no easier method of becoming disillusioned about Roses and no simpler way of parting with your hard-earned shekels. Rose enthusiasm has waxed to that point where the subtlest variation will throw catalogue writers into ecstasies and rob their pens of adjectives. Having been many times burned by these, I am thrice shy. I have reached the same determination about Roses that I have about investments: I want them seasoned and safe. I'm not interested in a Rose unless it has been on the market five years. In fact, the very next Rose order that leaves this house has a "stop" on it at 1900 and some of the items go back to the 1500's. Let others toy with the subtleties, idiosyncrasies and delicacies of the latest hybrid teas, we shall devote our Rose

space to Damask and Gallica, Provence and Moss Roses. And, incidentally, we will have fragrance.

If you find yourself surfeited with the beauty of the garden, leave it for a few days.

23. A HINT FOR LLOYDS. About the middle of June in these parts begins the open season for hunting flower show judges. Previous to that they are a little too tender to be gunned for. And since there is nothing in the law which says by what means they may be taken, they can be snared or lured or mercifully dispatched with a cold, sharp glance. The usual bait is a luncheon. If your quarry be a man, see that the trap is set with another male judge. The most hardened male judge will shy at a flower show lunch when he is the sole male to be present. Or if you whisper to him that Miss So-and-So will be there (and that person be a companionable soul, blessed with looks and a bright eye, and not *too* serious about flowers), he can be led into the snare easily.

It is customary for the president of the local club to be in at the death or, at least, to be awarded the brush. Consequently, the wily judge will secretly find out which are the president's exhibits and thereafter let his conscience guide him. It is also customary (at least I have found it so in my limited judging experience) to "play" the judges for a time: let them do their judging in peace as if all were well. Having judged, they are then usually fed. It is after luncheon that you spring the trap or ride them. They are then considered fair game for all those who have failed to win prizes.

I usually arrange to have a car waiting for me in a sequestered place, and into it I disappear as soon as the judging is over. Several of my judging friends, however, who have not been so forehanded, have had their susceptibilities ruined for life in these aftermath tussles with the unawarded. Some bright insurance broker, one of these days, will write a flower show judge's policy, guaranteeing them safe escape. Perhaps Lloyds might do it.

Already you should start lopping off the heads of flowers that are passé and about to set seed.

24. THE BROTHERS BAPTISIA. Flowers are like guests: some you have to entertain and wait on constantly; others are resourceful and independent. And since Heaven will bear witness that there are enough of the former in the world, it is with genuine delight that we welcome the latter. Among our many border guests have been the Brothers Baptisia: the blond Tinctoria, and the blue Australis. Accustomed to a wild home, they are grateful for the soil amenities of a border. (I've yet to see a wildling that didn't relish a good meal and wax fat.) Tinc, the yellow, is a native of dry sandy soil, but Austra has chosen the better part and prefers something alluvial. My preference is for this Australis, especially when he flow-

ers in the neighborhood of white *Iris Siberica,* and that fine, floppy, single maroon Peony, The Moor.

See that the early Lilies do not lack staking, but hide your stakes in the foliage. A stake should neither be seen nor heard.

25. FERTILITY. The custom of throwing Rice at a bride (frowned on by economical souls who would substitute old shoes for which they no longer have any use) is a grand old pagan habit that serves to remind the blushing maiden and her fortunate swain that marriage isn't just all beer and skittles. In Roman days, Corn was thrown over the bride, and in India, after the first night, the husband's mother and all the female relatives place on the young bride's head, as an emblem of fertility, a measure of Corn. The husband scattered some of the Corn on himself, with the same lusty aspiration. In old Poland, Rye, Oats, Barley, Rice and Beans were scattered at the door of the bride's house, symbolizing the fact that if she proved a good wife she would never lack these necessities.

Remembering these goodly customs and their meaning, I much prefer to give my old shoes to the Goodwill Industries and scatter my largess of Rice on the bride. For it would take a wild stretch of the imagination to read a hope of fecundity into my old shoes when they have passed from the respectability of Sunday wear, to the tappings and heelings of ordinary use, and from weekday service down the steep descent of scuffing through a season in the garden.

Lest you tire of its physical exactions, stop gardening at four, wash up and be cordial to the rest of the family.

26. If a Man Would Be a Titan. I'm sorry for a man who has never swung a scythe. He has still to discover the potentialities of his body, he has still to enjoy the noblest rhythm of labor, he has still to penetrate the past as one who lives in it. Most of us dip into the past only when we go into a museum or an old house—we go for an occasional visit: the man who swings a scythe is using the traditional tool of his forefathers and using the same muscles that countless generations before him used in this same task. When he props the snath against his knee to whet the blade, making a sweet tune with the emery stick, when he halts to flick the sweat off his brow and for a moment contemplates the hills or meadows about him, he might be a pioneer Colonial farmer, so little difference is there in his movement. With each swish of the blade, he enjoys the complete satisfaction of seeing the swath laid low beside him. Under this strenuous rhythm, the body begins to glow. Fore and aft his muscles slide. His pores gush forth as streams. He becomes Titanic.

"Heel down, toe up." That's the rule of the man with the scythe. And to every twenty swings the caress of the whetstone on the blade. After such a day a man eats like a giant, sleep wraps around him ere the lamp goes out, and the night is emptied of all sound.

Tomorrow make one more planting of Gladioli, and for final bloom, a last planting on July 4th.

27. ARCHITECTURE AND VEGETABLES. After working with both flowers and vegetables for a season, you realize that there is much more architecture to the one than the other. True, you find a classical balance in the stems of Garden Heliotrope, *Valerian officinalis,* Lilies have a columnar growth, and Tulips a mass-strain and a contour that would puzzle the best engineer, but these are naught compared with the architecture of the Cabbage, the decorative shape of the Kohlrabi, the flat planes of Fennel, the round plaiting of the Leek and the glorious fruiting of the Eggplant. The Summer Squash is a Baroque detail and the Carrot's foliage Rococo. Onions are positively Saracen and in any stalk of Corn you can find the curves and twists of *L'Art Nouveau* which promised to (but, of course, didn't) raise taste from its nadir of despair in the gorgeous 1900's.

If the season is damp, keep an eye for Iris root rot. Lift the plant and expose it to the sunlight for a couple of days.

28. CHRYSANTHEMUMS HOLD THE THIRTEENTH CARD. The business of making the perennial Chrysanthemum give its increase is a simple one, and we indulge in it regularly each year at this season. Some of the hardier sorts are

left outdoors over Winter, heavily mulched, and with hopes of their surviving the rigor of our Connecticut ice and snow. But since we have no illusions of what this ice and snow, this melting and freezing, can do, a sample of each kind is carefully tucked away under the glass of the cold frame after its blooming is over. The following Spring these are divided—the outside pieces potted up and the old center discarded. When a good ball of roots has formed, these are set in place in the cutting garden and borders, and are mulched with peat moss. Mulching is much easier than pulling weeds. Along in late June the heads are all nipped off to make the plants branch, and after that, save for staking (Chrysanthemums are amazingly brittle) and the occasional disbudding to get a big flower here and there, and spraying to annihilate the aphids that settle on the tips, we pay little attention to them. But after the White Frost has blackened other flowers, then, these Chrysanthemums play their winning trick. They remind me of sedate, bridge-playing old ladies who always manage, somehow, to have the thirteenth card. They take the last trick of the Autumn rubber.

The greenhouse should be given a thorough cleaning at this time.

29. VAIN PROMISES. This sort of thing happens every year. In the course of our perambulations we visit many gardens and see many things that arouse our floral concupiscence. There and then we say, "Yes, we'll have that next season." And

almost invariably when the season comes around, it is forgotten. In a friendly garden not far away the paved walk is spattered each summer with Portulaca that lift their multi-colored caps up to the sun like brave little chalice-bearers. And She says to me, "My dear, why *don't* we have Portulaca?" "We can have it very easily," I reply. This has been going on for fully five years now, and five Springs have I forgotten to order Portulaca seed until the very mention of the plant sends blushes of shame through me. The same has happened with several Irises and Peonies, most of the Lilies and no end of Roses. And I suppose the only way to make reparation for these sins of omission is to devote one year to growing only those things that I have said we could have easily. Wives seem to be endowed with most annoying memories, and the pathway to marital peace is never to forget.

Tomorrow begin clipping hedges and formal evergreens.

30. ELEGY FOR AN ELM. Having built this house for his bride, so we are told, the old master carpenter who set this Greek temple on a Connecticut hillside thereupon planted in front of it the dower Elms—one for himself and one for his bride. Through the years they have flourished, but the bridegroom Elm is gradually going. Tree surgeons have chained up his palsied arms and poured concrete into his hollow vitals with little avail. Each year we are obliged to take off a few more limbs that have died over Winter. Already,

against his going, we have planted a sturdy Wistaria that will cover the lifeless trunk some day. And when that day comes we can dispel our sadness with those noble lines from Cowper's "Yardley Oak"—

Time was when, settling on thy leaf, a fly
Could shake thee to the root—and time has been
When tempest could not.

In transplanting annuals at this season, take care that their roots never dry. Puddle them in a pail of mud before planting.

LONG PIECE
THE GOD OF KETTLES

THERE is an infinity of things on which men pride themselves, and perhaps the most boastworthy are their digressions. Any form of sport—golf, hunting, fishing, gardening even—is the open sesame to their pride. Some are craftsmen; they show their workshop with youthful pride and are highly set up when you marvel at their dexterity with tools. Some secretly practise one or more of the arts, and they display their amateur and apprentice attempts at painting and sculpturing with unconcealed joy. Others fashion pots; others collect queer and unaccountable objects; some are mighty walkers, and they scorn the convenient ride. But of all digressions upon which a man of the world either secretly or openly most prides himself is his ability to cook.

If circumstances oblige him to cook constantly, he may not mention it; if it is a hobby, then you need scarcely mention a stove but he is off into gustatory rhapsodies. Openly or covertly, there are moments when every man visualizes himself as a master of culinary accomplishments, a lord of stew-pans, a god of kettles.

This digression may first have come upon the male species in the very dawn of time. Home from the chase, his bag bursting with game, primitive man watched his woman spoil the meat he had snared with such great effort. He pushed her aside with a tap of his stone hammer—and the meat was cooked to his liking. Or perhaps there was a mighty domestic rebellion in those dim, far-off days; perhaps Neolithic woman told her Neolithic spouse that she was sick and tired of bending over a hot fire all day and that if he wanted any food he could cook it himself. Whichever way it came about, it is an indisputable fact that from the earliest times up to this palpitating present, the great cooks of the world have been men. Men have raised cooking to a profession, have given it the dignity of a great art.

Although many women take well-earned pride in their kitchen accomplishments, the majority look upon them merely as part of the day's work, part of the business of being a wife. They may attain dizzy pinnacles of gustatory delight, they may compose great dishes and write useful tomes on the art of cooking, yet the average woman cook, by her attitude toward cooking, seems to court sympathy, appears to enjoy her down-trodden rôle as Martha of the stew-pots.

On the other hand, man in his moments of amateur or professional recourse to recipes, rises to a state of great exultation. He has formulated a ritual for it and created distinctive vestments. As a chasuble to the priest and the mitre to the bishop, so are the apron and cap to the chef. As the doctor takes pride in his immaculate lancets, as the artist in his brushes and canvas, so the chef in his knives and cleavers and the diversity of his culinary equipment.

The great cooks of the world find an immortality that rarely comes to other professions. The architect who designs a cloud-piercing structure is content if he finally is paid his fee—the structure is usually named for the man or the company who financed it. The great general wins a battle, but the battle is known for the place at which it was fought. Wellington may have thrilled the world on the plains of Belgium, but the fight is known as the Battle of Waterloo. The chef, on the other hand, creates a dish, and thereafter it bears his name. Men in far corners of the world speak of this dish, and the name becomes a household word. The *cordon-bleu* never fades. The findings of the *Jury Digustateur* are remembered in countless homes and restaurants. In the ovens of Rocher de Cancale, Vèry, Voisin, Hardy, Vincent de la Chapelle, Boulanger, Robert, Meot, Roze and Careme, in these kitchens were created unfading immortalities.

Although of late years, in England and America especially, cook books have generally been written by women, the great classics of the culinary world were penned by men. From the early Italian volumes of Bartolomeo Platina and Roselle up to the comparatively modern work of Brillat-Savarin, the scholar must look to men as authorities on this art. They must also look to men to make the great experiments.

"The kitchen," says an old French authority, "is a country in which there are always discoveries to be made." Perhaps it is this lure of the unknown that leads adventuresome men to make strange and delectable combinations of food. Yet (we blush to acknowledge it), when there was compiled, some years back, a cook book of the favorite dishes of prominent men in this country, the majority of them were content with spaghetti!

In well-ordered households the cook has at least one night off. Also, it may be observed that in well-ordered households where peace dwells permanently, the men of the family are permitted to pursue their innocent digressions unmolested. Here is a chance to turn a digression to useful purposes. Why should not Thursday be known as the night when the men who boast their ability as cooks be given a chance to prove it? Let the man who prides himself on his campfire flapjacks and unsurpassed coffee see what he can do in the civilized environment of a tile-walled kitchen. Perhaps in this way we may raise up a race of men whose appetites attain heights nobler than spaghetti and fried eggs.

Perhaps, too, we will find more men appreciating the fact that to supply three meals a day to a hungry family is an accomplishment worthy of the highest award. Once he realizes this, even the humblest kitchen scullion becomes a minor deity and the cook herself, a veritable goddess of the Gastronomic Nirvana.

THE MONTH OF JULY

1. THE VAGARIES OF NOSTRILS. Strange are the ways of the human nostril and many's the trick that can be played on it. J. Horace MacFarland, that excellent Rosarian, puts his visitors through the blind-fold test—covers their eyes and walks them past his various Mock Oranges, and makes them guess what the odor is. The analogies which we are obliged to make to define scents are sometimes fantastic: *Iris pallida* to some is reminiscent of vanilla; Musk Roses of beeswax and honey; the Austrian Copper Rose, *R. lutea,* of either bugs or Coriander seed; *Humea elegans* of Russia leather and incense; *Clematis paniculata* of licorice; to one authoritative nostril (certainly not mine) the scent of garden Phlox is a cross between Walnuts and a clean pig sty, and the dried leaves of Valerian like an old dog kennel! Another ancient smeller—Topsell (1658-81) who wrote "Four-footed Beasts"—claimed that the roots of Valerian are beloved of cats, "for it smelleth moreover like a cat."

During hot weather Pansies grow straggly; cut them back and water freely.

2. BURNING BUSHES. Some things they order better in France. Thus for a garden party the average American hostess attains the zenith of her imagination by stringing up Japanese lanterns.

But in France, recently, the guests retired from the garden into the house for dinner. It was dusk. Dinner over, they came out to the garden again and found it a sea of twinkling lights. While they were indoors the gardeners had outlined the paths and the clumps of shrubbery and flower beds with candle lanterns made of tumblers. They took bar glasses (the short, stocky kind used for old-fashioned whiskey cocktails) and set in each a small carriage candle. The tumbler protected the flame from the wind, and, instead of hanging above the heads of the guests, the lights were at their feet.

Tomorrow begin collecting your own seed from perennials. Allow it to dry a fortnight before planting.

3. BOOK RULES AND SUMMER SEEDING. The sort of gardener who most quickly depresses me is the one who takes all his directions from books. "So-and-So's book says, etc." So-and-So in nine cases out of ten "lifted" that idea from Some-one-else's book and Some-one-else took it from a book written by an Englishman for English conditions and not applicable here. There is, for instance, the old book rule that you wait till August to plant seeds of perennials. What nonsense! Plant them any time you can make them grow or have space in your cold frame. We seed them into the trays as soon as the last of the annuals are set out and the trays are available. Early July is the usual season in this latitude. The seedlings aren't allowed to flower the first year and Autumn sees

them possessed of a robust root system. The same with biennials. All these are kept under slatted covers through the seedling stage so that the sun doesn't dry them up or encourage them to too much leaf growth. Commonsense is a far better guide to gardening than Somebody else's lack of it.

A handful of bone meal to each bush Rose will strengthen the summer growth.

4. OF THEE WE SING. The farmhouse stands at the end of a road, behind straight stone walls and a trim garden. It has no need for privacy, though, since neighbors are far off and people rarely pass that way. Such things as go on there are unknown because they are unseen. That was why the flag caught my eye as I neared the house on this July 4th tramp. It hung lengthwise from the porch beams—an old flag—and perhaps not a dozen people would pass that house to see its symbol of patriotism. The widow of a Civil War veteran lived there with the widow of a man who had made a name for himself years ago in one of New York's crack regiments. Two old patriotic crones, God bless 'em!

As I approached, a sound of music drifted down breeze. I leaned over the wall and peered through the open door into the front parlor. One ancient lady was playing the parlor organ; the other—a quaint old soul with a figure like a Noah's ark woman—stood rigid beside her. The notes wheezed and rambled along, and then drifted into the familiar air of "My Country 'Tis of Thee."

And with that the two old crones turned their faces to the ceiling and ecstatically began to sing.

I glanced down the road. No one in sight. No house near enough for neighbors to hear. . . . Behind that flag two old women at a parlor organ, two shaky voices at their patriotic orisons:

> My Country, 'tis of thee,
> Sweet Land of Liberty,
> Of thee we sing.

Give the Melons generous doses of liquid manure these days.

5. PLANTAIN LILIES. Though nothing could be more commonplace and nothing easier to grow, yet I do not blush when I voice my increasing admiration for the Funkia family. The Plantain Lilies, as old-fashioned as a red plush sofa, go on massing their mounds of leaves year after year and tossing their big bells into the July sunlight. We use *Hosta caerulea* to soften corners of steps of a brick path and to face down shrubbery along the kitchen. Here Tulips are set between the plants so that the Funkia foliage is all out when these Darwins open their cups. Later, they themselves give us their sticks of purplish mauve flowers. *H. subcordata grandiflora,* having smaller leaves, carries its white flowers a little later below the study porch. The kinds with variegated foliage, *H. lancifolia alba marginata, H. variegata* and *H. undulata media variegata,* I find especially interesting, even if variegated foliage is considered Victorian. Sun or shade suit these accommodating

fellows; in fact, all they ask is rich soil and dampness at the roots. With these at hand, they seem as contented as a fat old Chinaman asleep in the shadow of a compound wall or a pot-bellied joss grinning from ear to ear above the smoke of votive incense sticks on a temple altar in far-away Hunan.

Make the final planting of Gladioli tomorrow. This should flower before frost.

6. BEWARE THESE. May it not be held against me that once on a time I gave to grasping visitors what I hoped to be all my plants of Physostegia and *Anthemis tinctoria.* I had battled all summer to keep them in bounds, but they soon out-paced me. When these visitors came (merest tyros in gardening they were), my generosity appalled them. "What a prodigal!" they exclaimed. Confidently I watched them load the clumps into their cars and drive off. Some of them came back for more, but I've heard rumors that their attitude toward me has changed. Well, may they be at peace: Vengeance was soon turned on my own head. For scarcely had the clumps gone, than appeared a thousand seedlings and rootlets. Spring after spring they leap up at me like twinges from a bad conscience. Mention False Dragonhead and Anthemis within my hearing, and I blanch. I would sooner walk openly with a leopard cub for pet than let these two into my borders again.

Cuttings from hardy Pinks should now be taken. Cut with a heel, place in damp sand in the shade.

7. A BUTTERFLY GARDEN. From South Africa comes the story of a Butterfly Garden. It is laid out complementary to a building in Johannesburg designed by Sir Edwin Lutyens. From all over the world were assembled the flowers that would grow in that temperature and would attract butterflies. Since the butterflies of South Africa are famous for their beauty, this must now be a spot to ravish the eye. The same can be done to a certain extent in any perennial border. Collect from the meadows Butterfly Weed, and see how butterflies swarm to it. Humming birds seem to dote on Larkspur and bees love *Monarda didyma.* Small wonder that the common name of the latter flower is Bee balm.

Mangy foliage is the natural state of Oriental Poppy foliage at this season: Don't let it worry you.

8. A SOLUTION FOR WEDDING PRESENTS. Just about this time of year several thousands of June brides begin to touch earth, and look upon their wedding presents with a cool and appraising eye. The first flush of excitement over and life fast assuming its ordinary, jog-trot gait, they contemplate the generous gifts of their relatives and friends, and wonder what they are going to do with them. The ubiquitous wedding present is a problem. That lamp (there are always lamps), that vase (and their name is legion), that strange and unaccountable piece of pottery—what in Heaven's name shall they do with them?

We have gone among matrons and asked them how long one must be married before she can, without fear of hurting the delicate sensibilities of relatives and friends, assign these white elephants to the oblivion of the garret and refuse pile. Their answers range from two to five years. To a bride, five years will seem like an eternity.

There should be some solution for this. Perhaps an enterprising merchant will open a chain of stores to sell such unwanted gifts. In one ancient city of the South to which tourists go for antiques, is a shop in which the young brides put up their useless wedding presents for sale. And they sell like hot cakes, for the tale that goes with them is that these objects come from "some of the old families."

Unless you wish to pot them up for new plants, keep the runners cut off of Strawberries.

9. ROOTS BY THE MILE. Among the pet mendacities of horticulturists is to speak in exaggerated terms of roots. If a plant has a long rootstock it increases in geometric proportion to the labor entailed in digging it out. The common Butterfly Weed of our dry meadows is a case in point. Its subsurface migrations are a torment to those who collect it and their tales of its length and wanderings echo the tall romancing of Marco Polo. So do Oriental Poppies and perennial Baby's Breath. Another is Alfalfa, which will go down

fifteen feet and, according to the well-informed from South America, has been known to penetrate soil to the depth of forty-five feet! The root system of an ordinary Oat plant laid end to end will total four hundred and fifty feet. The classic example of root romance, however, is found in a report of an explorer who went into the Libyan Desert searching for its lost oases and who wrote at length on them in the dependable Journal of the Royal Geographical Society. He halted his caravan to excavate the root system of a tuft of grass growing in a dune. One rootstock he found to be seventy-five feet long and he estimated that the entire root system would total a distance of fifty miles. All of this was supporting a clump of leaves not more than eighteen inches high. Which shows to what lengths a plant will travel for drink.

A last planting of Golden Bantam Corn can now be made.

10. THE THYME BANK. Most of us are slaves to quotations. And quotations persisted in long enough are legitimate grounds for homicide. In our stone path, which is known as the Steep Ascent, grows a patch of *Thymus serpyllum*. Tell a visitor it is Thyme or let him recognize it, and invariably he rushes to Shakespeare and quotes, "I know a bank where the Wild Thyme blows." After ten years of this sort of thing my fingers itched to clutch the throats of such people. Or else I muttered under my breath, "You

may, but I don't." To spare myself committing justifiable manslaughter or (which is sometimes worse) being rude, I have planted a Thyme Bank. To the rear of it towers a Bush Honeysuckle of the Maximowiczi persuasion, and on each side, a *Diervilla florida venusta* with its tubular pink flowers. Flat stones make a step from it down to the level of a garden cross path. On this slope—a patch big enough for two large persons to sit on comfortably—is planted a mixture of the Thymes—*T. citriodorus, T. vulgaris, T. serpyllum* and *T. s. coccineus.* When quoters begin dragging Shakespeare into my garden, I merely lead them to this spot and let them quote their fill.

Begin dividing Irises this month. Enrich the soil before replanting.

11. A COLOR TRIO. Garnet, lemon yellow and blush pink may be three colors as distantly separated as the oil and vinegar and seasoning of a good salad dressing, yet if these three are combined in the garden or in a vase in the same proportions as one uses for the dressing, they mingle far more pleasantly than one would expect. One color should be used prodigally—the blush pink; one as a miser—the garnet; then salt and pepper with lemon yellow to suit the taste. Try it with blush pink and garnet Asters and lemon yellow African Marigolds. The effect isn't half as distressing to the eye as it sounds; in fact, it is a combination that will draw the eye again and

again. Placed together in a sunny window these three colors will fairly vibrate.

Snip off withered heads from annuals and thus prolong the bloom.

12. LEFT-OVERS. At an earlier age the big Sunday midday dinner was my idea of gastronomic Paradise. Any meal that followed it was a gross anti-climax. But as the years pass, my affection is turning toward Sunday night's supper. A bit of cold lamb from Saturday's dinner, a sliver of chicken from Sunday's midday feast, a touch of String Bean salad left over from the Beans of noon—of such tasty remnants is this supper compounded. Eating it brings the satisfaction of economy. It evidences good household management. It has about it a tidy air. As we grow older, I believe, we put more value on Life's left-overs—on old clothes that are too good to throw away, on an old love that has settled down from hectic ardor to placid companionship, on old habits that we have inherited from a speedier moving youth. So much of Life's worth-while things are second-hand anyway; each morning a second-hand sun rises on a second-hand world and lights second-hand people going about their second-hand work and play.

The soil around Lilies should be mulched these hot days with grass clippings or peat moss.

13. HEMEROCALLIS. We are on the threshold of a lively appreciation of Hemerocallis. So far this

Day Lily has either been taken for granted as a sort of wildling, or it has been treated casually in the scheme of garden things. Meantime, hybridizers have busied themselves with creating and fixing new tints, new markings and a variety of heights, and the next five years should see these new Day Lilies spring into popularity. Even pink and a red Hemerocallis are no strangers to the plant wizards, and they, doubtless, will soon be no stranger to intelligent gardeners.

The Chinese have long since cherished the old *Fulva* types. Many of the plants that line our Connecticut roadsides can boast a romantic heritage stretching back to the Orient. Brought from China by clipper-ship tars to their New England gardens, these roving plants ran away from the gardens' confines and have spread to the roadside banks. Now re-dressed, and refined, they return to us as new aristocrats for the garden.

Delphiniums that have finished flowering should be cut back to one foot; two weeks later feed them manure water to stimulate subsequent growth.

14. FORGOTTEN LOVERS. In one of Huysman's novels, *"A Rebours"* if I remember correctly, is a young gentleman who, having gone through all the normal pleasures, begins steeping himself in the decadent and luxurious, and his taste eventually turns to macabre and sinister plants and to exotic fragrances. I am reminded of him at this season of the year when Tuberoses begin to flower.

Now, frankly, the Tuberose is not the sort of thing a normal man would elect to grow to excess. I have only a few of them—the Double Pearl and the loose-flowered Mexican Everblooming—tucked away here and there in the borders. I grow them on request, and their scent has an almost fatal attraction to women. Their buds are parceled out, I find, to women callers who forthwith become romantic. Somehow, somewhere in the past of that sex, the fragrance of the Tuberose played a mighty rôle. From remarks about it, it appears to be the flower of forgotten lovers, lovers sufficiently forgotten to be safe.

Climbing Roses may now be cleared of the wood that has flowered this year.

15. SALES RESISTANCE. My gardener, whose opinion I have come to respect, stated the other day that he planned to take a correspondence course in sales resistance this winter. His reason for this choice of winter diversion he said was, "because slick salesmen are always selling me things that I don't want, don't need and can't use." And so this countryman, God bless him, has his back up. He has cluttered his house and his living with all manner of things that he bought because he couldn't resist the solicitations of glib-tongued solicitors. For the last and final time—when he had subscribed for those Letters of the Presidents in fourteen volumes—he had been taken in. Pity the salesman who approaches his doorstep next Spring, after he has mastered that course in sales resistance!

Sooner or later every one of us feels that way. Sooner or later each of us buys the "Letters of the Presidents" in fourteen volumes. In an unguarded or weak moment we capitulate to the slick arguments of the high-powered salesmen. With a sigh of relief, we sign our name on the dotted line. And when the merchandise appears, we wonder what manner of imbecile we were to have ordered it. We didn't need it, didn't want it, can't use it. We reproach ourselves for being so wasteful. Indeed, we all need courses in sales resistance.

Don't attempt to garden too much on these torrid days. Get the work over before ten in the morning.

16. MEN AND THISTLES. One of these days some learned psychologist will figure out what there is in Thistles that attracts the male—what subtle relationship between them; what accounts for the fact that men gardeners take such pride in Thistles. I have known fully half a dozen such men, and I have suffered patiently their rhapsodies over their pet plants—their gigantic size, their terrible thorns, their magnificent florescence.

Once I mentioned this coincidence in the bosom of my family. "All donkeys," She answered, "like Thistles. Have I not told you I loathe those Globe Thistles you insist on sticking into the back of the border? You are no different from the rest." Being thus properly chastened, I retired. . . . But the Globe Thistles are still there, and on these

July afternoons I find myself pointing to them with pride when visitors appear.

Keep the wheel-hoe and rake going these days to make a dust mulch after showers.

17. LEAN SOULS. Many are the misdemeanors, major and minor, that we pray our friends will forgive us as we hope to forgive them, yet in this category there is one exception—ingratitude. A subtle poison is ingratitude: it works from within and destroys slowly. We see the ungrateful wax rich, we see them acquire country places and vast gardens and all the material evidences of being justly rewarded, and we marvel that these things can come to pass. Then one day, when least we are expecting it, the importance of all this vastness and luxury crumbles before the puny character of the ingrate. The poison that has worked from within shrivels them into nonentities. Like the people David speaks of—God "gave them their request; but sent leanness into their souls."

The foliage of Peonies, which is necessary for the growth of the plant, should not be cut off.

18. BELLS AND STARS. Two summer bulbs give us great delight—Galtonias and Montbretias. The former you may call Summer Hyacinth if you like, or White Cape Hyacinth or Spire Lily. Their big bulbs are sunk six inches deep into the soil of the borders on the line of the Phlox. A dozen or more make an effective clump. For many weeks

they swing the white bells of their flowering. They revel in sifted manure and bone meal. Montbretias, on the other hand, are given positions nearer the front of the border—the line of the Iris and Lupins. Smaller bulbs, these go in only about four inches, in colonies of twenty or more. Some of the newer hybrids offer an amazing range of color. Like spattering of stars they are—stars that twinkle from July to September. Both of these bulbs in our Connecticut climate are lifted after the Black Frost has withered the stalk.

Any week in August is a good time to divide and move Madonna Lilies.

19. A BIG LILY AND A LITTLE ONE. To these foregoing Summer bulbs, I would add two others that we try—the Peruvian Daffodil, *Ismene calathina* and the Fairy Lilies or *Zephyranthes.*

A Loving Reader sent me my first batch of Fairy Lilies years ago, and I've been adding to them ever since. Delicate little white or pink Lilies, their place is in sheltered coves in the front of the border where they bob and nod to each other like polite boats in a quiet harbor. Three inches is the depth to set them, and a couple of inches apart. Being tender with us, they must be lifted in the Fall.

For the Ismene Lily I make up the same pocket of rich, rotted manure that I prepare for Tuberoses. This is forked in six inches deep and the bulbs are set about four inches deep, early June being the season. Action starts almost at once. By

July a deliciously fragrant Lily is unfolding. In groups of a dozen they make a perfect symphony of fragrance. Moreover their tribe increaseth very fast, so that by lifting them each Autumn we have managed to accumulate quite a store.

Sweet Peas should be cut daily and given an abundance of water to prolong their flowering.

20. MOSSY ROOFS. Invariably, when Americans go to England and see the moss-covered roofs of country houses there, they come home and demand that architects create them here. And the best the poor architects can do is to stimulate the color of the moss in painted or dipped shingles or in vari-colored slate. While these are excellent substitutes in effect, they are not moss.

In our pursuit of this subject we consulted Mrs. Elizabeth G. Britton, Honorary Curator of the Bronx Botanical Garden, and a well-known authority on mosses and lichens. Her reply was: "There are a few that withstand our adverse conditions and I have seen old shingle roofs green and rotten with them. Of course a thatched roof is easier, for that retains moisture and decays more quickly and contains more plant food. There are several families of mosses that grow on rocks and walls, notably the *Tortulaceae,* and *Tortula muralis* will even grow on lime and mortar. In S. W. Arizona and New Mexico they stand the climate, and have special modifications of the leaves that enable them to adapt themselves to changing conditions, like the Resurrection Fern and plant *Polypodium incanum* and *Selaginella lepidophylla* (see Bailey Enc. of Hort.). Of course, out West at Seattle, there are roofs covered with mosses, but their climate is like that of England. The *Grimmiaceae* also grow on rocks in mountain and forested regions." Perhaps some architects might experiment with these mosses and see if they would grow between the cracks of slate.

Some time this week lay yourself open to the temptations of the Autumn bulb catalogues.

21. THE GOURMET'S HALLMARK. Among the proofs of the veritable gourmet, the indisputable hallmark of his taste and discretion is salad, that course which "refreshes without weakening and comforts without irritating," as Brillat-Savarin hath it. Indeed you may know a gourmet among gardeners by merely walking through his vegetable patch and noting what salad ingredients he grows: Lettuce and Chicory, Endive, Corn-salad, Dandelion, Watercress, Radishes, Chives and esculents such as Tomatoes, Cucumbers, Beets, Potatoes, Carrots, Celery-root. With such delicacies does the gastronomic artist dream of titillating his palate. He has then merely to call on good olive oil, good wine vinegar, a corn of Garlic, a dash of salt, a powdering of black pepper and a dab of mustard. Find such salad ingredients growing in a garden and you may be sure of a good dinner. You may also be sure that here is a man who grows his vegetables with intelligence, since

he plants them with definite meals and dishes in view.

Make an extra planting of annual Gypsophila, Poppies and Sweet Alyssum in bare spots.

22. MEMORIAL CIMICIFUGA. Some plant names I like to roll round and round my mouth the way a small boy consumes a sour-ball. One is *Saponaria ocymoides,* another is *Ophioglossum vulgatum* and the third *Cimicifuga racemosa.* The last I like best of all. Nothing under the beautiful shining blue of Heaven could induce me to call it by so slithery a name as Snakeroot, for I grow it as a memorial to the man who brought it here years ago. A generous division from his own garden, it has multiplied and been distributed at the rear of a border that is backed by tall Cedars. A garden seat is close by, and we sit there on July afternoons and see the Cimicifuga toss its white spires toward the sky, while pink and white Astilbe gathered at its feet repeat in a more refined form its wild flowery grace. At such times I think these plants an even more fitting memorial to this man than the window the village put into the church, for his kindness, like the vigor of his plants, was abundant and perennial.

Annual Evening Primrose and Bachelor's Buttons make a pleasant combination these days.

23. THE JULY LET-DOWN. Most of us (since most of us cannot afford a host of gardeners to

prevent such an hiatus) pass through a flowery doldrums toward the end of July. The great Spring procession has gone. A gap comes in the parade before the big division of Summer appears. And invariably this is the time friends and other guests drop in expecting to see a fine exhibition. You have to explain that even in some of the best regulated garden families this lean season will happen. You rarely can explain, however, that it is a relief, this quiet fortnight. So abundant, so lush, so colorful is the Spring and early Summer blooming, that the eye and the nostrils and the emotions grow satiated and the perception of fine flower subtleties is dulled. This July period of rest before Phlox and Hollyhocks appear is like a restful dull Monday after a houseful of week-end guests has departed—a let-down to be sure, but a breathing spell gratefully received by a weary host. No, a garden that never ceases to bloom abundantly would soon become a bore. Much can be said against any emotional stimulus to which there "is no variableness, neither shadow of turning."

Feed Carpathian Harebells, and their blossoming flourishes through the summer.

24. UNENTHUSIASTIC THOUGHTS ON PLATYCODON. My sentiments on Platycodon, the Balloon Flower, are mixed. So are they on any plant that I do not grow well. And I envy the garden that can afford the space to make a display of it. My on-the-fenceness is due to the fact that its leggy habit requires both the supporting of the plant

itself and an immediate companionship of other things to face it down. All I have ever accorded it is a dab of Sweet Alyssum, growing there more by chance than by good intentions. Were I to try the dwarf forms—*P. Mariesii,* the blue, and *P. Mariesii album,* the white—my opinion might change. Perhaps my misgivings are due to the fact that it appears so late in the Spring that inevitably some of the plants are rooted up in early cultivation. You always have to remember that, and it's a nuisance. It's like calling on touchy people in whose presence you have to be *awfully* careful of what you say.

The shadowy reaches of a pergola may be brightened by planting Funkia subcordata.

25. SPORTS FOR DOG-DAYS. Three homely diversions for hot days I adore, and may I never grow too old to enjoy them. One is leaning over the pig sty and directing a gentle stream from the hose down the backs of my porkers. Their delight and mine is enormous. Another is to sit on a shady bank and watch puppies play, the while one is being defleaed rigorously by my wife. The third is to dig worms in the chicken yard. All I need do is to drag the fork, and the entire flock trails it to the spot where I turn up the soil. After that no worm is safe.

Order Autumn Crocus now and plant liberally under shrubs. Old writers used to call them "Naked Ladies" because their stems are never modestly skirted with leaves.

26. CUSHIONED PATHS. While the turf path kept in perfection is the sort of path all gardeners hope eventually to attain, there are others that are not to be despised, and among them is the path made of Pine needles. I encountered it first in a Rose garden near Portland, Maine. The owner had a Pine grove handy on the place, and each year a new layer of needles was laid down between the beds. The effect of walking on this was like walking on the deepest pile carpet. In the warm sun it gave off a balmy fragrance.

Or one might even put a proverb to test (a weakness of mine, incidentally). For countless generations old people have said of Camomile, "The more it is trodden the more it will spread." Why then not make a Camomile path? It might be roughish, but visualize it in a wild garden. Given an occasional cutting with a scythe, and constantly trodden, such a path would soon assume a rich and hardy verdure—unless the proverb is mistaken.

Arabis, Alyssum, Aubretia, Phlox divaricata, *Nepeta and the sprawly Veronicas can be trimmed back now.*

27. SERENDIPITY. Here is a nice word that collectors will enjoy—Serendipity. It was coined by Horace Walpole out of the title of the fairy tale, "The Three Princes of Serendip," the heroes of which were always making discoveries by accident. And that is its meaning—the faculty of making happy and unexpected discoveries by accident. When you wander into an antique shop in search

of a pewter candlestick and find a unique piece of Irish glass for next to nothing, you are blessed with Serendipity!

Mulching heavily with peat moss will save weeding in borders and beds.

28. PLANTS OF SUBURBIANA. Being country lovers, we assiduously avoid those plants that are definitely associated with suburbs. Mention Red Salvia, and I think of rows of dreary boxes into which people crawl at night—boxes set so close together as to make privacy impossible. The Catalpa tree is many a suburbanite's dream of arboreal attainment. However, it has virtues—it may be planted close and clipped into a pleached allée. The Barberry and the Privet are the hedges of well-to-do Suburbiana—and we let them have them, although all the tribe of Barberry is not to be sniffed at nor would I casually toss away my one plant of Pyramid-shape Privet—*Ligustrum vulgare pyramidale.* And as for the Japanese Maple —on second thought, yes, the suburbs may have that too, if they will let us rural gardeners have the exclusive rights to the Copper Beech.

Spraying should be as regularly done in the garden as dusting in the house.

29. MOSES AND THE CRAB GRASS. When Moses drew the Lord's attention to the fact that unless something terribly vile was done to the Egyptians, his Hebraic friends were going to lose out, the Divine Correction, on several occasions, assumed horticultural forms, you remember, plagues of

locusts and what-not. And one day Moses got beside himself and threatened to smite their borders with frogs. Of course this sort of warfare wouldn't be countenanced today. Imagine smiting your foe's garden with a plague of Japanese beetles! Compared with this, poisoning wells would be tame. Imagine visiting upon a foe's perfectly good lawns a plague of Crab Grass. Neither of these is so difficult to imagine; in fact, we've been fighting Crab Grass for years, fighting it with stolons of Creeping Bent, with destructive fork and various grass seed mixtures sown where the crab was dug out, fighting it by keeping it from coming to seed, since it is an annual. Spend weeks battling this greedy weed, and you'll think the Egyptians weren't so bad off after all. However, since we're not Egyptians, we can't lay the blame for this scourge on Moses, and since we try to be rational about such affairs, it would be insulting to think that a busy God finds time to take vengeance on our little patch of lawn. There remains only one person to blame—the nurseryman who sold us the grass seed. Like the good Lord, he, too, gets blamed for a lot.

Be sure to stake Cosmos with a sufficiently long and sufficiently stout pole.

30. CANNAS CAN BE GOOD. Give a dog a bad name, and he may eventually retrieve his reputation, but let a flower suffer the sneers of the gardening *cognescenti,* and all the fine hybrids of it that some faithful soul may create will flower to little advantage. Cannas are a case in point.

Mention them, and across the mind flashes unlovely memories of dreary park, prison and hospital flower beds. For years the Canna was an institutional flower, and that's enough to damn any plant. Yet some very beautiful hybrids have been created and at the sight of them we waxed ecstatic over their subtle pinks and yellows. They have ceased being institutional. We tried them first in the Cutting Garden to see if they were so terrible as we had feared and then, finding their real beauty, gave them a place in the borders, where, in late Summer, they mingle with starry Boltonia, with the prodigal flowering of the Phlox and the russet tints of Helenium. After frost they are dug up together with the other tender roots and bulbs scattered through the herbaceous planting.

Even though it has bloomed by now, Japanese Iris will be benefited by watering.

31. BANZAI—THE JAPS! One of the cheapest forms of gambling I've yet encountered is a package of Japanese Iris seed. It costs next to nothing, it germinates easily, and within two years you may have a fascinating crop of hybrids. If from this batch only one plant is worth saving, its glory when full blown will make you forget such little bother as you took with it. Japanese Iris sounds the final gorgeous note of the Iris symphony, a brilliant fanfare of color, a gusty roll of robust drums, a clash of myriad-tinted cymbals!

Order Evergreens tomorrow for August planting.

LONG PIECE

"AND SO TO BED"

WHEN that amorous Restoration worthy, Samuel Pepys, finished the day's record in his diary, he gave a last fine flourish of the pen and ended with, "And so to bed."

Millions before his time and millions since have gone off to rest with as light a conscience as he, yet Samuel Pepys' phrase will go down to posterity as the last exultant remark one makes as he stifles a yawn and switches off the light. "And so to bed" has a finality to it. The day is done. There are no more things one wishes to do or has to do. There are no more people to talk to and nothing more to be said. Work and play, trouble and laughter, earnest endeavors and inconsequential flippancies—all are over. That day's finished. "And so to bed!"

An amusing picture Pepys makes as he stumbles up the stairs. A young man (for the Pepys of the diary was in his thirties) often the worse for drink, and wearing the finery of his day—the silk suit with the gold buttons of which he was so proud, and the new periwig, that had aroused no comment when he first wore it, pushed to the back of his shaved pate. A candlestick is in his hand. One of the wenches of his household may be at his elbow. From the top of the stairs his sprightly French wife, in the petticoat that cost £5 and the patches that she favored, tells him in no uncertain terms what she thinks of him.

Whether sober or in his cups, whether bowed with the worries of the British Navy, of which he was secretary, or light-hearted over the last girl he had kissed, to Pepys going to bed was a ceremony. And so it was for many generations until, in our own era, people began to live on one plane. "And so to bed" meant going *upstairs* to bed.

Today, with innumerable people living in apartments or in bungalows, the act of ascending the stairs to one's rest is almost becoming obsolete. We merely walk into another room and tumble into the sheets. Going to bed has lost some of its fine old flavor. It has ceased being a luxury, and has become an efficient necessity.

My youth was spent in an old household in Philadelphia where going to bed still retained the atmosphere of quaint domesticalities. After dinner the family sat around and read or talked. Callers drifted in, chatted for a while, had their wine, and went home. At about half-past ten Bridget thumped up from her kitchen carrying the silver basket, which she deposited on the floor beside Grandmother's chair. Having bade a broguish good night, she disappeared. Then a yawn broke the conversation and bed was suggested. Grandmother went first, carrying the silver. The rest of the family trooped after her. Finally Grandfather, putting out the gas lights as he went along, began his slow progress up the wide stairs. He always seemed engrossed in deep thought. On the landing he stopped, compared his watch with the landing clock, wound it and stood there silently for a moment. Then he, too, mounted the last flight.

What he did in that silent moment before the clock always piqued my curiosity. One day I made so bold as to ask him. He was attending to a purely private affair, it seemed. That arrested position before the tall clock gave him a chance, so he explained, to say his prayer for a good death. It was the prayer of Launcelot Andrewes, the 16th Century English mystic: "Grant, O Lord, that the end of this life be Christian, without sin and without shame, and if it please Thee, without pain."

That perhaps gives us the clue to the old ceremony of going to bed. The darkness and uncertainty of night were akin to the darkness and uncertainty of death. The thought of one evoked thought of the other. The terrors of night were real terrors. Dreams were things to tremble over. There were no Freuds in those days to explain them pleasantly or unpleasantly away. The Compline hymn went—

From all ill dreams defend our eyes
From nightly fears and fantasies.

Today any psychoanalyst will tell us what our dreams mean; if we fear the dark we have merely to push a button and its terrors are dispelled. Night is divested of its apparent uncertainties. It is all safe and sane and explainable. It is difficult to visualize a man of the present generation living in an apartment and saying a prayer for a good death as he passes from the living room into his bedroom. It is impossible to believe that he fears the night when he has a telephone and a light switch at his elbow. This one-plane living has divested the act of going to bed not only of its picturesqueness but its faith as well. The mere act of ascending to a safe place and the sense of security that it gives are forgotten.

After one has lived for a while in a modern, convenient and thoroughly efficient apartment, he begins to realize that he is paying a heavy price for his luxuries. He is missing a lot of those domestic habits that go to make up the picturesqueness of life in a house. A house with an upstairs and a down requires attention. It presupposes responsibilities. There is the fire to bank for the night. There are windows and doors to lock. There is the business of going down to the kitchen to raid the ice-box for a pre-bed snack or an apple. There is the cat to put out. There is the final glance at the thermometer and a look up at the sky to see what weather lies ahead. Then comes the procession up the stairs. That, sirs, is the way to go to bed. And if, perchance, at the foot of the stairs is a table where you pick up your candle to light your way, then your joy can be complete.

Perhaps it is because of these things that more and more people are taking houses in the country where, for the summer season at least, they can enjoy the habits of living a little less efficiently, where things aren't all explained away, where life is lived closer to the uncertainties of Nature, and going upstairs to bed is a ceremony.

THE MONTH OF AUGUST

1. THE TEST. This is the month of the test of the gardener. Anyone will garden in Spring, for there's no resisting the allure of it, and in the Autumn it is likewise no effort to arouse interest, but August is the time when many a garden enthusiasm drops to zero. So much of the month's work is merely the grind of routine—keeping down weeds, pushing the scuffle hoe to make a dust mulch and seeing that plants do not lack water. Were I running things I would simply cut August out of the calendar, but, as it is, we accept the torrid circumstances of this month and lie about on easy chairs, our minds filled with vacant placidity, our lips blessing the first toper who discovered the gin rickey.

See that seedlings of perennials are kept shaded by a lath or cheesecloth-covered frame.

2. SCISSORS FOR VISITORS. Despite my resolution not to do a lick of gardening in August, the pride of possession often rouses me from lethargy. Yet there is one task I hand over to the female of the family: the business of snipping off the withered heads of annuals. It belongs in the same category as dusting, a low practice to which no man should stoop. Since it is a habit natural to women—one of the curses laid on them in Eden

or shortly thereafter—I keep several pairs of scissors hanging by the study door going into the garden and when any citified visitor in August elicits the slightest interest in gardening, I press one of these into her hand with my blessing. Of course, after the first hour, her enthusiasm melts, but by changing visitors every couple of days, we manage to keep the annuals tidied.

Having enriched the soil and given it some peat, set out the new Strawberry bed.

3. THE HOLE IN THE GROUND. The old fellow who sold us the lot was a true Yankee. He sold the barn in the rear of it first and left us a hole in the ground. And I suppose he chuckled in his beard. What can you do with a hole in the ground? Having no beard I didn't chuckle in it, but ours was the better part of the bargain, for that hole had been the old man's manure dump and the black soil went down three feet. Into this we planted Kansas Gay Feather, *Liatris spicata,* and Mallows in pink and white. Such Mallows! Such spikes of Liatris! The old man has gone to his fathers long since, but these plants flourish more abundantly each year. One of these August afternoons I'm going to pick a bouquet of them and seek out the old fellow's grave in the grass-grown cemetery down the road.

Any day now you can cut the old wood out of Currant bushes.

4. A PANEGYRIC ON TOMATOES. If you want to watch complete gastronomic delight, turn loose

an Englishman, fresh come from his native land, into your Tomatoes. He may protest that these huge beefsteak affairs we grow out of doors do not approach in flavor those grown under glass in England, still he rarely is reticent about his enjoyment of them. Lacking the Englishman, turn loose any stranger into a Tomato patch where you grow a variety of them—the little yellow Pear, the Cherry and even the sickly sweet Husk Tomato. These are one-gobble vegetables. We grow all kinds because they are needed for salads and they make pretty table decorations. The best of them all is the yellow Tomato. Cooked into jam with Lemon peel and Ginger, it makes a divine conserve. And if cream cheese be on the same plate (cream cheese mixed with thick cream) you have a dessert that will make any gourmet weep for joy.

Even this early you may start blanching the first crop of celery with boards or paper collars.

5. THE TRUTH ABOUT PIG WEEDS. During these years of gardening fully fifty-seven varieties of weeds that spring up on this place have been called "pig weeds." I have been informed that any normal pig will relish them. Well, the first season of my intimate association with swine, I put this to the test. Did these porkers fight for those weeds? They most certainly did not. Having rooted them around, they turned on me an icy stare. We starved them for a while, and then offered them more of those toothsome greens.

Their contempt was overwhelming. And thus it was we proved that the porcine name refers to the habit of the weed and not to the appetite and taste of hogs.

Tomorrow go forth for the fifteenth time and slay weeds. This warfare allows no respite.

6. EUGENICS FOR IRIS. There's got to be a conscience about this thing. I mean about disposing of old Iris. When first we came here the place boasted two clumps of mongrel kinds that, not being able to afford others, we religiously divided until paths and beds were literally crowded with it. Then, gradually, my Iris acquaintanceship and purse broadening, I longed for better kinds. For a while the discards went to neighbors, but today when I suggest a little gift of, say, a couple of wheel-barrow loads of Iris, they give me what, in common parlance, is called a dirty look. Consequently the common kinds go on the bonfire. No good is attained in increasing their progeny. The birth control of poor Iris is a worthy crusade for any gardener.

If you intend using a new piece of ground, dig it now and plant to a cover crop of Vetch or Clover.

7. THE PENGUINS. Great is the power of the dinner coat!

When first I came to this Rural Nirvana, I resolved never to deck myself in that habiliment. We were to live a simple rustic life—laboring in the garden in old clothes and few of them at that, and, when great occasions came, I should rise to the formality of a blue coat and white flannels—the "ice-cream pants" of youth. This resolve I have kept, and in this dress I dine under the dusk each night. When those who dress mightily in dinner coats ask us to their houses, we usually decline, for one must keep his resolves. Meantime, I have been watching this steady and silly penetration of the opera and city ways into our rustic simplicity. A near-by community, where living is very proper and precious, goes grimly into its dinner jackets each night like men in jungles, determined not to let the jungle overcome them. Presumably they do this lest they "go native." And along the July hay-scented country roads you meet them, prowling in their gardens under the August moon and the infinite stars, these precious little penguins!

Tomorrow, before breakfast, begin to thin the Dahlia buds.

8. MODERNISM IN BOUQUETS. Why not modernist flower combinations? We see so many sentimental and harmonious bouquets, so many studied and properly arranged flowers that they have become boring. Then, too, some people have a notion that there are definite rules about such things, and at flower shows there is a great to-do about balance and harmony. Some of the most pleasing combinations have been those that were never studied. For example, this one on a country house porch—lemon yellow Yarrow, pale pink Phlox,

with a dash of deep lavender Phlox. The bouquet was called "A Grandmother Who Smokes Cigarettes."

Clear off Sweet Peas in the Cutting Garden and fill the space with annual plants from the reserve supply.

9. MILLE FLEURS. When you have tired of being "arty" in your house bouquets, try a *mille fleurs*, after the manner of the mediaeval tapestry-weavers. Before me as I write stands a modernist brass vase, fresh from the mad and lovely imaginings of a Vienna atelier, and in it a loosely jumbled bouquet of white, cerise, plum and pink Cosmos, lemon yellow and orange Calendulas, pale lavender and white Larkspur, purple Asters, mauve and white Scabiosa and burnt-orange Zinnias.

Privet hedges and evergreens may be clipped and shaped these days.

10. FIVE ARGUMENTS AGAINST SHASTA DAISIES. Life would go on just the same for me if I never grew another Shasta Daisy or any of the *Chrysanthemum uliginosum* tribe. First of all, they demand a rich fare and take it from all and sundry in their immediate neighborhood. Secondly, they wilt at the slightest drought. Thirdly, their allure for aphids is as the magnet to the steel and the candle to the moth. Heaven knows there are enough aphid-loving plants without adding any more. Fourthly, why give over space in a border to white Daisies when the near-by meadow is packed with them? Fifthly, if you must have

a dab of white at that time and place in the border, there are a dozen other equally good things to use. These are five of many reasons why my soul never becomes enraptured over Shasta Daisies.

Cuttings of various woody plants can be set now in a shaded frame.

11. THE FIERY CARDINAL. Like Chickory, the red Lobelia, *L. cardinalis,* is a flower to enjoy in the mass and at a distance. How many of us have been deceived by the blue Cornflower! Pass a field of it, and you think to use it in the refined borders of your garden. But even a generous clump would make a poor showing and the individual plants are scrawny indeed. Leave it to the meadows. So also leave Cardinal Lobelia to the swamp lands. Sit upon a dry and distant bank to enjoy it. If you must use it, plant it generously in its beloved dampness in a wild garden. In the hand it is insignificant.

Each year I go into my favorite swamp to gaze upon it, where it grows under the shadow of old wild Apples leaning from the bank. And there I sit and hope no vandal eyes will ever light upon it.

Flowers of sulphur dusted on Phlox will help prevent mildew on the foliage.

12. DOING SOMETHING ABOUT IT. The other day a breezy Chicagoan came into the office and said, "I've just bought an old house. There's some Lilacs growing around the door. What shall

I do with them?" Trying to feel helpful, I asked, "What do you want to do with them?" He was nonplussed. He didn't really have any ideas about those Lilacs, whether they should be moved or pruned or cut down; he merely thought that something ought to be done about them. And his attitude is one that many people, on taking an old place, assume toward the things they find there. Especially old shrubs. Nine times out of ten they ought to leave them alone. Cut out the old dead wood and feed their roots—but otherwise leave them be. I hate seeing old shrubs dispossessed from the spot they have long enjoyed and made beautiful, just as I hate to think of old people being dispossessed from a house in which they have lived a long time.

See that the bird's bath is kept filled with water these hot days.

13. LEPROUS ROOFS. Like a Raspberry cane spattered with mosaic are those leprous roofs that jerry-builders are foisting off on an innocent public as beautiful. For some unaccountable reason roofs have burst out into plaids and checkers of violent contrasts, and all the tempering of the elements doesn't seem to soften their ugliness. A roof of many tones blended into mysterious shades can be a thing of great loveliness and a constant delight to the eye, but there's never a jot of beauty or the semblance of a thrill to be had from a roof that looks like the plaid of a Macpherson.

Coniferous evergreens planted this month should be watered daily until frost.

14. APHIDS. The aphid is to many plant diseases what the mosquito is to yellow fever and other afflictions of the Tropics—a cheerful and ceaseless carrier. He is even now suspected of spreading the mosaic disease which is turning strong Dahlias into pitiable runts. Consequently, I center my most vigorous efforts on his destruction. Other bugs there are, and Heaven knows there are enough of them, and a fellow has to be philosophic about most of their tribe, but I've chosen the aphid as my supreme protagonist. Slay that foe, and the others you can take care of with your left hand.

For big and constant blooms, cultivate around Heliotropes and feed manure water.

15. THE PATHOLOGICALLY MORBID. While any self-respecting gardener will fight plant diseases and plant bugs with lusty delight, too much should not be made of them. Some people become positively morbid over the ills that affect their darlings. Once that stage is reached they had better give up gardening, and join the great mediocrity who play golf. On the way to town the other day a garden friend sat beside me in the train. And she leaned my way and whispered, "I found a Japanese beetle in my garden yesterday!" Had she found a skull or had her young brother eloped with the cook, she could not have been more morbidly proud.

Order Alpine seed now and plan to plant it late this Autumn in an uncovered frame.

16. AS FOR BLACK CURRANT JAM. About this time of year we begin eating the Black Currant jam. Along in July comes the great harvest and the house is fragrant with the incense of these berries simmering. Then at night I am led down to the cellar to behold and admire Her housewifely attainment. Were we a well-disciplined pair, that jam would stay untouched till the Winter, but mid-August finds my palate lusting after it. Besides, many people, wretched sufferers from an arrested gastronomic development, never tasted Black Currant jam and we needs must let them sample it. Its gamy flavor is quite different from any other taste in the world. With duck or cold meat it is a splendid *obligato,* like a long-held high soprano note. Seeing that the bushes require very little care save for a Currant-worm spray, some bone meal in Spring and cutting out old wood occasionally, and seeing that they always set a liberal crop, we cherish them with pride.

Pot up rosettes of Sempervivums for gifts to garden visitors.

17. RIDGE TREES AND BEER. In the old country it is customary, when a new house is being built and the ridge pole is reached, for the carpenters to mark this topmost attainment by nailing up a small Hemlock or Cedar. Thereupon the owner opens a barrel of beer, and great rejoicing follows. The contemplation of this excellent habit fills us with sadness. Like the gift without the giver, the ridge tree without the beer is a hollow symbol. Still we hope goodly men here go on building

houses and nailing Cedars to their roof beams and clambering down to drink forbidden brews. For we love these human, kindly old customs as we beg God to love us—"not weighing our merits but pardoning our offenses."

Bowling, Archery and Badminton are the lawn games par excellence.

18. A PRIMA DONNA JOB. Among the lazy jobs that I enjoy none is more restful and yet capable of making me think that I actually have worked than disbudding. In early May we thin the Peony buds; in June, the scrub Apples and the Sweet Pea laterals are snipped off; in July and August the sidebuds of Dahlias; in September, the Chrysanthemums. As a breakfast appetizer, disbudding is supreme. Also it can be done when one is dressed in Sunday-go-to-meeting clothes. I always am seized with a disbudding urge about five minutes before guests are expected for dinner. Well, it's a good pose for a dressed-up gardener to be found in—the sort of thing you see in Sunday supplements when prima donnas are "discovered" in their gardens, gowned as for "Thaïs" and photographed registering tender affection toward a Sunflower.

Any week in August is a good time to divide and move Madonna Lilies.

19. PROFESSOR OF IRIS. A part-time gardener came to help us out that August, and I initiated him into the simple mysteries of dividing Iris.

There was quite a lot to divide and replant—several hundred feet of it that edged the Top Garden paths—and when he had finished he was quite skillful at the job. In his previous conditions of servitude this helper had made shoes, cut grass, done odd jobs of farming and tended the furnaces of the valley homes. This was his first plunge into the shoreless sea of flowers, and he took to it as a whale to water.

The week after he retired from my employ strange rumors came up from the valley. Otherwise sane and contented folk grew hectic and discontented with their gardens. Something must be done about their Iris. This worthy fellow, having graduated from my simple hilltop school, set himself up as Professor of Iris, went about from garden to garden, struck a solemn pose before every Iris clump he found and, with the judicial airs of the learned, handed down his opinion. Up and down the valley he went, lifting Iris, dividing it, replanting clumps and thus making jobs for himself until Winter. The next year these gardens made history for themselves in Iris time, which goes to prove that a little knowledge is not invariably a dangerous thing.

Bowling, Archery and Badminton are the lawn games par excellence.

20. ZINNIAS AND THE COMMON TOUCH. Among some of the more ethereal and esoteric of *cognoscenti,* the humble Zinnia is held to be of the

lower orders. Those who specialize in rare Gentians, for example, or the most difficult Primulas and alpine plants, contemplate the tip of their nose when you speak enthusiastically of the Zinnia. And here again Kipling was right: To walk with kings nor lose the common touch is as applicable to gardening as to society. I had far rather see a farmhouse front yard ribald with Zinnias than most of the Gentiana jewels I have been expected to enthuse over in English gardens. But, of course, that is purely a personal notion acquired after growing all kinds of Zinnias for twelve years and having had no luck with Gentians.

Watch Tomatoes for the green caterpillar and drop this noisome pest into a can of kerosene.

21. SELF-CONTAINED. Did we have on this Connecticut hilltop a salt mine, a Pepper grove, a Coffee plantation, an Olive tree and part of a sugar *centrale,* we would then be thoroughly self-contained. For now that the pullets can be slain and the Melons are ripening on their vines, we boast of dinners that come off the place completely save for the salt, the pepper, the coffee, the sugar and the salad oil. At the end of such a meal I feel like a patriarch, I feel Old Testamenty, save that I lack a beard, seven hundred wives and the customary assortment of concubines. Deprived of these evidences of prowess, I content myself with thwacking my sides and recalling the good fortune of the daughter of Zion, who was "left as

a cottage in a vineyard, as a lodge in a garden of Cucumbers."

Start making plans for Autumn changes in border. Tag Phlox you plan to move.

22. THE INCREASE IN NARCISSUS. Were we not a profligate race, we American gardeners, the dealers in bulbs would soon go out of business. I was meditating on this thought the other day as I forked up a patch under the lee of shrubbery where, several years ago, I had set a mere dozen each of Emperor and Empress Narcissus. The increase was four-fold. Having enriched the soil with bone meal, a dozen of each kind went back into that drift, and the remainder found other places. Considering the price we pay for Narcissi under the protective tariff of the Plant Quarantine, the discovery of this increase was like picking up gold. Thereupon I sought out other colonies and took their harvests. . . . My Narcissus order this Autumn will be reduced to zero.

By now you should have clipped off all the dried flower heads from your Lilac bushes.

23. THE SCARLET MALES. It is axiomatic: all men like red. They decorate their clubs in that fiery color; if they are gardeners, they use red abundantly in their borders; many of them, did their wives permit, would fancy themselves in red cravats. Which goes to prove that men are

close to the primitive. Red is the color the ancients held sacred to Thor, and all over the world you find it used to ward off evil. Highland milkmaids tie red worsted around their cows' tails and Chinese mothers tie a red string around a baby's wrist, and the red berries of the Mountain Ash are hung over stable doors in German villages, all for the same purpose—as potent talismans against unforeseen dangers.

Water Lilies reach the apex of their beauty this month. Plan to have even more next year.

24. LARKSPUR SHOULD BE BLUE. The habit of thinking that the Delphinium—or Larkspur, if you will—should be blue, mauve or white is as erroneous as thinking that the yellow and red members of this family are worth growing or can be grown with ease. (At this point I expect to be visited by a Come-to-California delegation.) Year after year I have tried to raise the *sulphureum,* the *nudicaule* and the *cardinale* kinds from seed. Either complete failure or puny plants attended my efforts. There was once an orange hybrid of *D. nudicaule,* I believe, that went under the name of *Aurantiacum,* but I never tried it. Nor have I seen many of the white kinds that didn't remind me of the week's wash before the laundress tackled it. Consequently, I shall hold to my erroneous azure opinions of perennial Larkspur.

At this season, pigs enjoy a bath. Wash them down occasionally with the hose.

25. BUT ANNUAL LARKSPUR. On the other hand, we bless the hybridizer who has given us such an abundant range of colors in the annual Larkspurs. Here are tints and tones and subtleties enough to satisfy the most exacting. With us they are a quick crop—quick to grow from the seedling stage, quick to flower and, unless closely cut, quick to reach their journey's end. A bowl of the pink kinds ringed about with tan *Phlox drummondi* is not hard to look upon, nor is a deepish low dish massed with all colors rising from a billow of Asparagus foliage a thing to be forgotten in a moment. For this very purpose one year we bought a great glass dish on the Rue Paradis, and it sits in the flower window these August days holding Larkspurian delights.

Begin harvesting Gourds. Pile them on a pewter platter for a table decoration.

26. A VINOUS BONEYARD. From a countryman I have it that a good vineyard starts in the boneyard. First you select the site, which should be a sunny slope. Having prepared the soil by diligent cultivation, then comes the work of setting out the vines. And it is at this point that the boneyard enters the picture. At the bottom of the hole, before the vine is set, dump half a bucket of broken bones—or the large crushed bone of commerce. The rootlets of the vine will anchor onto these and find their sustenance for many a year. So saith the countryman, and I did as he bade me, and even unto this day none of the dogs has un-

covered those thirty-two caches under my thirty-two vines.

Watch these days for the first flowering of Cobaea scandens, *a late-flowering vine with distinct beauty.*

27. MADONNA COMPANIONS. Now that they have ceased flowering, and the basal leaves begin to wilt, is the time to move Madonna Lilies. Lift them carefully, and plant afresh after the soil has been enriched with leafmold, sand, rotted manure and bone meal. At this time scales can be taken off the bulb and planted in damp sand kept in the shade, where they will soon afford an increase. When resetting these old Madonnas try to make some other flower combination than with Delphiniums, which has been done *ad nauseam*. Try them with Hemerocallis. Slip them into a shrubbery planting. You might even face them down with groups of Regal Lilies, which are shorter and more sprawly of stem.

Tomorrow begin scouting around the countryside for a farmer who has manure to sell.

28. THE SPIRE FAMILY. During three seasons of the year some one of the Veronicas is making its presence felt around the garden, and a very welcome presence it is. *V. repens, teucrium* and *amethystina* come along in May, some in the borders, some in the rocky path that we call the Steep Ascent. Scarcely have their colors faded when *V. incana* of the gray foliage contributes its

violet spikes. July sees *V. spicata* and *spicata alba* adding blue and white where none was before. In August and September the lusty *V. longifolia subsessilis* punctuates the Long Border with clumped blue spires, whilst at the back, *V. virginica,* a taller and lankier member of the family, assumes white and holds its seed-heads until the Black Frost of October cuts it down.

As annuals in the Cutting Garden are finished, sow the row to a cover crop.

29. KITCHEN COLONIAL. At this season of the year all the world and his wife are a-hunting antiques. On the roadside lawn the farmer places a Windsor chair, which to the antique-seeker is as sure a sign as a bunch of mistletoe over a Brittany inn door is to the drinker of cider. Up in these parts anything homely, curious and sufficiently worn passes for an antique and eventually finds a purchaser. The current notion regarding New England antiques today is that they must be crude or savor of the kitchen. That our forebears ever aspired to live like white folks and have beautiful furniture and good pictures and fine linen is a presumption none of these visiting antique-stalkers venture on. When they visualize the Colonial they think only of Kitchen Colonial.

Grapes may be bagged about this time and the bunches thinned.

30. DEATH TO MOLES. The summer after we had mulched the lawn with Tobacco stems, no moles

appeared; the year we neglected to do this, they came in droves. Evidently Sister Mole belongs to the Anti-Nicotine Society. She is said also to dislike Castor Oil Beans and cyanogen gas. Both of these we have tried without success. Traps? In ten years of setting traps I've never killed a mole. Our moles are clever fellows. The dogs are the best exterminators, but they also exterminate the lawn. Poisoned bait is dangerous where you have pets around. So I had almost come to accept moles as among those least of God's mercies, that we have to bear with, when my friend, Doc Lemmon, gave me his receipt. The mole, he avers, travels at 11:30 A. M. and 5 P. M. At these hours take your stand near his run, spade in hand. Where you see the soil begin to hump, drive down the spade. *Sic Semper Tyrannis!*

Grass clippings may be allowed to lie where they fall and mulch the roots of the plants.

31. THE WARNING. On these late August nights we listen carefully, like men awaiting an inevitable doom, for the music of the katydids. The date is set down and as surely as day follows night, in six weeks' time the Zinnias will curl and brown at the first touch of the White Frost and many another tender plant will shrivel in the cold that devastates our hilltop. On these first katydid nights we realize that the Summer laziness is drawing to a close: soon will come the busy Autumn.

Start disbudding hardy Chrysanthemums and stake them at the same time.

LONG PIECE

COLLECTING SMOKE

A STERN parent got me into the habit. He had come to witness my folly in spending vast sums on the rehabilitation of this old country house. Late one night—an August night after a long drought that left the countryside bone-parched—there drifted down breeze the smell of smoke—a penetrating, persistent smoke. It blew in the bedroom window where I lay reading. With it came the terror of fire. Lest I should waken the household, I crept noiselessly downstairs. No sign of fire in the house. To the barn. No sign of fire there. No glow of fire showed on the horizon.

The next morning the breakfast conversation went something like this: "I thought I gave you a good pair of nostrils," said he, gazing at me with stiff disapproval; and I, "I thought you did." Then he, with mild scorn, "I heard you go downstairs to search for that fire last night. Had you as good nostrils as I thought, you'd have known it was Cedar smoke from more than two miles away."

Kipling once wrote an essay on traveling with smells—the odors of foreign places and peoples—but collecting smoke is even more poignant and fascinating. For most smokes have the quality of incense, a statement not true of all smells. There is, for example, the smoke that comes from cannel coal. It is omnipresent in London, now and again you sniff it in the Beacon Hill section of Boston and even along Park Avenue in New York. The soft coal smoke that curls out of house chimneys in St. Louis is akin to it. Hard coal smoke is unpleasant. It has a metallic quality, in contrast to the soft dirtiness of cannel coal. When you smell hard coal smoke you think of factories; when you smell the smoke of cannel coal, you think of pleasant morning rooms in Mayfair and of chilly countryhouse bedchambers in Surrey.

Of wood smokes the variety is legion. Start with a French Canadian town in late September. From the chimneys issue the plumes of Birchwood smoke, an unforgettable incense. Applewood, which is often burned in New England fireplaces, makes a spitty fire, but its smoke is not distinctive. Cedar, on the other hand, seems to vary according to localities and kinds. Red Cedar smoke in Connecticut strikes my nostrils quite differently from Red Cedar smoke in Santa Fé. The dryness or dampness of the air definitely affects both the quality of smoke and its movements.

The Deodar, which you find burned occasionally in California, has a rare fragrance, and so does the Eucalyptus—a hard, smouldery wood. Palmwood and Bamboo give off a pungent dry smoke, reminiscent of Chinese laundries and the odor that hangs over Chinese inland towns. In Arizona and the Southwest you find the smoke of the Cottonwood Tree. A lady sort of tree, this, with feathery foliage and a noble head. Its smoke smells as though there had been scattered onto the coals fragrant knobs of gum Olibanum and the flowers of dried Lavender. The smoke of Magnolia, too, is unforgettable. I collected this recently on the roof of a restored plantation house in Louisiana.

It has a saltiness to the nostrils, the same saltiness that Louisiana sorghum leaves on the palate.

The reeking peat fires of Ireland and the dung fires of Egypt both provide dry smokes. So do the fires of burning Autumn leaves swept up by profligate and too-cleanly suburbanites. In California, instead of these little leaves, you encounter on the side streets the fires of huge dry palm branches which give off a fragrance quite distinctive. And who of us can forget or mistake the smoke of a burning abandoned Christmas tree?

Like most fragrances, smoke must be fresh to catch its full bouquet. Nor should you have too much of it. There is only one exception to this statement, and that is in the case of stale incense in an old church. It is usually tinctured with the acrid odor of gutted candles and the miasma of unwashed humanity, kept damp by stone walls and pavements. Stale incense in a house lacks this quality; in fact, incense seems out of place in a house, however Bohemian its occupants may be. Besides, church incense, being made mainly of fragrant gums, has much more body to it than the punk sticks and pastels supplied by the Orient to Greenwich Village. On the other hand, this same punk incense smoke gone stale in a Chinese temple has a "body" of its own because, here again, the unwashed East flavors it.

For an amusing diversion let me recommend this collecting of smokes. Most of us, when we travel, use only one sense—sight. Now and again touch is tried, when we feel the patina of old paneling, and taste, when we drink the wine of the country. But the sense of smell is mainly used for turning up our noses at the primitive sanitation of other lands.

Collecting smoke brings you into strange places. There was that afternoon, not so long ago, when we climbed ladders and finally stood on the topmost roof of an Indian pueblo in Taos. With us was the learned dean of a woman's college, fresh initiated into the custom. From chimney-pot to chimney-pot we went sniffing. Leaning against the wall, sunning themselves, two aged, toothless Indians watched us closely. When we had diagnosed the smoke they broke into a merry cackle—for what we solemnly pronounced as burning Mesquite Bush proved to be only one of Mr. Armour's ham boxes!

THE MONTH OF SEPTEMBER

1. THIS YEAR OF RAIN. Everyone has been saying (and they said it last year, too) that they never saw such a year for rain. Never has there been such a rainy summer. Over those who live in houses where the trees grow close and the bushes thick has come the sadness of monotony. The dismal days were hard to live through. And yet, as some wise person has said, it is a sure sign that we are over-civilized when we grow afraid of rain.

Harvest Onions now, allowing the bulbs to cure in the sun before cutting off the tops.

2. "ARTISTIC ARRANGEMENTS" AND A GREAT HATRED. After judging at numerous flower shows this year I have acquired a fierce and devastating dislike for those "artistic arrangements" that members of garden clubs make according to rules. Into my nervous and irritated ear have been poured such words as "balance," "color harmony," "suitability of container" until I was ready to commit justifiable homicide. It seems that some one, with worthy intent, once made up rules about arranging flowers, and ever since, women have accepted them in the same category with the Ten Commandments, the Apostles' Creed and the Volstead Act, as inspired, irrevocable and irrefutable. This is something that sadly needs debunking. When, the

other day, we saw a bowl of the flat planes of yellow Tansy lying above a cloud of pink Columbines, we wept with joy, for the woman who made it declared she had never heard of the rules. She it was, too, who put a great mass of the feathery Josekae Lilac in with sprays of the brilliant red Paul's Scarlet Climber Rose, in defiance of every rule ever written about bouquets.

It is about time we returned to the Directoire type of bouquet, when you took a bowl or a series of vases one above the other and packed them tight to make a pillow or a column of color. At least these would be a relief from the single flower stuck in a scrawny vase that people insist on being "so Japanesey!"

Tomorrow order Roses for Fall planting and begin preparing the soil for them.

3. TAGGING PHLOX. The gardener who thinks he can remember colors is deceiving himself, especially when those colors are in Phlox. The flower head in full bloom of August or early September is one tint and the faded head of late September another. Moreover in the jungle of plants growing in a border, well-filled and broad, who has the prescience to select the right plant to move? To avoid this confusion we resort to tags when Phlox is to be transplanted. The color and height of the variety is marked on the tag, and thus Autumn moving becomes a simple matter. No longer does the Lilliputian Tapis Blanc hide its snowy trusses behind the rangy stems of scarlet Fire Glow, nor

does Mahdi plant its purple heads in the front line of the Summer border.

Always burn any leaf or stalk that shows signs of disease. Never put it on the compost heap.

4. THE DYSPEPTIC'S TEXT. Search the Scriptures, and you'll find in them almost anything you want. When the noise of city traffic gets unbearable, you have merely to open the second chapter of Nahum and read "the chariots shall rage in the streets, they shall jostle one against another in the broad high way." When you are overstaying your welcome, remember Solomon's tip on good manners: "Withdraw thy foot from thy neighbor's house lest he be weary of thee and hate thee." For the dyspeptic and those who cannot relish such delectable foods, there is a gorgeous text in the Book of Numbers (read the eleventh chapter and you'll find it): "We remember the fish which we did eat in Egypt freely, the Cucumbers and the Melons and the Leeks and the Onions and the Garlic."

Begin cutting out the old canes from the Blackberries and burn them.

5. PEOPLE IN BOXES. What can be done, I wonder, about those rows and rows of uniform, dreary and usually ugly boxes that line the poorer quarters of our towns and are sold for homes. Here and there some proud owner, with a vision, plants his front yard and curtains his windows prettily and makes a garden in the rear. One by one his neigh-

bors, not to be outdone, begin improving their places. In a short time the street has been transformed. It has become a pleasant place to live in and real estate values begin to rise. Give us one owner in each block with a real love for home, and these boxes will blossom like the Rose.

Autumn is an ideal time to seed down new lawns. Water after seeding or pray for rain.

6. SINGLE ASTERS. It is an indication of subtle taste when gardeners, as they are now doing, show a preference for single Asters. We have about run the gamut of doubling in flowers. Perhaps the final stage in this decadence was reached when someone announced the production of a double Iris. The tissue-paper powder puffs that are double Hollyhocks, the woolly, tousled-headed pompons that are Asters fall in the prodigality of their bloom. They have a tawdry air, like a stout woman plastered over with too many jewels: whereas the beauty of the single Asters—somewhat reminiscent of the flowers of Gerbera—are slim and modest maidens, content to find their attractiveness in set of head and blush of cheek and quiet laughter.

Begin transplanting perennials tomorrow and if the day is sunny, shade and water well.

7. FOR A FALL BORDER. Unless it can be kept strictly in bounds, the Michaelmas Daisy is no plant to venture into the herbaceous border. A rapacious and ravenous fellow, he soon robs the

soil of all its sustenance and elbows other things out of place. Better have a Fall border for him and his kind, a border where the plants can be massed. For the beauty of Michaelmas Daisies is best seen in masses and at a distance—mauve and purple and pinkish clouds set against a rear wall or fence, with Jap Anemones placed before them; midway, Heleniums clustered here and there to give a golden contrast, *Lilium Auratum* in clumps before the purple or royal blue of the Asters, and the front of the border faced down with hardy Chrysanthemums. In such a border you would find color from the first week in September till nearly mid-November.

By now the chickens have finished molting and the egg production should pick up.

8. TURTLEHEADS. Among the herbaceous perennials that should be classed as more curious than beautiful is Chelone, Shell Flower, which blooms with us from late August through September. It makes a well-shaped bush in time, and if given a dampish location, deep rich soil and a manure mulch for the surface roots, spikes of flowers come out like the head of a turtle from under its shell. A large clump of Chelone in a turn-around on certain kinds of places is better than the Cannas of a previous generation and it has the advantage of being hardy. C. *Lyoni* bears purplish red flowers: C. *obliqua* is taller and the flowers a deep rose; C. *glabra* is white. These Shell Flowers or Turtleheads are cousins of the Pentstemons and, of

course, American in origin, natives of our Western states and the Southwest.

If you intend enlarging your frames, order the sash this week.

9. THE VIRGIN'S BOWER. Were I a poet I would write it an ode; were I a painter I would immortalize it on canvas; being merely a gardener I bring to it the best my talents afford—manure and lime. The Virgin's Bower, *Clematis paniculata,* even the Latin of it is pretty. For weeks in Summer we give its twining tendrils a hand until one end of the upper porch is embowered. Early September sees its stars appearing—here a star and there a star, as the light of the heavens twinkle through dusky mists. And when that Milky Way has come down to dwell with us, it brings also a divine fragrance. What a prodigal return for our poor offerings of bone meal in Spring, lime in Summer and a manure mulch over the Winter months! Bittersweet is spread above its roots, for the Clematis wants its feet covered from blistering sun, and the Bittersweet branches support its lower tendrils.

Finally, having poured out flower and fragrance, it leaves us with a laugh—curls up feathery seed pods that cling to the vine for a fortnight, like bits of old-fashioned jewelry. And far into November its foliage remains green, as though it were loath to leave.

Any day now you may start planting Narcissi: they appreciate early intrenchment.

10. PILLOWS OF FRAGRANCE. From a lovely old Devonshire garden came a box of fresh Lavender, and with this as a base She started one of Her pleasant harvestings. By this season the Lemon Verbena can be cut back for bringing indoors, and each leafy twig is carefully saved. These are spread on newspapers on the attic floor, and when the leaves are dried and stripped off, She mixes them with the Lavender and this goes into small pillows that are slipped between the pillows on all the beds. We, who are used to them, fall to sleep breathing their quaint fragrance, and the delight of guests who discover whence the perfume comes is among our pleasures of having them here.

Straw flower for Winter decoration should be cut in the bud, bunched and hung up side down to dry.

11. A PLEASANT SLAVERY. It is good for a man to become slave to some sort of dumb animal— to have a dog to look after and a canary to watch. How strange a house would seem without them! How lonely and untenanted! Imagine starting the day without a bird in its cage singing to you! Imagine going to bed without a wee dog at the foot of it! These things are hard for us to imagine, She and I who are slaves to our dumb nuisances; only the next time I build, a dog-door will be in my study, such as Sir Walter Scott had in his, and the canine tribe will be taught to use it. Next to being without a dog, I cannot imagine sitting still when one is scratching on the door outside.

Keep high grass cut away from buildings and fences and be alert for grass fires.

12. SEVEN LITTLE ENKIANTHI. Seven of the Enkianthus family have found a place here—*E. campanulatus Palibinii, cernuus rubens, latiflorus, pallidiflorus, pendulus, recurvus* and *tectus*—a grand line of botanical Latin, and may I be forgiven if I sound highbrow in naming them. Being of the line and lineage of Erica, they ask a peaty soil, in return for which they grow architecturally in whorls bearing bell-shaped flowers. When Autumn arrives they turn a vivid red, like carmine Catherine-wheels. Cochin-China, Japan and the farther hinterlands of the Himalayas are their native homes. A long way have they traveled to reach our Connecticut hilltop garden! By the time I'm an elderly person, I hope, I shall stand under the 15-foot shade of *Campanulatus*, and pluck long branches of the scarlet-flowered *Rubens*. As yet they come only to my knee, so, for the present, my sight must be lost in faith!

Begin harvesting Gladioli bulbs as soon as the foliage begins to turn brown.

13. THE SPECTRUM ON THE FLOOR. Our immediate ancestors in the Victorian Era found pleasure in simple things, and when we revive them, strange to say, the pleasure loses none of its innocent tang. To our flower collection we recently added a little glass prism found among the treasures of a Philadelphia antique dealer. The meeting of the two rear planes is cut to form the image of a vase and above it are painted sprays of flowers, so that looking into the front plane you see a silvery vase spilling Roses and Fuchsias. Now why in the name

of sanity do two grown-up people want to spend their hard-earned money for such a gewgaw? Well, we remarked that, too. Then the other day I happened to step into the Morning Room—and there, like a jewel on the rug, lay the spectrum! Our silly prism was playing the same pretty trick it did for the Victorians. Callers who see that spectrum on the floor wax ecstatic over it. What children we are!

Autumn Lilies are at their best now, compensating us for all the care we have given them.

14. TORCH LILIES. My ardor for the Torch Lilies—Red hot Pokers, Kniphofias, Tritomas, or whatever you will call them—began as a spark in Kew Gardens, blew into a roaring flame for several years on this farm, and was finally extinguished after we became surfeited with them when our experimental patch took on the semblance of a Pineapple Field. Twenty-seven varieties in a space 24′ by 80′ are a little too much for one place. Recently, however, I have returned to Torch Lilies, and with satisfaction. They are not all vulgarly scarlet, as some would suppose, for the *Gracilis* types boast dwarf dainties in citron and tones of yellow; the *Modesta* hybrids combine creamy white and coral red; the *Multiflora* a white, and Solfaterre, soft yellow in Autumn. Of the scarlet and reds, *Erecta* runs to orange scarlet, Lord Roberts is a giant five feet high, *Quartiniana*, another tall kind, scarlet shading to yellow, and *Rouge-et-Souffre*, as its name indicates, half red and half

sulphur. While one may not care to introduce the colors of the larger kinds into a respectable and well-ordered border, a bed of mixed Torch Lilies and grasses is not to be despised. One little gem, *Kniphofia Nelsonii,* scarlet and gold, has a refinement of flower and foliage that recommends it for the rockery.

The hardiness of the Tritomas is doubtful north of New York, but if a few plants of each kind are laid away in soil in a damp-proof cellar over Winter, these will carry bloom the following year. Feed these Torch Lilies generously, and their floral response and increase is amazing.

Cover crops of Rye should be broadcasted over each part of the vegetable garden as it is cleared.

15. DUSK DEW. There is a quality to Autumn dew that cannot be found in the dew of Spring or Summer—it sharpens the nostrils, the way a dab of bloater paste on toast edges the appetite of a cold morning. Dusk is the time to enjoy it. In the valley the mist softly gathers and mauves steal across the farther hills. From the ground rise faint and penetrating fumes—the honey aroma of late Phlox, the pungent spice of Yarrow foliage and of Helenium flowers from the near-by border, the saccharine fragrance of a late Clematis star, and overlying all these subtleties, the persistent, sweaty spice of wet soil and damp fallen leaves.

Let your neighbors know that you are dividing the garden spoils and are willing to share them.

16. Satisfaction in Obesity. This may not appeal to what Keats called "elegant, pure and aerial minds," but my desire for satisfaction these days is amply awarded by the increasing obesity of the pigs. When they first arrive, I delight in their cute tricks, their squealing and running around the sty. Through the summer, I rejoice in their sensuous mud-wallowing. With Autumn my thoughts turn to size and weight. Their ration now includes Corn, with an occasional bucket of windfall Apples for dessert. Soon we shall start feeding them Peanuts as they do in Virginia, to add (so I hold the childish faith) a nutty flavor to the meat. Like condemned men awaiting execution, they are given a rich and abundant cuisine.

Examine all trees for dead or dying wood.
Cut it out and paint the wound.

17. A Note on Gaillardia. The reappearance of Gaillardia in September is like an old lady popping in to say good-bye before she starts on a journey. By that time the plants are just a bit frowzy: they sprawl more than in the youthful Spring, but their flowering is none the less vigorous. Between us, Gaillardia is known as Nigger Flower, because of its gaudy tints. I've often wondered why some of the pastel-shades devotees haven't launched a crusade against it. Certainly the new Portola hybrids, so loudly tooted by seedsmen, are no shrinking Violets in color. Nor is one sure of maintaining a desirable kind from seed, as Gaillardia "throws back" almost as speedily as Columbine and as surely as Pyrethrum. To keep

up good blooms, the clumps should be divided every third year since, after a time, the aged plants become blind and their flowers are few and far between. Rooted cuttings set out early in the Spring is the surest way to obtain dependable bloom. It is advisable to pot up both seedlings and rooted cuttings because, in this stage, the roots are delicate and resent disturbance.

Keep an eye on the Christmas Rose for its first blooming. Likewise for Chrysanthemums.

18. "RIDICULOUS TOYES." When old Gerarde in his "Herbal" wanted to indicate things as beneath his contempt he called them "ridiculous toyes," and so I used to classify most of the garden statuary of the gnome and naked-boy-holding-a-fish variety, until my heart melted for Bertha. We found her in a Berlin shop and brought her home to sit placidly on the top step of the Steep Ascent behind a clump of Pumila Iris. A terra-cotta terrier (or maybe she's a sheep dog), she placidly contemplates the world from her flowery height, scares near-sighted old ladies, throws children into gales of laughter and is absurd enough to exist without having to be explained. . . . My next ambition is to own a Nigger Boy hitching post.

Toward the end of this month you can divide and move Peonies.

19. EUPATORIUM AND TWO COMPANIONS. Once in a great while I like mixed parties, and just

about as often do I like border sections that are mixed parties, and bouquets wherein the butcher's boy dances with the lady. One such bouquet was sent recently to a friend—the refined color and form of sulphur Souvenir de Claudius Pernet Roses mixed with common hoyden purple Eupatorium. Now this commoner Eupatorium has a place in our Long Border, and a few hundred feet away its first cousin, Joe Pye Weed, *E. purpureum*, flourishes in August by the meadow gate, and its white brother, *E. ageratoides* or White Snakeroot, I gather in the rich bottom of the woods across the road. The refined member of this family appears to be the Lilac *E. coelestinum*, or Mist Flower. It comes into bloom about the time the Gaillardia at its feet are making their red and yellow Fall notes and the Coreopsis affording a few late yellow Daisies. The combination of these three is not undesirable at this season.

Watch for the first White Frost and, lest it destroy them, cut all tender annuals for house decoration.

20. BOILED GREENS. After several weeks of traveling through the English countryside, the mere thought of boiled greens is enough to cause a gastronomic revolution. Rural England's cuisine has not yet emerged from the mediaeval stock-pot. We had eaten boiled greens—a few lonely cabbage leaves floating in tepid water—from the chalk cliffs of Dover to the Grampian Hills and we publicly vowed on the docks at Southampton that a boiled green would never again pass the threshold

of our lips. Then we arrived home to find that, by one of those miscalculations gardeners will make, enough Endive to feed a township was flourishing in our truck patch. It appeared that we were in for a Nebucadressarian diet from July till frost. We discovered the cook and the gardener gazing upon that magnificent Endive display. Muttering covertly, they were. That night a dish appeared upon the table, and instinctively I reached for the fire tongs to bear it out lest its sight revolt us. Boiled Greens! However, since no man should be hanged without due trial, no dish should be cast into the Jehoshaphat Valley of the pig sty without due tasting. So we tasted—gingerly, remembering our solemn vow of the Southampton Docks. We tasted more. We heaped our plates. And ever since then boiled Chickory greens have been among our gustatory Autumnal delights.

Tomorrow bring out, examine and repair all sash for frames.

21. The Balloon of Country Gossip. One September morning I leaned out my window to gaze upon the reaches of the lawn and Long Border, and found that spot strangely peopled. From somewhere, a herd of cows had broken loose, and hearing that Zinnias and Auratum Lilies and the tips of Pompon Chrysanthemums made good eating, they just wandered in to sample them. What they did to the lawn and the border in that gustatory perambulation need not be told in detail. Devastation on all sides, and my wrath thundered up and down the valley. I told to every

listening ear that I had worked on that lawn ten years, and now look at it. Consider my masticated shrubs! Gaze upon that half-eaten border! And having let that steam escape, we set about to repair the damage. Soon the valley was filled with quaint rumors. Those cows had eaten up $5,000 worth of rare Lilies that no one else possessed. They had ruined an entire crop of Dahlias. They had dealt destruction to ten shrubs that were the only shrubs of their kind in the country. People stopped by to sympathize with us. Farm wives hinted that if, perchance, we could spare a slip of one of those rare shrubs, they'd like to try it. A nurseryman put in a bid for those imaginary Dahlia tubers. The balloon of gossip that hung over our garden swelled to enormous proportions, and in its sympathetic shade we rested, laughing, for many a day.

Young perennials that have not been given their permanent places should be placed in the cold frame now.

22. NO GOOD COOK STACKS HER POTS. By this time the environs of the cold frames are beginning to look less like an Italian slum. Since July, the array of flats and pots of seedlings has constantly increased until they overflow the frames and spread around on the grass. Slats shade the frames but for the others we use bagging on sticks, sewn together with string in that inconsequential way men sew. Now that September is upon us, begins the business of setting out. Flat after flat is emptied. Beds and borders begin to fill up. Some are set aside for friends, some to carry over the

Winter in the frames—each empty flat being cleaned and stored away as it is finished. In a fortnight those frames emerge from their slums, hygienic and orderly, because we clear up as we go along. This habit I learned from a red-headed sister (God bless her!) who is likewise an excellent cook. She gave it me as a solemn rule that no good cook stacks her pots—she washes each one as she is finished with it.

Hardy biennials saved in trays for next Spring's planting should be congregated in a protected corner.

23. A BLUE FOR AUTUMN. A valiant little plant is *Plumbago Larpentae,* and when it begins flowering in September my thoughts turn Chinaward where coolies crowd the Shanghai streets—or used to—in deep blue. In Shanghai it was first discovered, being among the treasure brought back to the Occident by that intrepid plant stalker, Robert Fortune. In rock gardens and borders it makes its display until the frosts of October have cut it down utterly. It wants full exposure to sun and a deep rich loam: with these it thrives, and its clustered deep blue flowers put to shame the weary and worn Sweet Alyssum that drifts in shoals near it.

Clean all flats, trays and pans as they are emptied and stack away orderly.

24. THREE ARISTOCRATS. Of two of "Chinese" Wilson's 'aristocrats' have I become enamored; nay, three—*Ligustrum vulgare pyramidalis*—Pyramid Privet; *Daphne Ghiraldi;* and Beauty

Bush, which has to stagger through life under the load of *Kolkwitzia amabilis.* The last is an arching shrub not unlike Deutzia and much more beautiful. The first—the Privet—describes itself in its name, and a fine pyramid it makes, a worthy upright shrub to plant with others not so erect. *Daphne Ghiraldi* is a little gem. Not over three feet at most, its leafage is reminiscent of a Palm and so is its clustered orange fruit hanging from the axil of its whorl of leaves. Like all the Daphnes, it is satisfied with scant fare, and asks only to be protected from too much northern wintry breezes and given a modicum of lime.

When the Asparagus foliage begins to turn, cut it off and heap on the bonfire.

25. PREMATURE FROST. While it is customary to become lugubrious over the approaching end of the outdoor flower season, I am unable to grow *triste* about it. I welcome any premature frost. By the end of September one becomes surfeited with garden beauty. Since the early days of Spring our emotions have been tugged at, and now, with Autumn at hand and much beauty still to come from coloring leaves and the harlequin countryside, emotions are almost tugged out. It's like sitting through the Ring day after day: by the end of the week Wagner has palled on you. So come quick, sharp early frost! Obliterate some of this beauty! Clear decks for the majesty of Autumn!

Excavate next year's Sweet Pea trench and fill with all the manure you can spare.

26. THE CELLAR TEST. From the way I enjoy the domestic autumnal rites, one would gather my real vocation to be undertaking. The pride of the mortician at the well-turned-out corpse pales before my pride at the final obsequies of Summer. I go about the business of taking down screen doors with the grim determination of a man facing the inevitable. The dismantling of awnings, the secreting of porch and garden furniture in the bowels of the barn—these are acts of finality that bring me complete satisfaction. With Autumn also I begin to appreciate cellars—the shelves of preserves, the barrel of cider, the wine in its cask, the coal in its bin, the rat trap baited. Show me a man's cellar in Autumn and I'll tell you the sort of man he is.

However busy you are these days in physical labor, spare a few moments to enjoy the beauty of the flowers that remain.

27. THE PUPS AND THE PEONY STICK. Like a child who has been too often told what it must do and what it mustn't, I approach Peony-planting with singular caution. For if you set the eyes of these blessed roots more than three inches below the surface of the soil (so all the Peony Solons state) their flowery children are bound to be blind; and if you set them less than two inches, all the diseases in the Peony pathology will descend upon them. You're damned if you do and damned if you don't. That safe margin of an inch is, indeed, a narrow path to tread. However, being a credulous soul, I follow directions exactly and, lest I should

sidestep to the right or to the left, each Fall I make a Peony stick. Two pieces of lath nailed at right angles to each other and one of them sawed to the exact three inches.

The hole is dug. The root set on the bottom. The Peony stick then measures the depth of the eyes by laying it on the soil with the three-inch arm swung into the hole. And year by year this was my habit until we took up wire-haired foxes, and Gina and Judy came to make life amusing. Helpful little beggars, they assisted in digging every hole. When I laid down the name tag to pick up the measuring stick, said name tag disappeared into the forest of the Michaelmas Daisies. And scarcely had I captured the tag than the Peony stick went flying down the garden path. Thus, in the course of canine events, my prized Jap Ama-no-sode came to be labeled True Love and Kelway's Wild Rose went blind and Mistral wilted before the onslaught of illness that comes to those whose noses are too near the surface.

More Celery should be banked and the Brussels Sprouts crop harvested and taken to the kitchen.

28. CHANT FOR SASH. Two Autumnal rites we perform on the same day, the one being the signal for the other. First the screen doors and screens are taken down to be stored into the space that is emptied by bringing forth the cold frame sash. Like the final inspection of a ship before she goes to sea is this emergence of the sash. Putty is tested, new glass put in where panes were cracked and the paint pot produced to give an extra coat on the

frame. This sash-before-Winter work ought to be accompanied by song, the way sailors are said to carol before setting out to sea. Perhaps, as we dab on the paint, we might chant antiphonally,

"Comrades, pour the wine tonight
For the sailing is with dawn!"

The windfalls from the Apple trees will be relished by pigs, but don't give them too many.

29. GARDEN GIVING. I have yet to meet a mean gardener. The veriest miser in other things, the pinch-penny and the dollar-squeezer will burgeon forth prodigally if you show intelligent interest in his plants. And therein he is a wise man, for much of the joy in gardening comes when we share it with others. Yet the Scotch-Irish in me stiffens perceptibly when those who are not intelligent in the ways of plants come trooping up in the Fall for some "cute little Calendulas and Zinnias" to transplant into their gardens for next year. Such people we usually pacify with Iris, put aside especially for such inconsequential beginners. Every gardener should keep on hand a stock of give-aways, just as druggists in Philadelphia, when I was a brat, kept sticks of licorice root and candy to give children who patronized them. The especial treasures—the fine Lupins and the uncommon Kniphofiae and Sedums and Peony divisions and such—should be preserved for those callers who know a good thing when they see it. The gift without the giver may be bare, but the gift without the receiver is a total loss.

Go around the garden and, for the good of your soul, contemplate the variety and color of fruits it contains.

30. THE COMPLETED CYCLE. Toward the end of September the garden looks strained and distraught and awry, like an old monk who shows the wear and tear of having resisted temptation a long time. Most of its plants have served their purpose; their life cycle is completed. They have flowered and set the seed of a new generation of their kind or their hybrids. Their legacies are ready for the future. At such a time we should not expect too much of the garden. Were there armies of helpers to move in potted plants as they do in England, then the succession of color might be maintained up to the very eve of the killing frost, but lacking these, we must be content with what we have. Instead of lingering over those memories, which are the pain of the past, let us turn our eyes to the rich panoply the trees are beginning to put on and the multitude of colored berries the bushes now hang out to indicate that their cycles also have been completed.

Corn stalks can be chopped up and heaped on the compost pile.

LONG PIECE

THE RISE AND FALL OF BELLS

THERE was a spot on the walls of the Kremlin at Moscow where, once on a time, you could have heard such strange music as is rarely found elsewhere, save in Italy or Spain. When dusk crept down the streets, you climbed to the battlements and waited under the bell tower. Suddenly, a whine of ropes. Into the dusk far above muttered a throaty diapason. It spread over the city like a fog, touching other towers. The bells of Moscow's two hundred-odd churches began to speak. Thunder and clash, tinkle and rattle, they rang out the Angelus. For five minutes the air rocked with the cacophony. Then peace came down again. You passed into the murky streets.

The same, perchance, you may hear if you stand at dusk on the Butte de Montmartre at Paris under the lee of the Sacre Coeur, or on the Pincian Hill at Rome or beside the bell of Our Lady of Guadeloupe at Mexico City when she speaks from her throat of eleven tons.

Other sweet bell tones flash across the memory, and with each comes a strangely beautiful, or peaceful or picaresque vision. A church bell ringing to Evensong in a sleepy English village carries quite a different air from a church bell ringing to evening service in a sleepy New England town. The bells of China somehow tinkle differently from the bells of Spain. The big bull bells at the throats of elephants in Indian jungles speak a different tongue from the cackling bells at the throats of cows wandering through New Jersey meadows. The bells on a troika dashing down a Russian city street are distinctive, and so are the bells on sleighs in northern countries, as distinctive as the ominous clatter of bells on a fire engine or the persistent articulation of bells aboard ship.

We still have bells aplenty, and yet their sweet

conversation is swallowed up in the noises made by the machinery of our modern civilization. Hearing a church bell in a busy American city is as pleasant a surprise as unexpectedly meeting in a crowd the girl you love. So fast has the automobile with its raucous horn supplanted the gentle horse that even the sound of sleigh bells brings an unwonted delight.

From the earliest time, bells have played their part in the music of the household. In Eastern countries, they were an item of the dress of women. Women wore bracelets, ringed about with little bells, that tinkled every time they moved, warned others of their approach and apprised lovers when they were at hand. In his story of Will Kemp, the Elizabethan actor who danced across England, Alfred Noyes tells of Kemp being joined by a country lass who danced along with him, and, to make music for their going, Kemp hung bells about her ——

"I fitted her with morrice-bells, with treble, bass and tenor bells;
The fore-bells, as I linked them at her throat, how soft they sang!
Green linnets in a golden nest, they chirped and trembled on her breast,
And, faint as elfin blue-bells, at her nut-brown ankles rang."

Once on a time, the door-bell was a distinctive feature in the noises of the home. It had a tinkle all its own—a tinkle preceded by the screech of the wire that pulled it. This was supplanted by the electric bell, which gives no warning before its alarm. Then came the buzzer. Our grandmothers may have been bothered by the noises of scratchy wires, but what would they think of our muttering buzzers? Would they miss those strange coils of spring on which the bell nested in its dusty corner up near the ceiling of the rear hall? Or the congregation of little bells gathered on the wall of the kitchen that were sounded by tugging a bell-pull? Nowadays we have the bell-pull, because it is decorative, but its wire is attached to a buzzer.

Then there is that whole symphony that was associated with meals. Dinner was announced by a gong or bell and the courses ended and began with the tinkle of a table bell. Today the meal is announced secretively and the hostess fishes around with her foot to touch the kitchen buzzer when she sees the courses coming to an end.

In my own house (having a horror of buzzers) the table bell came from the harness of a pony I rode across the Siberian steppes. The bell that hangs on the back porch and calls me in from gardening sounded the hours on a fishing vessel in Cape Cod waters. Along the shelf of my study ranges a collection of all kinds of harness bells gathered from a dozen different countries. Each has a music of its own. At one Adirondack camp I visit, the call that summons the household from the lake is uttered by a bell that once called the slaves on a Southern plantation: there is silver in this bell and its tone consequently is soft. On still another place has been adopted for a fire bell an old wagon tire, as is the custom in rural towns.

In our endeavor to hush the noises of the household we have lost the sweet music of bells. Aren't they worth reviving? There is one household in a suburb of New York where the servants toll a rising bell. At all other times of day it stands mute in its niche; only with the rising does it speak to awake the household. A quaint and lovely custom, and one worth adopting.

One family of bells alone we have not forgotten, and they will be associated with that season so long as men live to celebrate it—Christmas bells. On that day they reign supreme, free from the competition of the buzzer, kings of all joyful sounds.

THE MONTH OF OCTOBER

1. VERSES FOR A NIGHT WALK. Autumn brings me closer impacts with reality than any other season. The balmy airs of Spring and Summer breed in my mind only pretty pantheistic sentiments, but let a tang spill into the air, and my comfortable and easy-going soul is spurred on to great adventure. On nights such as these I disappear over the back wall and head across country. The stars are sharp and brittle. Odors of dying vegetation rise from the ground. I tramp on, searching for what Vaughan said he saw ——

> I saw Eternity the other night,
> Like a great Ring of pure and endless light,
> All calm as it was bright.

And turning toward home, my feet slogging along a little slower, my head in the heavens, I wonder at Vaughan's other verse ——

> There is in God, some say,
> A deep but dazzling darkness, as men here
> Say it is late and dusky because they
> See not all clear.
> O for that Night! where I in Him
> Might live invisible and dim.

As soon as frost blackens the tops, harvest Dahlia roots. Allow them to dry off in a shady place.

2. BLACK NARCISSUS. I have always held to the theory that cows should be named from Greek mythology, bulls from the Roman Emperors, goats after Irish saints, chickens after Egyptian goddesses, ducks after the minor prophets and pigs after one's more intimate friends. All types I have tried and only the porcine compliments were resented. People, after the manner of people the world over, tried to find resemblances and I discovered that even intimates are touchy on some matters. So I took refuge in absurdities and next year the litter will be named after French perfumes—*Quelques Fleurs,* Black Narcissus (a horrible stench), Ashes of Desire, *Qui-es-Tu?*

Tomorrow begin top dressing the slopes of the Rock Garden with stone chips.

3. PLANTING THE TIDES. Bulbs should be naturalized in grass the way tides creep up a sandy beach—irregularly, in soft curves, with the crowded waves at a distance. Mere careless flinging about of Narcissi and planting them where they fall only makes for a spotty effect when the bulbs are flowering. Like any other planting, the area intended for naturalizing should be studied, its irregularities marked, its hills and dales noted, its background taken into account and the trees and shrubs that break its surface turned to good advantage. Watch the tide creeping around the buttress of a bridge—that is the way to have bulbs swirl around shrubbery. Let them break in waves against the hill crests and go spilling in broad drifts down the dales and yonder where a wall or

fence or massed shrubbery afford background; mass the bulbs as breakers mass. However poetical this analogy may seem, yet it is eminently practical and it applies equally to Narcissi, Grape Hyacinths, Snowdrops and the other bulbs that lend themselves to naturalizing.

Pot up some Parsley plants and keep them on a sunny kitchen window sill.

4. RHUS TOXICODENDRON. Whenever on these October days I pass a wall ruddy with the leaves of Poison Ivy, I share with Adam and Eve their coveting of the Forbidden Fruit. How tempting —and how disastrous! Even Virginia Creeper wears no such scarlet as does this vine, whose touch to most of us brings pain. The Scarlet Woman Vine! She treads our highways with alluring beauty, and yet what a vicious trollop she can be to those who touch her unawares!

Among our friends was one who looked on her beauty to lust after it. He brought home great quantities of it, stripped from the stone walls of the countryside, and decorated the balustrades of his porch with it for an Autumn dance. The next week seven debutantes and sundry young gentlemen had learned their lesson from Rhus toxicodendron!

Recently in an English book on vines I came across one of those superb pencils of enlightenment that English gardening books sometimes direct toward our American plants. In this country, it solemnly states, the planting of Poison Ivy is forbidden. Indeed, yes; neither do we plant poison

Mushrooms or choose mountain lions for household pets or give our babies rattlesnakes to play with.

As garden stakes are pulled up, grade them according to size and place in their proper racks.

5. COQUETTE. In Japan, it is said, the coquette follows the Autumnal practice of handing her lover a tinted Maple leaf, indicating that as it has changed color so has her devotion. Imagine the consternation of these Nipponese swains were they to see our Swamp Maples in October! They blush a fiery red. Summer's ardor is cooling. It no longer warms to us with its wonted smile. Our gardens pass into the chill nights properly jilted. . . . In the Tropics grows a vine that the natives call the "Life of Man" because thrice in a day do its flowers change their character. Happily for lovers, tropical coquettes have not yet adopted it as their favorite flower.

Maintain the slaughter of weeds, especially in beds and borders and edges of the Cutting Garden.

6. THE STRANGE BEHAVIOR OF L. SULPHUREUM. I am not sure if the ladies of Upper Burmah and the Shan States bind their feet as do—or did—their Chinese sisters, but a glorious Lily from their land seems to enjoy this treatment. *Lilium sulphureum* bulbs came to us plump and promising, and we gave them large pots to grow in. Midway in their progress they faltered and hesitated.

Such perversity not being their habit, we forthwith repotted half of them into smaller pots. As September succeeded August those in the large pots showed no signs of throwing a flower stalk; those with the cramped feet shot up a five-foot stalk and by mid-September their promise of flowers was well on the way to fulfillment. In my notes I find it recorded as of October 6th, that we moved the flowering *Lilium sulphureum* into the house. They made a gorgeous show in a corner of the Morning Room, but so heavy was their fragrance that we had to move out all but one. Meantime, their sisters with the unbound feet of the Occident waxed fat with foliage and nothing else.

Shrubbery will begin arriving soon; see that the soil is thoroughly prepared and mixed for it.

7. STRAWBERRY HILL. When Horace Walpole first moved into his famous little house, "Strawberry Hill," he amused his friends with letters describing it. In one of these famous epistles he tells how "it is set in enameled meadows, with filagree hedges." And that he has about "land enough to keep such a farm as Noah's, when he set up in the ark with a pair of each kind; but my cottage is rather cleaner than I believe his was after they had been cooped up together forty days." He also says that "two delightful roads, that you would call dusty, supply me continually with coaches and chaises; barges as solemn as Barons of the Exchequer move under my window. . . .

Dowagers as plenty as flounders inhabit all around."

Beets, Carrots and Radishes should be pulled before they grow woody.

8. THE PREVARICATING DENTIST. The gardener after my own heart is a dentist in Boston. For years, so I'm told, he drew teeth and filled fillings and made humanity suffer, until, one day, he took up gardening and began making atonement for all the misery he had caused. And he did it in a strange way. He had lettered seven excuse cards—one for each day of the week. Let the slightest horticultural event break upon his horizon, and teeth can go hang. He merely puts on his door the card for that day and deserts dentistry until the whims of Flora and Pomona have been served. The Monday card reads something like this: "Called Away on Serious Consultation. Will Return Thursday." The Thursday card announces a death in the family. Wednesday tells the toothachy world that he has just become a grandfather. What a superb fabricator! What sublime audacity! And despite this, they tell me, he has a large practice.

Narcissi, Crocus, Hyacinths and Tulips intended for indoor growth, should be put in pans now.

9. SHRUB MIGRATION. In September dig the holes, in October and into November—or as long as the ground is open—move shrubbery. But the hole is the most important step—and yet it comes

midway in the work. For acquiring shrubs begins with the desire for them. Then follows the study of catalogues. Next a study of where to place what you order. Always vow that you are going to live to see these shrubs reach maturity, and space them far enough apart so they won't crowd each other when they do attain their full growth. Then send in your order and go to preparing the holes.

Once when we were putting in a shipment of shrubs, my old gardener remarked, "When those roots begin to taste that soil they'll be mighty glad they came to this garden." If your garden table is well-laid you need never fear moving shrubs so long as the ground can be worked. A mulch for the first year may be advisable; after that you have merely to watch those bushes being glad they came to your garden.

Tomorrow scatter lime on the compost heap and water it down well.

10. WINDS AND TILTH. Borrow's remark that there is sun and moon and wind on the heath, Brother, is a rule for gardeners, if they only knew it, for by taking advantage of them, soil can be built up to a fine tilth. We have tried it for several years now, this depending on sun, wind and rain. The Melon patch started as an area of starved soil that would support nothing save Poverty Grass. This was turned under one Fall and the soil left in rough ridges until well into December. Then it was forked again into fresh ridges. By Spring that earth had been turned a dozen times, and nary a drop of fertilizer put on it. Its crop of

Melons was astounding. And each year that is all we do—let the sun and the rain and the wind and the snow continuously break it down, ridge after ridge. For air in soil works a rich magic, and rain tinctures it with sweet liquors, and the sun's heat cooks it into a fine tilth and the wind across the heath crumbles it.

When the sky, the barometer and the thermometer threaten a sudden cold night, cover your hardy Chrysanthemums with light cloths or newspapers.

11. EATING EXHIBITIONS. It would be of great assistance to judges at flower shows, whose work requires them to pass on decorated tables, if the person decorating and setting the table should give some hint of the menu designed to go with the decorations. I have often stood before these tables and wondered if the creators of them exhausted all their imagination on the flower piece, or if some was left for the courses. Man may not live by bread alone, neither can he survive merely on a decoration that answers all the forty-seven ideal points established for judges. If we could only be assured that one's glimpse of that delightful bowl of fruit was to be accompanied by a substantial breakfast, we might have a more comprehensive basis for judging the exhibit. Perhaps the time will come when the good ladies who set and decorate these tables will be obliged to supply the meal, and the judges will be invited to try it. Judging then, might become more arduous but certainly it would be more enjoyable. My ar-

tistic (?) sensibilities always melt toward that table which is set for dinner with candies and nuts. It is pleasant both to eat and judge an exhibition at the same time.

Mulch heavily with manure those spots where you intend planting Lilies which arrive very late.

12. REMARKS ON HYACINTHS. Among my few garden aversions is the Hyacinth. Though bulb dealers may plead their cause violently, they always sound like Devil's advocates. First of all the bulbs are not cheap. Secondly, their flowering is stiff and suitable only for making patterns such as gardeners made in Victorian days. Thirdly, the bulbs give only one year of mature and satisfactory bloom. Three years are required to bring a Hyacinth bulb to the full flowering stage. The next season it gives that mature and complete flowering. However carefully lifted, dried and replanted, its subsequent bloomings will not be as good; in fact, it dwindles each year. I would much rather raise a few in tall green glasses, the way our grandmothers raised them, treating them as amusing house bulbs, and let them go at that.

Drain the Lily pool, bird bath and other water receptacles and cover with light boards.

13. HORNET HIBERNATION. I have a sneaking admiration for hornets: they take what they want when and where they want it. The first sharp bite in the air, and they calmly enter the house

as though they owned it, go to bed for the Winter and never wake up till Spring. Their ways of forcibly entering a tightly screened house are past understanding. We catch them on the wing with towels (which are rarely fatal), with the back of a hair brush and the sole of a bed slipper (which sometimes are) and we gas them with noisome fumes. Nevertheless some survive, and for this persistent clinging to life, I admire them. Yea, even did I admire the bold hornet soul who chose for his Winter residence the bottom of my woolen pajamas. Before he met my inevitable wrath he made his presence felt. . . . And that night I slept on my face.

See that plenty of firewood is stacked in the cellar and on the back porch.

14. STANDARD HELIOTROPES. There is nothing complicated about making standard Heliotropes: one needs merely the plants and patience. In early Spring start either with plants or well-rooted cuttings, giving them a light compost in their pots. Select one strong central stalk and lop off all sides. Tie this to a stake. Discourage the slightest sign of side growth until the desired height of stalk is reached, meantime seeing that the plants never lack water. When the height is reached, repot them into more spacious pots, mixing plenty of leafmold and a sprinkling of lime with the soil. Thus established, the top of the stalk should be pinched off to force top side growths, and as these appear they should be tied until able to stand by

themselves. Manure water is given during this process. When frosts are over they may be planted in the border. Before Fall frosts, they should be taken up again and the roots squeezed into the smallest possible pot without injuring them, in which close quarters they spend the Winter in a cool greenhouse, with occasional waterings, until they are wanted again in Spring.

By this time you probably have eaten the last of your broilers. Now give the chicken house a thorough cleaning.

15. BLACK FROST. Among the refined cruelties practised by the Tsars in ancient times was to condemn a man to death and then, as he stood on the scaffold with the halter around his neck, reprieve him. Many a Russian malcontent clung to that hope of pardon and went mad awaiting it. I think of those poor devils these days when we're waiting for the Black Frost. Other frosts—White Frosts—have come and gone with their petty destructions. The mercury has danced up and down its tube like a coloratura soprano running her scales. We've had brisk days and days languorously warm. What remains of the garden is very precious because it has so short a time to live. We hope for a reprieve all the while, knowing that the Tsar of Winter must visit his wrath eventually. . . . And then one night it comes—sweeps down from the north silently on a still night. We awake to find the garden blackened. The miserable cadavers of our flowers hang with

bowed head on the scaffold of Winter. The Tsar has not been pleased to extend us his mercy.

All naturalizing of bulbs should be completed by now although the smaller fellows can still go into protected coves.

16. THEN RAIN. Invariably after frost comes rain, and after the Black Frost heavy rain. Year by year I have been noting this down and year by year we have enjoyed the sense of enclosure this Black Frost deluge brings. It drops down like a curtain between the show of the garden and the audience of the house. The play is over; our thoughts turn indoorward. Night and the rain wrap us round comfortably like an old coat. We sit beside the fire and listen to the drum-beat of the rain drops on the tin roof of the kitchen, and the staccato slash against the window panes. On such a night desires become a mere memory. We are safely harbored. We sit in peace, assured that no danger can befall us—little boats in calm harbors riding out a storm.

All foliage cut from borders and beds should be burned and not allowed to lie about.

17. THE APPROACH TO GARDENS. I have a theory (which may or may not be tenable) that gardens should be entered by slow degrees; that one should never be able to burst upon them entire and that the paths to their glories should also both reveal and conceal the garden's hidden secrets. Through a low gate massed with shrub-

bery or laced with vines, down or up easy steps, by winding ways that give no hint of whither they are leading—by such means should we approach a garden. And there is reason for it. The enjoyment of a garden's design and colorful delights constitutes a spiritual and emotional experience, and such experiences should never be entered at one full swoop, the way a diver goes head first off the deep end; rather they should be neared slowly, deliberately and with humility of approach. . . . Had I a garden of a thousand acres, its gate would be narrow and low-set, and those who entered it would pass with expectancy and uncertainty of what lay beyond.

If your climbing Roses are in an especially windy spot, lash them in place with rag bands.

18. MIDGET GARDENS. By degrees gardening has entered a Lilliputian phase. It began with those rock gardens made on tables that are so popular at English flower shows. Then it shrank to smaller proportions and the "sink" garden came into vogue. This is a garden planted in an old stone sink or trough. Now it has dwindled down to a little patch of the desert and we have Cactus gardens no bigger than a plate and Japanese gardens in a saucer; and from Spain, recently, have come little ceramic pieces showing a house, a bit of terrain and a wall that one plants with living material—gardens not much bigger than an ink pot. Rough-handed nurserymen who used to struggle over ceiling-high Palms now have gone

into growing midget plants. We may soon expect magnifying glasses to be classed with garden tools.

Tomorrow see that all tender bulbs and tubers are brought into a frost-proof place.

19. REASONS FOR HAVING A MICROSCOPE. However absurd the foregoing sentiment may sound, let me state that the gardener who does not include a magnifying glass among his garden tools is missing a lot. And if he cannot aspire to using a microscope he is missing even more. For a world of hidden mysteries unfolds beneath the eye when once we penetrate the superficial appearance of a leaf, a flower, a bark or a fruit.

Years ago my first college assignment with a microscope was to make a study of the structure of Bamboo. Under the lens appeared those curly wires that give the Bamboo its strength. They are like the wire that used to be wrapped around the old-fashioned gas hose leading from the chandelier to the table light. I remembered how I marveled then at this sublime and simple cell structure. Years afterward I was not so puzzled when I read that in Japan and China feeding powdered Bamboo is a refined method of dealing with one's enemies. Those microscopic wires are far more effective and less easy to detect than ground glass.

Plant Roses as soon as they arrive, water well and give a light manure mulch.

20. FLOWERS AND FURNITURE. It would be amusing, one of these days, to study furniture

history in the light of the house plants used with each period. The earlier eras of furniture were eras of very limited heat. The Elizabethan manor hall that gave us Tudor furniture was so meagerly heated that no tender plant could have lived there. Nor am I sure that the various styles of the Louis in France made any improvement. It was not till we reached the age of stuffiness and stoves that our forebears could keep plants alive indoors over Winter. And since then the style in house plants has patiently trailed the style in furnishings. Read the old catalogues of nurserymen who supplied our Victorian grandmothers—their stock was positively blowzy, their plants went with bustles and red plush sofas. Now that we are waist-deep in the angles and strange contours of Modernism, Cactus is the house plant supreme—Cactus of macabre shapes, Cactus that will live untended in a room whose sunless walls are aluminum, whose ceiling cork and whose furniture is covered with snake skin!

Have all flower vases scrubbed thoroughly and put away for the Winter.

21. DISAPPEARING ARTISTS. Oriental Poppies, *Dicentra spectabilis*—the old-fashioned Bleeding Heart, and the equally old-fashioned Virginia Bluebell, are the disappearing artists among common garden flowers. They put on their little show —and bob off the stage. And, frankly, that's what I like about them. *Dicentra formosa,* on the other hand, clings to its ferny foliage and grows more

and more mangy as the days pass. It is an anticlimax. The only bother with these disappearing artists is that one is apt to forget them—forget where they disappear, so it were better to plant them in a Spring border or corner that can be forgotten during the other seasons, or else to mark them so permanently that there's no danger of rooting them up.

Of these three, Mertensia is really the cleverest artist. First purple foliage that turns to gray green, the flowers, in their turn, wearing sky blue in the first part of their act and pink in the second. You really couldn't expect more of a plant than this, could you? With a few card tricks and a couple of rabbits out of hats and gold fish out of pockets, Mertensia could go on the vaudeville circuit.

Begin now buying those garden books you intend giving away for Christmas; in the meantime you can read them.

22. FERNS IN THE FALL. Even as late as this, Ferns may be moved, since Autumn is the ideal season for transplanting these collected wildlings from fen and meadow into the garden. Three rules apply to Ferns and all transplanted native material: (1) Dig them with enough earth and roots; (2) If plants are scarce take only one and, when they are very scarce, take only a rooted part of one; (3) Give them, in their garden location, the same kind of soil, exposure or protection, dampness or dryness as they had in their

native spots. The Fern can't any easier change its habitat than the leopard his spots.

See that one frame is filled with hardy, early blooming plants to give you the first outdoor blossoms of next year.

23. THE PEREGRINATION OF GARDENERS. It is a pretty coincidence that those who enjoy gardens and gardening also enjoy travel. To be eternally contented to stay in one spot, satisfied with one's immediate surroundings, is a sure sign of old age, decay and slowing-up of ambition. Every so often it is good for one to go into voluntary exile from the things and people we love—children, wives, pets, friends, gardens. Robert Burton, who wrote the "Anatomy of Melancholy," and was wise in his generation (his generation being from 1577 to 1640) set down the same thought thus: "Peregrination charms our sense with such unspeakable and sweet variety, that some count him unhappy that never traveled, a kind of prisoner and pity his case, that from his cradle to his old age beholds the same still, still, still the same, the same."

These final warm days of October are very precious; lie out in their sun as long as you can.

24. PERSISTENT BLOOMERS. Some flowers, like steadfast friends, stay with us to the end, and to these we cling when the less robust and more showy have gone down the Autumn wind. One year, under the shelter of the Top Garden wall, a line of Pansies continued their unceasing bloom

from mid-April until almost the first of the New Year. I picked flowers three inches wide from that bed on the fifth of December. Verbena will do that sometimes, too, and in a sheltered spot *Phlox subulata* goes on cheerfully throwing a flower—the same Phlox that threw flowers abundantly in Spring. I have even had a Sweet Pea, planted at the same time as the others, give me bloom in late October. For such vagaries may Heaven be praised.

Young fruit trees should be protected from the depredations of mice by wire-cloth collars.

25. HARVEST. Among the serenities that no money or honor or acclaim can ever bring is one that defies the worries of the world. It is to sit in front of your own fireplace of an Autumn night and, before going up to bed, to eat apples from trees that you have planted with your own hands, you yourself have pruned and sprayed, you yourself watched grow from mere sticks to fruitful abundance. And if a wife be by your side (and not talking too much) and a dog at your feet (a dog not too intent on fleas!) you may dismiss all else with the ease and inconsequential gesture with which you fling the cores into the embers.

Seeds of rock plants intended to be planted in November should be ordered now.

26. EMERGING ARCHITECTURE. Among the multitude of beauties that make Autumn very much worth while is the manner in which the archi-

tecture of deciduous trees emerges from their cloaking of leaves. The wine-glass Elm in leafage is a glorious sight and the noble Oak and the Poplar —upon these we have feasted our eyes these many months. Leaves fall. Limb and structure step forth. An intricate and entirely different beauty offers itself to view. The tree enters on a rational, scientific phase. We see the why and wherefore of its noble posture, its vast spread, its seemly contour. It becomes a thing of bone and sinew, a magnificently articulated mechanism. We now understand more of its workings. Like a conjurer who has mystified us, Nature shows how simple the trick is. And yet even the mightiest among us cannot turn it.

Light brush should be gathered now to lay over Foxgloves and Primroses before putting on Winter mulch.

27. NEW ENGLAND GROWS YOUNG. A flapper came into the garden the other day (a good looking flapper) and remarked that what amused her about this New England countryside was that the old houses all looked as though they had had their faces lifted and their hair dyed.

There has been a mania for restoring and remodeling old places. Even old barns are being given a new lease of life. And it is rather a thrilling experience to ride along some by-way or back-country dirt road and suddenly come on one of these old places that stood abandoned for years and now has entered into its second youth. Generations ago, when New England farmers, tired of the heavy taxes and the unyielding, boulder-strewn soil, left these farms for the richer lands of the Ohio Valley, they surrendered their homes to the ravages of Time, little suspecting that another generation would bring them back to life. Wherever you go you find them—their rock-held terraces spilling Roses, Hollyhocks leaning against a house that is newly painted and its quaintly-curtained windows looking out on gardens made by men and women who, for a time at least, have abandoned the city that they also might grow young again.

Check up on that farmer who promised, two months ago, to deliver manure this Fall.

28. CHRISTMAS ROSES. Under the lee of a big Forsythia bloom the Christmas Roses, a cluster of waxy white single flowers held above the tough green foliage on thick fleshy stems. In that sheltered spot they have bloomed through eight Autumns and Winters with no more care than a Spring feeding of bone meal, a Fall saturation with manure water and, when snow flies, the protection of a small frame. From late October till April we gather little bouquets of these flowers. Virginally white at first, they later grow pinkish around the edges and then purple. One day, I enthused over them to a prominent nurseryman and his reply was characteristic: "Don't tell anybody about them. People will be trying to buy them from us, and we haven't a plant of *Helleborus niger* on the place." Seeing that seven years

pass from seeding to flowering in this particular plant, it is rather expecting too much of gardeners to raise them from seed, and, of course, the Federal Horticultural Board has laid its pest-petting hand on their importation. So it seems futile to discuss the desirable varieties of Hellebore— the *H. Orientalis,* which is the Lenten Rose, bearing white, purple, red or crimson flowers; the *H. foetidus,* with small green flowers tipped purple; *H. viridis,* the British species, with clustered heads of bright green. These beauties we might possess some day if a miracle could happen; meanwhile we are content with our one variety the common *H. niger* and, despite the anxious solicitation of that nurseryman, I would shout its glories to the four corners of the earth as Gerarde did when he first brought it to England in 1596.

Side roots taken now from hardy Chrysanthemums can be set in the cold frames for next year's supply.

29. THE ESCAPE. The terrible wailing of the siren at Sing Sing when a human being escapes from his cell, the bay of blood-hounds tracking down a runaway nigger through the swamps of Louisiana—these are warnings of search never to be forgotten. These and the shout that reached our ears one placid October dusk—"Pigs Out!" With a scamper and thud, past us shot a ton or more of pork, ham, bacon, spareribs and sausage meat. Under the pressure of their speedily increasing strength the fence had given 'way. They had tossed heavy stones aside as though they were

pebbles. Freedom lay ahead, and they were making for it with the speed of express trains. Why have whippet races, I thought, when you could race hogs? One might lure them to the goal just as we lured those hogs back from a mile away, just as prisoners are often caught—by the thing that lies nearest their hearts. Find the woman, and you eventually find the prisoner. Fill a bucket with hog feed, and freedom palls instantly on escaped hogs.

Ere night fell they were back in their gilded cage, safely snoring in that perfect pig house, on mattresses of clean leaves. Like the wise creatures they are, they probably grew philosophic, the way we do after a journey—it's good to go, but better to come back home.

See that culverts and drains are kept free of fallen leaves that might choke them.

30. BLUEBIRDS AND MUSH. Late October, and a family of five bluebirds is wheeling around the garden and across the pinky-dun of the dried Poverty Grass on the hilltop meadow. They seem to like this spot. They are loath to leave it. Some, indeed, never leave. For several Winters the gardener has kept a couple about the place by the simple expedient of dumping his oaten meal mush pot each morning on a fence post near the house. Any one can keep bluebirds, he insists: all you need do is to maintain a steady diet of oaten meal mush.

Begin forking up soil that you want to leave rough over the Winter.

31. FALL FREEDOM. Now is the season when urbanites think Fifth Avenue the most beautiful spot in the world, and we do nothing to disabuse their minds of this notion. To country dwellers, late Autumn brings a peculiar freedom. By this time all the people one should invite to the country have been invited. The house grows still of nights. We no longer need be dressed up to our company. The grocer's bills drop down to the reach of our purse. There is still a little wine left in last year's barrel. We begin afresh to gather the fruits of solitude.

Save space in an open frame for planting alpine seeds.

LONG PIECE

AROUND THE OLD MELODEON

THE time was (and it's not so far distant but many of us can remember it) when a favorite amusement in many American homes was to stand around the old parlor melodeon and sing gospel hymns. Moody and Sankey had dragged their revival nets up and down the country, and the catch of souls was prodigious. Not satisfied with singing in tabernacles, people were swept along by pious excitation into making gospel music a part of home life. The melodeon became the domestic altar and the rhythm of the household was gaited to the lachrymose words and airs of "There is a Fountain Filled With Blood," and "Throw Out the Life Line."

How strange these hymn-singing homes appear to the latest generation, which has not known them. They are one with the plush sofa and the cosy corner, with men who took pride in the variety of their whiskers and women in those caudal appendages known as bustles.

Some people like to think (and they are entirely wrong, of course) that the American home was safer, purer, nobler, more firmly established in those days than it is today. They attribute it partly to the fact that the father was still the overlord of the household and partly to this custom of singing gospel hymns. Nevertheless whilst one generation found satisfaction in tunefully declaring that Heaven was its home, the others were learning the ribald words of "Everybody Works But Father." For this gospel hymn era, if the truth were told, was the last stand of the old patriarchal guards, the last vestige of that parental aloofness, of that Tsar-like fatherhood, of that Old Testament conception of what a man should be when he became head of the house; a cruel and unyielding doctrine, fetched here by the Puritans and extending, with gradually lessening force, to the very threshold of today.

Father is a different person today from what he was forty years ago, and we have a notion that giving up gospel hymns had something to do with it.

The mistaken notion about this gospel hymn era was the idea that it was closely related to religion, whereas it was merely a phase in the evolution of music in the home. True, it afforded an outlet for emotion, religious and otherwise, and it was a goodly custom of united household endeavor, but, more important than these, it proved that music was the heritage and right of even the humble and the unsophisticated.

In the early days of America, music was a genteel custom for the better-educated ranks of society. The music of the harpsichord, the flute and violin, and the part-singing of old songs, were drawing room accomplishments that went with fine clothes and richly endowed households. The commonalty were satisfied with folk-songs and ballads printed on broadsides and sold by peddlers; music, "classical music," as it was sometimes called, was a diversion for the gentry. Before the Revolution and afterward, such centers of culture as Charleston and Philadelphia had their St. Cecilia Societies and New York and Boston their subscription concerts, at which the better music was heard, and New York supported its "gardens," where catches of the day were sung. But even with these opportunities for those who could afford the entrance fee, music was still mainly a home product and its making and appreciation carried an aristocratic air.

The manufacturing of cheaper pianofortes and the introduction of the melodeon brought music down to the reach of more people. The presence of one of these in a home marked the progress of that household. Keeping up with the Joneses in those days meant having a piano. Aspiring and socially ambitious parents subjected their children to music lessons, and the less worldly learned to play and sing gospel hymns. Music was made in the home, and it could be made in more homes than it had been.

Then man devised many inventions. The talking machine lowered the price of music and made its production effortless. The radio has carried on this work. The grandchildren of those who once stood around the old melodeon singing hymns now dance the black bottom before a loud speaker. The parents of these dithyrambic offspring applaud their efforts and try to emulate them. This ease and universality of music in the home has helped break down that last wall between parents and children. It has brought father off his pedestal, it has loosened his joints, it is keeping him young. The two-stepping parent cannot wear a dour face for long. He understands youth better than he used to.

There are those who consider jazz the final corruption of the home, and yet it is merely the last step in the evolution of domestic music. Having made home music a common possession of all, the next step is to develop an appreciation of good music. And today we are in the full tide of a very wonderful musical evolution. We are developing a taste for good music. The better cinema orchestras play Beethoven and such masters because the people demand them. Our concert halls are packed. In thousands of households when jazz comes over the wire some one jumps up and finds a station that is sending out better music.

The next step—and it is not far off—will be the realization that making this kind of better music is an accomplishment that gives the highest sort of satisfaction. Music made without effort affords very little outlet for the emotions, hence people have to dance. But let us once realize that playing some instrument well gives a complete and satisfying emotional "kick," and we will make it an accomplishment essential to a full and rounded education. When that day comes, the American home will be richer, and parents and children will have even more bonds in common. We will have household music of the sort that bound us together when we sang gospel hymns.

This will come; I am sure of it. Meantime those of us who *had* to eat Irish stew because our father made us and who *had* to sing those maudlin gospel hymns can contemplate this new evolution with a sympathetic and kindling eye. And yet—and yet what wouldn't I give once more to hear a freckled-face, red-headed, rangy sister in pig-tails lift her wavering voice to sing, "The King of Love My Shepherd Is."

THE MONTH OF NOVEMBER

1. IN MEMORIAM. Of your charity, on this Day of All Saints, remember her to whose memory these pages, a meagre and inconsequential offering though they may be, are dedicated. May she be enjoying (as surely her saintliness and great sacrifices did warrant) that Garden where the

"Gallant walks
Continually are green,"

where the vineyards and orchards are "most beautiful and fair," "where Cinnamon and Sugar grow" and "Nard and Balm abound!"

She used to sing of that Jerusalem, her happy home . . . I can hear her singing still.

Get out heavier gardening clothes and take no chances these days when overheated.

2. NIGHT RETURN. In Autumn when the days shorten and commuters dress by artificial light, and come home in the dark, then are the times when this journeying to the city to earn one's bread becomes dreary and irksome. Perhaps the going isn't so bad as the coming back—the coming back tired and sleepy and with nerves on edge. And those are the nights when, to bolster up my flagging spirits, I recite into the herbage of my

scant moustache the consoling lines of Thomas Lovell Beddoes:

The earth may open, and the sea o'erwhelm—
Many the ways, the little home is one;
Thither the courser leads, thither the helm,
And at one gate we meet when all is done.

Begin preparing feeding stations for birds. Lay in a supply of Sunflower, Hemp and Millet seed.

3. THE BALANCE SHEET. About this time of year, I read over my garden notes and make up a profit and loss statement, and if my failures don't go above 40% I'm satisfied. Compare what you planted in Spring with what you brought to successful flowering, and you are amazed how many things have been forgotten and how many simply didn't work. Again, each year's balance sheet will show some strange behavior by some hitherto dependable standby. For no accountable reason Stocks will show a loss or Verbenas stood still or Corn was inconsequential. These failures I note to give special attention to next year, the way a merchant "pushes" a slow line of goods.

This week is about the last in which to do Fall plowing.

4. FIRST BLOOMING. Another tabulation I make at the end of the garden year is the list of first bloomings. These are set down day by day as they appear and now go in a big set of columns that cover, so far, the first bloomings for ten years.

Whereas annuals fluctuate according to the time they were first sown, there is very little fluctuation in the perennials' dates. When one of the natives tells me that the weather ain't what it used to be when he was a boy, I listen politely and think my own thoughts, for these tables show that it really changes very little. A deviation either toward earliness or lateness may be marked in one year, but over a decade they about strike an average.

Election Day offers an excellent opportunity to plant Tulips.

5. EVERLASTINGS. Except for Honesty, *Lunaria biennis,* very few of the Everlastings appeal to me in Winter. In late Fall, after the garden has gone, a few bouquets of them for a time are refreshing to have about, but my prejudice against Everlastings is that they *are* everlasting. One soon tires of them. They collect all the stray dust that comes their way. I'd prefer an occasional vase of flowers from a florist in Winter to a dozen mangy, grimy, dried bouquets of the best Helichrysums ever raised. And even Honesty, by the first of the year, goes into the fireplace. Its silver shillings are too annoyingly reminiscent, by that time, of my lack of them.

All shrubs and trees set out now should have the soil well-firmed around the roots, and be staked where necessary.

6. THE AWARD FOR SANITY. A medal of the First Class for Sanity should be awarded one of

my neighbors. Most of his land is under the dense shade of Hemlocks, and he doesn't expect to grow grass there. How many gardeners fuss and stew about shady spots, and write to garden editors and curse garden-book writers because there is no way of making perfect lawns in dense shade! They try Pachysandra, English Ivy, Periwinkle and such ground covers, and it never occurs to them to treat such soil as soil. This neighbor, on whose broad breast I would pin the medal for Sanity, First Class, treated the soil beyond the perimeter of his trees with peat and other acid-inducing means, and then he went into the woods and collected Moss of the kind that grows in the sort of shade he has in his garden. It is thriving. Eventually he will have mossy stretches—soft, gray-green drifts spreading between his Hemlocks.

The pruning of Grapes can be done any time now that the sap is down.

7. QUAINT POSSESSIONS. In the dingy shadows of a New Orleans shop we came across this strange little object. What it was, the dealer didn't know, nor had we the slightest idea. But taking the gamble, we carried it to the hotel, sacrificed a tooth brush for the cause, and out of the filth and dust emerged as quaint a little toy as ever you would wish. It was a little press made of ebony and ivory. Two ivory posts hold the screws and ivory forms the knob and the decoration on the top lid. In this, ladies of an erstwhile era pressed their mitts and handkerchiefs. Today callers grow curious about it and when She is away, I press flowers

in it for Her letters. . . . Just another gewgaw; just another thing to dust! But how precious are quaint possessions, how much a part of us do they become, how necessary they are to those of us who are odd sticks!

Tomorrow begin putting a manure mulch around bush fruits and on the Asparagus bed.

8. SEX INSULATION. Cap, my indefatigable garden aid, began missing his garden when scarcely the Black Frost had come. He looked on the extra hotbed sash with envious eyes, and a great thought was born. Excavating a foot or so into the earth, he began making himself a greenhouse. A friend had contributed a stove. The sash would furnish the necessary light, but the side walls stumped him. Finally he solved them in a novel fashion—he made double walls of boards and for insulation between them stuffed several years' accumulation of sex, mystery and romance magazines, doubtless on the theory that hot-stuff will never die. The things he brought to flower between these sex-lined walls astounded the valley. His flowers fairly leaped and his Tomatoes ran riot. One of these years I'm going to try it myself with that set of unexpurgated Arabian Nights and the pudgy red volumes of Rabelais and Boccaccio.

By this time all salt hay and straw necessary for mulching should be delivered to your garden.

9. MADONNA OF THE SWINE. She sits on the shelf of the Summer dining terrace, a quaint

ceramic peasant maiden with ruddy round face and blue plaid apron. One arm is around the neck of a goat. With the other she clasps a sheep. And crowded around her are deliciously fat pigs—big pigs and little pigs. Because of my fondness for pigs, she caught my eye in a Munich shop and carefully I carried her all the way home. When she was set in place, the cook, pious soul, asked me if it was the Virgin and I, impious soul, assured her it was the Madonna of the Swine. Ever since then she has always kept a little bouquet of fresh flowers in front of her.

Begin hilling up Roses. Lay manure between the hills.

10. SNOWBERRY. Commonplace though it may be, we find great delight these days in the white berries of the *Symphoricarpos racemosus* which, planted in a sheltered spot, still holds its fruit snow-white. Usually by this time the berries have turned brown, bitten by the cold, or birds have gobbled them up. What an accommodating shrub this is! It tolerates a certain degree of shade, it has a good form and is not exacting as to soil. While its pinkish flowers are inconspicuous, one has to accept this defect with grace so long as it serves its purposes admirably. Like a great many people, it doesn't make a show in a crowd, when all the other shrubs are glorious in flower, but it can be depended on to give complete satisfaction when the others have finished their work, washed up and gone home.

Go over the lawn and fill hollows and inequalities with rich loam.

11. A Good Riddance for Temptation. Making plans for gardens that never will be built is a form of innocent diversion wherewith gardeners may keep themselves satisfied through the Winter of their discontent. It involves spending thousands of imaginary dollars and is, perhaps, the cheapest way available to satiate that craving to buy plants that you've never tried. In the odd moments of one Winter I worked on plans for a sunken garden in the new German manner—stone-supported terraces with an oblong pool in the bottom—a sort of miniature hanging garden. Into it went a vast assortment of plant material that I could never afford and much that I'm sure I couldn't grow. The following Spring, when the new catalogues arrived, I found it much easier to look at them with a complaisant and satisfied eye. If this could only be applied to grocers' bills, club dues and accounts with the tailor, how simple living would be!

These are days when you sigh for a greenhouse. Begin saving for one now.

12. Crumbs for Mice. There is always great talk, at this season of the year, about protecting young fruit trees and newly planted shrubs from the depredations of mice. Precautions are necessary at times, but the Winter of the biggest freeze in this locality, when food for mice and rabbits grew scarce and many an orchard and hedge was girdled, found ours untouched. We had trimmed water suckers out of the old Apples that Autumn, and were too lazy to do more than heap them in piles.

A long Winter of heavy snow followed. The following Spring every brush heap was consumed, but never a tree was touched. Consequently, though it may be the better part of wisdom to cut weeds and grass away from young trees and further protect them with galvanized netting, I'm satisfied with leaving a few crumbs around for these poor little devils to gnaw at over Winter.

A collection of varicolored fruit cut from shrub and tree makes a vivid decoration these drab days.

13. THE NEW ORCHARD GENERATION. After several years we agreed that even in orchards the old must give place to the new. When first we came here there was, on a gentle slope behind the house, the remnants of an old orchard—rheumaticky, twisted, gnarled old Apples, gorgeous in their blossoming but lean in fruit. Season by season these were trimmed and sprayed and their branches chained and their crippled parts supported. And each year they have contributed more and more to our wood pile and our bills, and less and less to our table. That old generation of trees has been going these many seasons and there is nothing more to do for them. Consequently, this year we replanted the area to dwarf trees of many kinds—Apples, Cherries, Plums, Peaches, and we only wish we had done it in the beginning. It is really a waste of money to try to bring back fruitful bearing in an orchard after once it has passed a certain stage of neglect and decay. Even tree sur-

geons, who are usually not frank about such matters, express their doubts when a tree is a mere hollow shell. It were better to harvest the wood and start all over again. And that we have done, with the fond expectation that we shall live long enough to enjoy the fruits of this new generation of dwarfs.

Lime powdered on soil that needs sweetening can be left to wash down with the Winter's rains.

14. AN ORCHARD GARDEN. But having set out these new fruit trees is only one part of a dream we have for that orchard. Eventually, it will be incorporated into the garden itself and the trees become an item in a plan that calls for winding paths lined with Iris and Peonies and Hemerocallis, backgrounds composed of collections of Mock Oranges and Deutzias and shady areas where Rhododendrons can be induced to grow. Such is the quality of our dreams, and by attaining them piecemeal, that orchard will eventually attain its full stature. At present, Spring finds it a Milky Way of Narcissi, and at times we are tempted to let it go at that, but gardeners are ever discontented, and the sign of progress among them is that they change their gardens continually and reach out for more and more wild spaces to make blossom like the Rose.

The first pots of Tulips can be brought indoors and put in a dark closet to start growth.

15. WINDS OF NOVEMBER. The winds of the months have as many moods as the men whose faces they lash and soothe. A promise of good things to come is borne on the March wind and the April breezes toss the evidence in scattered catkins and ruddy Elm pollen. May brings the first zephyrs, and with the June wind, spreads the fragrance of a thousand perfumed flowers. The siroccos of July and August, blown across the sunbaked soil, come as a warning to the less robust to stay in shadowy corners. September carries the fragrance of Clematis and October's winds tear the panoply of color from the trees. Then comes November.

A different wind from all of these is November's wind. Trees and bushes are bare. They stretch gaunt arms against the darkening sky and sway helplessly and wail and creak as the winds race down upon them. The saddest wind of all, this.

Today a wind from the West out over the hills
came blowing—
Ah, how it made dim dreams and memories
start!
And I thought that I smelt in my room the Wild
Thyme growing
And the scent of the sweet Bogmyrtle filled my
heart.

Inspect fruit and vegetables in the root cellar and take out those that show signs of decay.

16. MANURE AS DIAMONDS. In some ways gardening folks are a stupid and helpless lot. I'm impressed with this every Autumn when a load or so of manure (sometimes ten or twenty, according to the state of my purse) is hauled up this hill. Visiting gardeners contemplate it as though it were diamonds and make vague remarks to the effect that they can never get manure, and the automobile is cutting down the supply. Then I always ask them, "How hard do you try?"

The time to arrange for Autumn delivery is in the Summer. Scout around the countryside a bit. Jingle a little real money. You'd be amazed how much manure is available and how anxious farmers and dairymen are to sell it.

Sawing wood, that sport of ex-emperors, may be started any day and continued any day hereafter.

17. ROOT CELLARS. There are a myriad odors that make the mouth of man water, and not the least of them is the smell of a root cellar. Dip down into its shadowy depths, and fine aromas tingle the nostrils—the overpowering sweet fragrance of Apples, the subtle scent of Pears ripening on shelves, the stout earthy reminder of Potatoes, the insistent smell of Onions and the abundant effluvium that arises from Cabbages stored against the winter. He who has a root cellar still his appetite keeps.

Since too much of any good thing is irksome, resolve to forget gardens and gardening for a week.

18. November Cleaning. If ever you have owned real estate you will appreciate the kind of tenant who, when she finally departs from the house, leaves it swept and garnished. If gardens could speak their opinion of many of us, I'm afraid they'd have scandalous things to say. Only the fastidious among gardeners really cleans up in the Fall, really leaves the garden he had tenanted, in seemly order for its Spring occupancy. And yet these last garden rites are so simple. They require no horticultural knowledge. Common sense and the ability to rake and run a wheelbarrow are all they demand. When I finally leave them, toward the middle of November, I like to feel that if, when Spring came, another gardener should have these seven acres more or less, he should remark of me, "He gardened like a gentleman."

Cross-country tramps are a fine diversion these days and calling on isolated farmers even finer.

19. Acknowledging Another Failure. Failure having been my lot after several years of struggling with Blueberries, I have finally concluded that growing this fruit to success is not among my gifts. I refer to those Blueberries that are as big as your thumb, over which the horticultural world got hot and worried some years back. We gave them the acid soil that was required and tried to keep them damp, which amounted to reproducing a bog condition on a dry hilltop—a silly effort—and finally the third

year when they set fruit and I watched it expand and take on color, my friends, the robins, dropped in and ate every one of them. After that, I was convinced that Blueberries on this dry Connecticut ridge were never intended for my scheme of things. I have put the experience down in the list of those foolish efforts on which we, as gardeners, waste time and money. Alas, that list is appallingly long!

In all the world's vast library there is no better reading for a countryman than the catalogue of a mail-order house.

20. THE PERCENTAGE OF SUCCESS. And since we are on the subject of failures, let me observe that you may know a real gardener by the fact that he doesn't mind acknowledging them. Keep on trying new things—new flowers, new vines, new trees, new shrubs—by all means keep searching for these new experiences. Give a new plant at least a three-years' trial in various soils and locations, but don't be disappointed if you lose when you are gambling with the odds all against you. Sooner or later, you realize that there are certain things you can't grow. Sooner or later, too, you will realize that Nature is appallingly wasteful.

In the commercial world, a man is considered successful if he brings to fruition 50% of his efforts. Certainly a higher percentage cannot be expected of the horticulturist.

Cider, having now attained a ripe hardness, may be offered to those who call.

21. 3800 OF THEM. It has been estimated that there are no less than 3800 different catalogues issued by seedsmen and nurserymen the world over. Three thousand eight hundred beginning with Abies and Abronia and ending up with Violas and Zinnias! From this appalling flood of "literature" most of us are splashed by half a dozen drops. What the total circulation of these may be one can only guess. The money spent on their production must rise to a prodigious sum. So much effort, so much expense, so much thought and study! Indeed, we gardeners are citizens of no mean country.

Look into the career of Uzziah, of whom it was said that "he loved husbandry."

22. FIRST SNOW. It should come after nightfall, the first snow. You should step out on the porch to consult the thermometer and through the darkness a stray flake should touch your hand. You go indoors again, grateful for a warm house and a secure roof. Cold frames were long since covered, beds mulched, Roses hilled—all that is done. The Begonia in the window, against the night-sheeted pane, stands comfortable and prim. Embers die on the hearth. You go to bed. That is the way the first snow should come—with faint warning, quietly in the night, so that you awaken the next morning to a sense of great stillness and peace and the virgin radiance from snow-covered lawn and meadow and housetop shining through the air.

The wise householder has, by this time, bespoke her Thanksgiving turkey.

23. Some Birds Roost Al Fresco. To the mysteries which I shall never understand let me add the mystery of why some of the chickens these cold nights go to bed on the roosts like sensible folk, and some insist on roosting in the highest tree exposed to all the winds of the world. It is positively eerie to wander out into the garden these starlit November nights and see the leafless tree above the chicken yard inhabited by those black blobs that are Rhode Island Reds and Plymouth Rocks. Nor all my coaxing will bring them down, for the blood of a wild ancestor must run strong in them and they will stay wild until they reach the pot.

Tomorrow begin fattening hogs for December killing. Feed them lavishly.

24. Huddling Houses. Once the leaves are off the trees the valley houses come very close, as though huddling to keep each other warm. Houses we never see in Summer emerge in the panoply of their architecture—some stark, some amusing, some grubby, some well-kept. And how welcome are the lights in them these nights when night is long! How pleasant it is to watch the family's progress in them—the dining room light at supper, then just the living room, finally the first floor lights go out and lights appear up-stairs. Then even these are switched off. And that is the signal for me to switch off mine.

One of these spare days count up what your garden has cost you this year—and draw your own conclusions.

25. THE LOVERS OF FLORA. When a boy, of his own volition, begins to wash behind his ears, then you may know that he is in love; or, if he isn't in love, he's about to sit up and take notice. When a gardener begins to give up slovenly habits of cultivation in his garden, then you may know that he has passed the childish stage of dabbling in green growing things. Clean tools, clean borders, clean edges—by such marks may you know the man who has finally been smitten by Flora. A gardener's tool shed at this season and the condition of his cold frames are a certain proof of his devotion.

Having taken a week's vacation from gardening thought, see that your house-plants are given adequate watering.

26. VARNISHING DAY. Toward the end of November, we shellac the gourds. Harvested before frost, they are now brought down from the barn, and, the kitchen table covered with old papers, we start the varnishing process. All manner of gourds are grown along the back fence by the pig yard and their variety is past recording. Give them a coat of white shellac and they will hold their brilliant colors and shapes indefinitely. Let them dry thoroughly and then make a table decoration of them—heap them on a big pewter platter with sprigs of oak leaves stuck between. Fruit can be shellacked this way, and so can the berries of fruiting shrubs and the hips of Roses. Before me, as I write, is an old brown Chinese bowl holding stiff sprays of Silver Moon and Tau-

sendschoen hips, the copper and vermilion berries of Bittersweet, the tiny purple fruit of *Callicarpa japonica,* and the garnet umbels of Highbush Cranberry—all shellacked to hold their color and shape through the flowerless days of Winter.

Choose some phase of garden lore to read up this Winter: you'll be surprised at your ignorance.

27. A THANKSGIVING WINDOW. A little bay window in the hall serves for an altar to the goddess Flora. Ivies are trained against the window frames and in the Spring and Summer big bowls of flowers fill the sill, changing with the seasons. Finally the Black Frost brings death even to Chrysanthemums. Oak leaves and Evergreen boughs are then massed here. One Thanksgiving, we hung the frames with ears of Indian Corn—red and yellow and blue—grown from seed sent us by an Indian friend at Taos. Varnished pumpkins and squashes ranged along the sill. It made a fine pagan display.

Keep plucking the Christmas Roses as they bloom under their little glass frame outdoors.

28. VINEGAR FACES. In my Winter tramps hereabout, I have been encountering the dour faces of the natives, the grim look of men and women on isolated farms far back in the hinterlands. And I'm wondering why people must be so grave and sour and vinegary. Certainly our coming into this world is painful enough, and the manner of our

leaving it is, in most instances, nothing to boast about. Between these two momentous events, Life spreads no bed of Roses for us. To some it's a springless couch. To most it's a humpy one. A rare few find it pleasantly circumstanced, like an old bed with curtains to keep out draughts. The best of us seem to lie unprotected, in all the night winds of the world. Since so unfairly does Life deal the cards, let those of us who can, laugh: let girls giggle and boys shout and old men chuckle in their stomachs and old ladies titter behind their fans.

Oil the secateurs and garden scissors, and lay them away in a safe and easily remembered place for the Winter.

29. DR. TITFORD HOLDS FORTH. A day in London, once when we were there, coincided with the time Wall Street threw its bonnet over the wall. The next morning I sallied forth to splurge my infinitesimal profits and met up with W. J. Titford, M. D., Corresponding Member of the Society for the Encouragement of Arts. He was introduced for the price of a quid between the dirty green covers of "Sketches Toward A Hortus Botanicus Americanus." This worthy medico, having studied (so he infers) the plants of the West Indies, and North and South America, and of Africa and the East Indies, wrote an amusing and learned book on them in the Year of Grace 1811. He appears to have missed Cyclamen in his study of Jamaican plants, but many another thing he doesn't miss, for his medical, commercial and

economic suggestions have the universality and placid seriousness of a Munchausen. The native orchid of Jamaica *Orchis Habenacia,* he states, makes excellent eating and should always be carried on shipboard to prevent famine at sea. Fourteen of his plants make good beverages, two cure baldness, ten can be compounded into cosmetics, five will make hats, seven will preserve the teeth, two afford excellent umbrellas, one will attract rats and three can be fashioned into excellent walking sticks.

Dr. Titford may have made his little mistakes and been twitted for them by other members of the Society for the Encouragement of Arts, but how much more amusing and entertaining is his kind of flower book than the strictly correct, unimaginative and sterile compilations that our presses vomit forth each Spring!

Surprise the local parson by appearing in church on Thanksgiving Day. After all, this is our big feast.

30. WINTER MULCH. There is nothing that will so quickly make a garden look like an abandoned farm as hay and straw blown about, and yet our garden writers tell us to Winter-mulch flowers with Salt hay or Rye straw. True, having laid it on the borders, you are supposed to hold it down with boughs or boards, but I've yet to see the bough or board that did its work completely. Gardens so covered soon look like women who have just washed their hair and can't do anything with it. We've tried them both, and for weeks

in Spring we are kept tidying up the place. Elm leaves and peat moss we prefer for this Winter mulch.

A supply of weather stripping is the countryman's ever-present help in time of Winter draughts.

LONG PIECE

THE QUEST OF TRANQUILLITY

AT THE end of that long gallery of the Louvre where the Venus de Milo stands, and in that little corner room of the Königliche Gemälde Galerie at Dresden where hangs the Sistine Madonna, you may witness an unusual phenomenon. Children can always be found there. All sorts of children from all walks of life. The smudgy-faced peasant rubs elbows with the clean little aristocrat. The tatterdemalion with the smartly dressed.

Their mere presence is enough to cause wonder. But even more wonderful is their behaviour: no wriggling, no whispering, no uneasiness, none of the fidgeting and scuffing to which children are given when told to be very good. Of their own accord, apparently, they conduct themselves like little angels.

The reason for this amazing transformation is not far to seek. It is the supreme quality of any great work of art that it imparts an air of serenity to those who behold it. Tranquillity issues from it with the overwhelming penetration and persistence of fragrance from a flower. In its presence the beholder must adapt his mood to this peace or else flee the place. Whatever stimulation, whatever exaltation may follow after a time, the first effect of such a great work is to impart serenity. The mind and the spirit are quieted, as though someone had lain a stilling hand upon the shoulder. The problem of the hour, the worry, the anxiety, drop away, as an old cloak slides off. No desire, no ambition, no want, nor need make themselves felt in the presence of this perfection.

Among children this is especially pronounced, for—although we may think of them only as roistering and noisy—children are very susceptible to tranquillity. They react more favorably and quickly to the tranquil parent than to the nervous and raw-edged. The tranquillity of a grandmother can work magic on them. For this reason no guard is needed to keep these youngsters quiet in the presence of the Venus de Milo or the Sistine Madonna. Moreover (though this may sound strange), they seek these great works of art of their own volition. They are not told to go into such-and-such a gallery and sit before such-and-such a picture; they visit these because they want to. The attraction is as true, direct and unerring as steel to the magnet. This is one of those verities which are hid from the wise and prudent and revealed unto babes.

The search for tranquillity in some form is the most important problem of our contemporary life. Amid the rush of every day endeavor, in the conflict of ambition with circumstances, in the gruelling persistence of necessity by which our lives are goaded, we dream of serenity as though it were a land that is very far off. We yearn for it, we talk about it like men who are ahungered, we hope some day to attain it. Yet few of us are willing to start in quest of it.

We are unwilling to start seeking it, because we don't know where to look. We are fearful, we city-worn and work-tired people, lest when we find it we will be disappointed. That which we most need we are afraid of because it must be bought at a price, and the price is more than many of us are willing to pay.

Nor are we all gaited for the same kind of tranquillity; the state that is tranquil to one will be nerve-racking to another. Each man must seek this perfection after the manner of his own heart. To some there is tranquillity in the quiet, rural scene, and some find it on the restless sea. On some this peace descends when they are in the garden, on some when they are among books or pictures or listening to music. Some need to be alone before it comes to them and others want companionship. There is no one highroad to this blissful state—the ways thither cut across the rude and ugly heart of the world, through its turmoil and its noise and its bewildering complications.

Mere contrast does not bring serenity. The occasional exchange of the town for the country, the hilltop for the flat lands, is not enough. It is not enough to give up a few entanglements, resign a few responsibilities, throw off a few of the cluttering encumbrances that surround us. This quest must be so direct, so simple and complete that it appears childish. Indeed, that is what it is —we must seek tranquillity as children seek out the Venus de Milo and the Sistine Madonna. Nor shall we find it save in some place or object or condition that approaches perfection, the way those two supreme works of art, in their spheres, approach perfection.

The Christmas picture as it has come down to us through the ages offers the perfect study in tranquillity. The Babe, the Mother, the wondering cattle, the adoring simple shepherds against the humble rustic background—of these commonplace things is it composed. The star that stood still, the angels who sang, the wise men who worshipped—with such uncommon elements is it embellished. But even with all these the picture is not complete. The faith of a vast number of humanity holds that under these unwonted circumstances Divine Wisdom came down to dwell with men. It brought peace to the earth and good will between those who lived on it. Such faith, then, makes this first Christmas the very apotheosis of perfection and its remembrance the perfect tribute.

Whether we be tired or poor or defeated or entangled, whether we be brilliant as the star or beautiful as the angels or dumb as the cattle, simple as the shepherds or learned as the wise men, from it extends to us a serenity nowhere else to be found. In its presence the fidgeting of our ambitions and the scuffing of our necessities are stilled. Its quietude engulfs us and overwhelms.

What happens beyond that none of us can know nor needs to know. Perhaps there is nothing more to seek in this quest of tranquillity than that we bring to Perfection our imperfection, that we offer simplicity to Its wisdom, that we remain very still whilst It looks upon us and we look upon It.

THE MONTH OF DECEMBER

1. INTEMPERANCE IN GARDENING. The gardener who makes gardening his sole interest in life may soon develop into a bore and a fanatic, dreaded by his family and avoided by friends. When I meet such people, I blush for my hobby. For gardening is not the whole of life: it is merely part of a full life, and the other parts are just as essential. Some other hobby or hobbies besides gardening should be pursued at the same time—dogs or collecting or travel—each pursued temperately. Intemperance in gardening is the bane of horticulture. It can cause as many heartaches and bring on as much evil as intemperance in drinking or intemperance in eating. Among my acquaintances are violent Prohibitionists who are the veriest sots in gardening, lamentable, incurable, horticultural drunkards, whom I would respect more did they drink a little good liquor and garden less.

If you plan to use the services of a landscape architect next year, consult him now when he is not so busy.

2. GERVASE MARKHAM LENDS HIS SUPPORT. That very wise old writer on horticulture, Gervase Markham, in his "Farewell to Husbandry" set down sage advice, as of December, for those melancholy souls who are temperate in only a few things:

"For your health, eat meats that are hot and neurishing, drink good wine that is neat, sprightly and lusty, keep the body well clad, and thy house warm, forsake whatsoever is flegmatick, and banish all care from thine heart, for nothing is more unwholesome than a troubled spirit."

Tomorrow put the top mulch on Roses —manure, straw and evergreen boughs.

3. PIONEER WOMEN. Some years ago a competition was held among artists for a statue to the Pioneer Woman, the typical female who trudged the dreary plains of the West and helped found our empire beyond the Mississippi. She made a picturesque figure, this woman. Historians enjoy praising her fortitude. We are told that her like will never be known again.

Yet of late years we have encountered a new race of Pioneer Women who, in their way, are building up another empire, breaking down another kind of frontier. These are the wives of those men who willingly give up living in cities and undertake all-year country existence.

More and more people are acquiring country homes. Each year longer and longer stretches the period they stay there. Finally a day comes when they decide to forsake the city and its ease of living altogether for the health and tranquillity of the countryside. Then it is that the challenge is given the new Pioneer Women.

The women of the plains acquired self-reliance and assurance that ever since has been proverbial. They were prepared for any eventuality. They had contempt for fear. Their resourcefulness could laugh at unexpected demands. They learned to do things with their own hands—and no nobler skill than this can any man or woman attain.

This same assurance and resourcefulness are found in the new Pioneer Woman. She knows the necessity of turning to, cheerfully, when servants desert; she must be able to meet demands made on her. She is as quick on the self-starter as her sister of old was on the trigger. Distance and loneliness hold no terrors for her.

You encounter her on snow-chocked roads skidding along to the station to meet her husband, or taking the children to school, or fetching the milk the milkman forgot or the groceries the groceryman said he couldn't deliver. You hear of her staying alone at night in isolated farmhouses just as the Pioneer Woman stayed all night alone in isolated cabins. You see her foregoing theatres and easy shopping and the pleasant contact with friends, strong in the belief that country living will bring strength to her husband and children.

And would she swap her place for all the ease of cities? Ask her, and hear her laugh! Would she exchange the peace of the country for the bedlam of steam drills and traffic? Would she live the standardized life of people in apartments? Would she surrender the crisp, cold morning, the huge open fire, the homely meal, the bob-sledding on the hill, the skating on the pond?

One of these days artists may compete for a statue of the New Pioneer Woman. For a calico gown she'll wear a short skirt; for a shawl, a leather wind-breaker; for a poke bonnet, a little pull-on hat. But her eye will be as clear as the eye of the Old Pioneer Woman and her cheek as rosy. And when the inscription is carved, the praise of her fortitude, her patience, her endurance will be spelled out in just as noble words as were applied to the woman of the plains. For this Pioneer Woman of today is steadily opening up the frontier of saner living. May her tribe increase!

When the ground has frozen, the mulch should be laid on all beds and borders.

4. THE IMPERMANENCE OF PERENNIALS. Whereas we usually think of perennials as permanent, quite a number of them pursue a very definite existence and, having reached the end of it, simply die. Conditions of site, soil and draining may conspire to shorten their lives, but when their course is run, the end is reached.

To assist in the longevity of these herbs, the border where they grow should be redug, renourished and replanted every five years. At that time the perennials may be divided—the outside, lively, young shoots put back and the aged hearts discarded.

We worked on this sort of job constantly for three weeks one Autumn—tagged several hundred plants, lifted them, heeled them into a shady hollow and then set about re-trenching the old soil. By November the border was replanted and by December it was under mulch. The first season after that the bloom was sparse—these newly set plants were just getting their anchorage, but the following year and in years since the revigorated border gave an amazing increase.

Provide a metal barrel for the storage of wood ashes from open fires.

5. PAINTING MEADOWS WITH DELIGHT. My old Scotch-Irish friend on Long Island has an eye for beauty, but he wants it served up in big mugs. Crocus by the thousand, and all that sort of thing. Last year he set out an orchard on a sunny slope and had the good sense to sow it "with delight," as Shakespeare says. He bought several pounds of mixed flower seeds and broadcast them under the trees. By midsummer that hillside was a grand Persian carpet of jumbled flowers. Next year, when our meadow is sown afresh, a pound or two of these mixed seeds will go into the grass—and if the farmers hereabout don't want that hay, don't want to feed their stock on

> Daisies pied, and Violets blue
> And Lady Smocks all silver-white
> And Cuckoo-buds of yellow hue

then we shall feed it to the pigs and bed them down with it. Lucky pigs, to sleep on Persian carpets!

Collect Oak leaves and Pine needles for mulching Rhododendrons and other acid-loving plants.

6. RUNNERS. To the antique business of London belong strange figures which, apparently, are peculiar to that city. They are called "Runners."

Their official and self-appointed costume consists of top hats and Prince Albert coats, the age and condition of these garments being no criterion so long as a man wears them. Their business is to scour both London and the adjoining countryside for whatever antiques may be available. They go from house to house blandly begging for antiques. And when one is acquired, off they trot to the dealers with their prize. Men of rare discernment, these, and their knowledge of antiques and antiquities is profound. Some of the contemporary runners represent the second and third generation in the business. Where they live, and how they manage to exist no one knows, but their colorful Cockney and sly ways give a picaresque tang to London's antique underworld.

Plant one fresh batch of Paper White Narcissi every ten days for a succession of bloom.

7. THE SMUGGLED GEM. While for women smuggling may be their second oldest profession, for men it is a nasty business. And yet I stand confessed of it. Once in the Tropics a friend gave me the bulb of a flower that seemed so rare and precious that I was willing to perjure my immortal soul for it. I, who had refused time and again to smuggle, was thrown by my floral Achilles' heel. The bulb traveled safely, unsuspected and unseen, in my wash rag. And I brought it up here and carefully planted it in rich soil, watched it throw up leaf and stalk, moved it from sun to shade, fought off its insect foes and finally

reached my crowded hour of bliss when it flowered. Was there ever such beauty! Such fragrance! How sweet, that stolen fruit!

The same week it flowered, we chanced into the greenhouse of a nurseryman not five miles from here, and there on a bench were hundreds of my precious bulbs in bloom! My smuggled gem was merely a commonplace.

Grape-vines that have been pruned should be lashed securely to their wires and posts.

8. YUCCAS. How that Yucca came to this New England dooryard garden I could never guess. We stopped one July day to admire it—hung over the fence in a scandalously bold fashion—and the old lady popped out. In the Autumn she gave us the plant, and ever since our interest in Yuccas has been growing.

Native to our Southwest, Yuccas like a well-drained location fully exposed to the sun, and here they will defy the worst drought. Though they usually are petulant over being transplanted, late Spring is the time to move them. The six kinds worth trying are *Y. gloriosa* or Adam's Needle, so called because of its sharp terminal spike; *Y. filamentosa,* which is fairly dwarf although its flower stalks will shoot up to six feet sometimes; *Y. recurvifolia,* with longer leaves and shorter spikes than *Y. gloriosa; Y. flaccida,* somewhat similar to *Y. filamentosa* in its habits; and *Y. angustifolia* which is not so overpowering that it can't be used in large rock gardens.

See that the feeding stations for birds are kept supplied with seeds.

9. TIME-TONED BRICKS. Next to old damask, old bindings, old vellum and old wine, I love old brick walls—walls laid up in no especial fancy bonding, just common, ordinary straight courses laid on a sturdy foundation, and given a patina by the elements of many generations. Here and there a soft brick grows pink and a header holds the crisp black given it in the kiln, and the mortar turns a soft gray, and moss creeps over the face of the wall where trees shade it.

Such a wall was turned to the road by an old mill on the river below us. How long ago it was built I had no need of asking, for Time had scratched her date upon it. And in idle moments I used to saunter down there, sit on a shady bank and contemplate those soft, time-toned colors. They added one more item to my list of those things which make life worth living.

Palms in the house appear to enjoy a monthly bath of soap and water.

10. THE USELESS ARRAY. One of the domesticalities that is very precious is the custom we keep a week before Christmas, of laying out all those things that are valuable for Christmas presents—those extra cravats bought in Vienna, that indecent shirt picked up in Paris, those water-jugs lugged home from Porto Rico, that utterly senseless box which meant so much to us in the dull town of Axminster. We set them out and decide who will accept them gracefully. Such is the irony of gifts. Next year, we vow, we shall not collect

this junk; next year we'll give everyone an Edam cheese or a coffee-pot.

Seed that you are saving for next year should be kept in a dry place, preferably in a tin box.

11. HOUSE PLANTS AND PLEASURE. House plants are an exacting pleasure, and if we are not willing to meet their exactions we need not wonder if the pleasure be short. Sun is needed and daily care should be shown them. After a time, certain of them take on a personality: they flourish or are stubborn or pine away unless we give each one what it requires. In the limited sunlight of the modern city, where tall buildings and narrow streets afford merely a wan glow, it is useless to expect these lovers of sunshine to thrive. We must content ourselves with remembering those sunny plant-filled windows where kindly old ladies grew their Palms and Azaleas and Cyclamens to envious perfection. I remember watching such an old dear all one Winter—watched her fuss over her pots as though they were children. When she went into that sunny bay window to water and spray and pull the faded leaf, she entered into a new and blissful world. She was like those old crones who toddle into church each day for their gossip with the Infinite.

Before heavy snow falls, wrap the Box bushes with burlap.

12. THE GREAT DISILLUSIONMENT. My heritage having fallen in fair ground (which is to say I was born in Philadelphia), my taste for scrap-

ple comes naturally. There are times when I hunger for it as a man long starved. One such day came in mid-December, after we had moved to town. Now I might have asked the cook for it, or suggested to Her that the cook supply it, but She, coming from Boston, thinks baked beans and fish-balls the highest attainment in foods; scrapple is unknown in Her Yankee cuisine. So having found an excuse to take me back to the country, I went boldly to a butcher and asked for Philadelphia scrapple. He wrapped a package and handed it to me and I fled for the train. All the way countrywards I thought of scrapple, and in the bouncing, rural taxi to the house, I thought of scrapple, and I thought of it as I lighted the kitchen fire and heated the pan.

This was to be a meal of meals, this solitary Saturday night supper. I would gorge on that scrapple and think pleasantly of Philadelphia and Pennsylvania and Apple Butter and the quaint Pennsylvania Dutch and my Scotch-Irish and Quaker ancestors. This night I would dine with them, with those fine old souls who had brought me up in the fear of the Lord and of the Yankee.

These thoughts cheered me as the pan grew hotter. The great moment arrived. I opened the package—opened it, and wept. On the cover was stamped, "Philadelphia-Type Scrapple, Made in Boston, Mass."

That night I dined with my forebears off scrambled eggs.

A Wardian case—a little box made of glass—can be turned into a fascinating indoor garden.

13. PENTSTEMON FRONTIERS. Next year, *sans faut*, I shall go exploring into the hinterlands of the Pentstemon world, cross the civilized frontiers of *P. barbatus Torreyi*, *P. Digitalis* and *P. laevigatus*, and push on into that wilderness of new kinds our plant explorers have been turning up in the Rockies. The Pentstemons are mainly an American race, indeed, as American in origin as Phlox, and yet the average gardener knows little of this great and interesting family. Herbert Durand writes of them tantalizingly and here and there a western catalogue offers a few new names. What fun to explore that family in its ramifications! And even though failure and disappointment may lie ahead (for I've no illusions about all of the Pentstemons being beauties) yet the experience will be worth the trouble. Even the mere sight of a reed shaken by the wind will repay us for going into an unexplored desert.

See that all garden tools are thoroughly cleaned before they are put away.

14. ANNUAL MALLOWS. Looking back on the past year of gardening, one of the annuals that gave us most return for the little trouble we took with it was the Mallow, *Lavatera*. Planted where it is to grow, thinned out to a foot apart, and given water in dry seasons, it flourished abundantly. The clearness of its pink and the clean virginal tint of its white kind, seen both in the garden and in vases set in our sunny flower win-

dow, have won it a place among those annuals that we shall continue growing year after year.

It is advisable to keep the soil of house plants stirred; use a kitchen fork.

15. OBITUARY. The time having come when my pigs were prepared to fulfill their ultimate destiny, I caused to be prepared and distributed among friends and neighbors the following obituary:

SOME PENS ARE MIGHTIER THAN OTHER PENS

RICHARDSON WRIGHT

announces
(though reluctantly)

the imminent demise of his two favorite hawgs

WEE-WEE AND FANNIE

the progeny of John Held, Jr.'s prodigious boar

FANNIE'S SENSATION

Those desiring succulent morsels of these gargantuan swine, should place their orders (and right soon) with S. E. Guthrie, Silver Mine Avenue, Silver Mine.

PURE PORK — FED ON FLOWERS

Tomorrow order a live Christmas tree in a pot and plant it out of doors after the holidays.

16. Ode for Pigs. The foregoing obituary having been sent in good faith, it brought the sincere sympathy of many good folks. To my desk came telegrams of condolence, memorial verses, letters of porcine sympathy. Out of this great flood of memorials one ode deserves immortality:

Listen, Wee-Wee, while I wonder!
Were flowers all your belly's plunder?
Was Dickey Wright so mean to you?
Was pollen what he made you chew?
Did Agnes ne'er your thirst assuage
With aught but Rose or Scarlet Sage?

Were those gay stunts,
Those piggly grunts,
Those seeming mastications,
One big pretense—
One brave defense
Jaw-bone gesticulations?

Were such the fate of you and Fannie
No man could hold my raging Nannie.
I'd haunt the house upon the hill
And all night long shout—"Daffodil!"
And when the owner sought for me
I'd ne'er disclose where I might be.

But knowing pigs
And having raised 'um
I close my ode
With "Pax Vobiscum!"

The golf-playing husband may make reparation to his gardening wife by giving her, for Christmas, an order for those plants she couldn't afford this year.

17. Early American. A protest has been raised against the exclusive application of the term "Early American" to the architecture and furniture of the original thirteen Colonies. What about the rest of the country? Why isn't the French of New Orleans just as "Early American" as the English of Georgia? Or the Spanish of the Southwest and California? Or the native Indian? Perhaps these sections were not sufficiently quick to take up the antique business. Tradition is carried on by substantial proofs. Their claim to the title, however, is just as legitimate as any that came out of Connecticut or Virginia. America was a large place to have been early in.

Wire suet to trees where birds can gormandize on it.

18. Monkey Puzzles. One thing for which the suburbs of America may be devoutly thankful is that the Monkey Puzzle Tree, *Araucaria imbricata,* has never been accepted on this side the water as it has in England. There the peak of suburban garden pride is this monstrosity, and the owner's pride lies in the fact that the plant being tender, he constantly gambles with the Winter elements on its survival. Since it is not hardy, only the area south of Washington and in southern California would sustain it outdoors. Various forms of Araucaria are raised for house plants, especially for the Christmas trade. They appear to survive indoor neglect with patient gallantry.

Let the family know that instead of the usual cigars or silk stockings, you'd really prefer a new thermometer or pair of clippers.

19. TRANSPLANTED LADIES. That world, which is too much with us, early and late, must be escaped from now and then if we are to retain our sanity. One of the by-paths that gives me freedom is trying to naturalize flowers in secluded wild spots where none grew before. In late Autumn, I take the surplus of the tamed, civilized kinds, and seek out hidden, protected spots behind walls and in woodsy glades, and plant them there. In August, I tramp around to see how they are coming along. My effort to naturalize Red Hot Pokers into the meadows of lower Connecticut met with dismal results—they perished to a man. Oriental Iris has been more successful and the few Peony roots and long-spurred Columbines I could spare have flourished and waxed fat. Transplanting these pampered denizens of the borders to the wilderness of bog and meadow has been not unlike that strenuous trek some of our grandmothers took when they journeyed overland and helped settle the opening West. It offers rude contrasts, and only the sturdy can survive. Yet those that do survive have such a valiant air that when I go to visit them I find my troubles flee. The world and its exactions fade into dim distance in the presence of these civilized folk flourishing in a new land. I return from my calls on them renewed, refreshed and with soul washed clean.

Don't be too practical in the choice of a gift for your gardener: a couple of detective stories is often more acceptable than a pair of wool sox.

20. INSIDE SUMMER HOUSES. One of the Winter-study subjects that has been interesting me of

late is a survey of bowers and garden shelters as they have been evolved through the centuries and in various countries. Practically all peoples, Oriental and Occidental alike, have used them as garden features from time immemorial. They are the calm harbors in the tossing sea of vegetation. Into them we go and are safe: secluded spots for rest and meditation, for casual chatter, for making love, for clandestine rendezvous, for writing or composing, for the meal *al fresco* and the forty winks snatched on hot afternoons. Some may even be used for prayer. I like to think, as I scan the pictures of these vine-clad bowers and houses, some humble and some noble, that in them all those pleasantries and purposes did come to pass —that men knelt to pray, and charming ladies succumbed to kisses, and the leafy walls looked down on happy family teas and artists in the throes of composition, and wicked people plotting sinister infidelities, and old men and women contemplating that end of life which is the beginning of another.

Fruits and berries from garden trees and shrubs will mingle prettily with holiday greens.

21. IMITATION SNOW. Once upon a time (which is the way all Christmas stories should start) my childish eyes were entranced by a certain type of realistic Christmas card. A Winter landscape showed a church prominent in the foreground. Its windows were lighted and toward it from all directions trooped happy people wading through

drifts of snow to early service. There was snow on the church steeple and on the window ledges and on the hats of the congregation, unbelievably real snow. Nature cast that snow around with prodigal hand. On these cards she always made Christmas the sort of day Christmas should be.

It was a distinct disillusion to discover that this really wasn't snow, that it had just been put there. Christmas lost some of its tang when I found that the snow was only imitation.

Recently, in an effort to recapture some of that old-time innocence, I set out to find cards like those, only to be informed that the Postal authorities frowned on them because the snow, instead of melting as respectable snow should, clogged the stamp-cancelling machines. Thus illusion went down before efficiency and another Yuletide idol was smashed. I wanted to believe once more that this imitation snow was real. As one grows older this is the hardest sort of thing to do. To a child, illusion can be reality, but the sophistication of years snatches away illusion. Age brings us to Christmas with minds stripped of such pretty fancies. And it's all a great pity.

Buy only those Christmas greens that do not rob the country of plants that are fast disappearing.

22. FOUR CARDS IN PARTICULAR. So heavy has become the trafficking in Christmas cards that very few illusions are left us. Once, only kings and the very rich afforded their own cards; today, one is quite out of the swim unless he can find or

devise a card to call his own. And how clearly does their selection indicate personality! Show me a man's Christmas card, and I'll tell you what he is.

They seem to fall into four groups—the pretty and innocuous, the smart-aleck, the very personal and—a small section, indeed—the religious.

The pretty and innocuous are usually the "boughten" kind, as they say in New England, those made up by the thousands and on which one either scribbles his message and name or has his name discreetly engraved. These usually run to English scenes of the Pickwickian Era. England and Germany used to produce the majority of them. Of late, however, France has broken into the market, and the modernist and smart stationers over there make up cards that are pretty but strongly redolent of fashionable dressmakers' shops. They have, to use that cryptic word, "chic." And while their intentions may be perfectly good, they would serve just as well for Yom Kippur or Thanksgiving Day.

For the smart-aleck card, I have a fierce and destructive dislike. It reminds me of the type of man who "shows off" at parties. Invariably he displays his worst characteristics. Petty cynicism, conceit and the mind bereft of illusions make a poor showing in cold print on Christmas morning. I feel like blushing for people who send out such cards. Are they that way the other three hundred and sixty-four days of the year? Or are their hearts so shriveled and their minds so twisted that they aren't capable of grasping what Christmas is all about?

The humorous card, on the other hand, is generally a jolly burst, and the more healthily Rabelaisian it is, the better I like it. The world sorely needs the purge of ribald laughter. I like to think that the wondering shepherds, having paid their reverence to the Child, retired to the bar of the inn and drank deeply and noisily to His health.

In the personal card are still more evidences of the infinite variety of human beings. The labor and expense they represent are appalling. Some are beautifully presented, some breathe warm and tender sentiments. I like them because they show that these people, for one day at least, are not afraid of wearing their hearts on their sleeves. Children and family groups, houses, fireplaces, the front door, the window with the lighted Christmas tree—we may tire of them, but of such stuff are the eternal verities of the home compounded.

When I find a religious card in the Christmas mail, I'm reminded of the poem Henley wrote about the little old women who came around the wards of the hospital where he lay sick—old women bearing cheerful messages. He likened them to neat housewives sweeping the Bridegroom's path. Scarcely have they swept the path than the dust and débris of the world clutter it again, and yet, day after day, they go on sweeping, constant in the belief that they are making the way clear for His coming. We may disagree with their theology but the quality of their faith can never be questioned. They hold it in the face of bitter discouragement and disillusion. Perhaps it is because of these that they can hold it.

There is a fifth class—the practical card. Lately

these have appeared in the form of maps. They come from people who own country places and are intended to be used in summer when you set out to find them. Of course by that time the card is mislaid or lost, but the sender's intention was good, anyhow.

Rolls of string in various sizes and strengths will be appreciated by gardeners in their Christmas stocking.

23. IMITATION SNOW MELTS. The dismal end of Christmas cards is sad to contemplate.

Having opened all the packages under the tree, the shoal of cards is lifted into the lap and you open them one by one and pass them around. At first they are greeted with sprightly remarks and exclamations, which gradually trail off into dumb acceptance. Finally, when you come to the last, your glance travels from the heap on the floor to the fireplace. Yes, burning is the neatest way to dispose of them. The names of the givers are laboriously set down in the Christmas list, a few are laid aside as too pretty or touching to destroy. Then the rest go into the embers. . . . Eventually there comes a Spring day when housecleaning turns one's possessions upside down. From hidden drawers out tumble these old cards we saved as being too pretty to destroy. A moment's hesitation, and they, too, go the way of the cluttering.

Since they live such a short while, since they often are accorded merely a passing glance, is this business of sending Christmas cards worth while? After all, isn't it just a big imitation snow storm?

Yes, perhaps the snow is imitation, perhaps its illusion is soon dispelled; but one thing is very real—the urge that makes people send these cards. The material ways in which we express the Christmas spirit may be ephemeral; the spirit itself is everlasting. The paradox of that glittering imitation snow is that it symbolizes something always fresh and genuine and so utterly splendid that we need but a moment's glance of it to carry us through the year.

Tomorrow distribute bottles of home-made wine to elderly gentlemen who should have them.

24. THE HECTIC EVE. There was a time in Massachusetts when a man went ignominiously to the stocks or the local jail if he dared celebrate Christmas. The Pilgrim Fathers suspected that Christmas smacked of Popish origins and therefore ought to be suppressed. Besides, it caused otherwise sensible people to spend money on presents that they ought to spend on food and clothes or put into their savings accounts. For weeks previous to the day, household chores were interrupted by women making and worrying over gifts. Men were known to stop their profitable labors to celebrate. So the worthy Fathers clamped down the lid on Christmas.

Samuel Sewall was one of these pre-Volstead Prohibitioneers who helped make the law. In his diary he records being shocked by people who were bootlegging presents and surreptitiously having a good time on Christmas Day. If he had his way he'd punish them to the limit, just as his descendants feel about those millions of good Americans who defy the liquor taboo.

Looking back on those times I feel that Samuel and his stern friends were rather quaint old parties and, perhaps, future generations will look on our own as the same. For taboos of this sort lose their edge when truth enlightens the people. When the average John Doe New Englander learned there was something to Christmas that wasn't of Popish origin and that it was a splendid act of Christian character to give presents and make children and wives and friends happy, and that it was well for man to break the dreary stride of labor with an occasional jamboree—when he learned these things, Samuel Sewall and his taboos were relegated to the shelf as curiosities.

Yet many a mother and father on Christmas Eve swear they'll never do it again. Secretly—and sometimes openly—they agree with Sam Sewall. For weeks their lives have been disturbed by this hectic rush for presents. Bills mount up. Some one's always forgotten. Christmas might find many a heavy heart. And think of all those who couldn't afford to celebrate Christmas! Yes, the rich can afford what's denied the poor! Money is wasted. Men come staggering home under loads of useless presents. Women have nervous breakdowns. Something ought to be done about Christmas—forbid it, prohibit it, see that it is curbed and obliterated by constitutional amendment.

People may feel this way when Christmas is over, but suggest taking them at their word, and you'd start a revolution.

For we know, as surely as we know anything, that happiness which comes without effort, without sacrifice, without bother, without disturbing the even tenor of work and living, is rarely worth either the giving or the receiving. The Christmas that hasn't caused bills to mount isn't worth celebrating. If it doesn't leave one tired, it isn't worth remembering. If we ordinary mortals cannot stoop from the godhood of work to assume for one day the frailties of man, then something is wrong with our godliness. If we cannot reincarnate in ourselves the heart of a child for one day, then we had better cease boasting of manhood.

House plants make excellent presents for old ladies.

25. THE ASS. Among those that stood around the manger in Bethlehem, so the Christmas story tells, were not only adoring shepherds and wondering cattle, but an ass.

The ass is a lowly bearer of burdens fast being supplanted by the motor truck. When its working day is done, it will have naught else left it save to be a butt for jokes and a symbol of the Democratic Party. And yet, who can resist having a tender feeling for this ridiculous beast? It is typical of so much that Christmas represents. The world is filled with ineffectual people constantly being supplanted by more efficient people. It has hosts of men and women at whom the sophisticated writers of this age poke fun—rustics and the "boobery." Nevertheless we find them at the nativity of most of the great things in this world.

Their hands fashion the crude beginnings of our arts. They open the wilderness to civilization. They sing the songs from which great musicians compose their works.

Meditating on this lowly ass and its presence at the Christmas manger, I am reminded of that quaint line in the Psalms: "Though ye have lain among the pots, yet ye shall be as the wings of a dove."

The girl who shies at Mistletoe may never know it as Viscum album.

26. FIVE THINGS TO LABOR FOR. If it be true, as some preacher has said, that there are only five things in which a man may interest himself and labor for, then all of these are found in gardening. The five are pleasure, power, money, learning and God. Certainly we derive pleasure, pleasure of all five senses. Certainly a sense of power comes to the man who works in his garden—power over his body—power over the soil. For money we labor hard and long that we may spend it aplenty on the garden. Learning is ever the aim of our work—learning more and more of that vast, complicated world of green growing things. And if at the end of the garden path some starry, still night we hear the rustle of His coming and the dusk wind blows the hem of His healing robe across our wearied face, then we attain the final and noblest thing a man may labor for.

To the Romans, our Christmas feast was the Saturnalia or thanksgiving celebration for harvests.

27. LEGEND AND SCIENCE. One of the amusing reliefs about gardening is that you can be as simple and old-fashioned as you wish, or as intellectual, modern and scientific. If you really prefer old wives' names for plants you may use them, and there's none to forbid you. You may call it Baby's Breath or *Gypsophila elegans*. Or you may follow old practices because their legend has been handed down; and sooner or later, along will come some learned scientist who finds a rational basis for them. We put salt on Asparagus in the Spring, for example, because it originally was a maritime plant, and we figure that it likes salt, the way an American in Paris occasionally likes a good cup of coffee. Recently Science discovered that the chlorine in salt really has a definite fertilizing value.

Finish the last of the turkey hash.

28. FROSTED PANES. All night long frost ferns had been growing up the window panes, their feathery fronds uncurling against a sky that was starless. I awoke suddenly, chilled, and felt the daylight shut out. Cold had drawn its blinds. The room was icy, the floor frigid. . . . My thoughts ran to frozen pipes and a furnace that needed stoking and mercury that lay at the bottom of its tube like a poorly digested supper. And having thought of these matters, I leaped from the bed, went directly to the window and scratched "*Amo te*" with my nail. Then I descended to the frozen pipes and the dying furnace fire. When I returned, my tender sentiment had melted and the Ferns

were gone. The sun is no respecter of amours or *Cryptogamia.*

By this time you should have paid all this year's bills from seedsmen and nurserymen.

29. In Exile. We had been in town only a week when She remarked, "D'you know, when things go against me, I think of the Top Garden." I blessed her for those words. All day long, things had gone against me and I, too, had thought of that Top Garden, now shaven and shorn by the Winter winds. The next morning we took the first train up there—we and the dog. And had the gardener not been in sight most of the time, I know we would have knelt and kissed the blessed earth.

Lest you weary of your horticultural environment, plan to take a trip some time this Winter.

30. Procul Este Profani. The words that are now written at the end of this ephemeral chatter should have been set down at the very beginning. For these pages are a snare and a bitter delusion. Dr. Johnson would have called them "a long-winded and multifarious dissimulation." Very little actual gardening is recorded here. Those who seek for information about this and that should consult the practical books, of which, Heaven knows, enough are available.

No, these odd bits and pieces are merely inconsequential thoughts about gardening and country folk, gathered over a decade by two people who collect queer things and fuss with their flowers and are domesticated and whose doings and sentiments mean very little beyond a narrow circle. The wise and sensible, having read this far, need read no farther. We take refuge in the thought that "there is a pleasure in being mad which none but madmen know!"

The final magnificent gesture you can make outdoors is to turn the compost heap over for the last time.

31. Finale. "Blessed be God," I write at the end of my garden journal, as I did in the beginning, and for a final fillip, this grand sequence of thanksgivings from the 33rd Chapter of Deuteronomy:

"For the precious things of heaven, for the dew and for the deep that coucheth beneath, and for the precious fruits brought forth by the sun and for the precious things put forth by the moon, and for the chief things of the ancient mountains and for the precious things of the lasting hills."

About the Author

Richardson Wright (1887–1961) was the editor in chief of *House & Garden* for nearly thirty-five years, beginning in 1914, when he was twenty-eight years old. He was the author of numerous books, among them *Another Gardener's Bed-Book, The Gardener's Day Book, A Small House and a Large Garden, The Bed-Book of Travel, Truly Rural, The Story of Gardening,* and *Hawkers and Walkers in Early America.* He lived in Silver Mine, Connecticut.